Jung

W
FROM STOCK

C000256656

BOURNEMOUTH LIBRARY

610322263P

Jung

A Feminist Revision

Susan Rowland

BOURNEMOUTH

2003

LIBRARIES

Polity

Copyright © Susan Rowland 2002

The right of Susan Rowland to be identified as author of this work has been asserted in accordance with the Copyright, Designs and Patents Act 1988.

First published in 2002 by Polity Press in association with Blackwell Publishers Ltd

Editorial office:
Polity Press
65 Bridge Street
Cambridge CB2 1UR, UK

Marketing and production:
Blackwell Publishers Ltd
108 Cowley Road
Oxford OX4 1JF, UK

Published in the USA by
Blackwell Publishers Inc.
350 Main Street
Malden, MA 02148, USA

All rights reserved. Except for the quotation of short passages for the purposes of criticism and review, no part of this publication may be reproduced, stored in a retrieval system, or transmitted, in any form or by any means, electronic, mechanical, photocopying, recording or otherwise, without the prior permission of the publisher.

Except in the United States of America, this book is sold subject to the condition that it shall not, by way of trade or otherwise, be lent, re-sold, hired out, or otherwise circulated without the publisher's prior consent in any form of binding or cover other than that in which it is published and without a similar condition including this condition being imposed on the subsequent purchaser.

ISBN 0-7456-2516-9
ISBN 0-7456-2517-7 (pbk)

A catalogue record for this book is available from the British Library and has been applied for from the Library of Congress.

Typeset in 10.5 on 12 pt Sabon
by Best-set Typesetter Ltd., Hong Kong
Printed in Great Britain by T.J. International Ltd, Padstow, Cornwall

This book is printed on acid-free paper.

Contents

Preface

This book is designed for the new reader of Jung, for all those engaged with feminism and for researchers. Two chapters sketch the man, his life with women, and then carefully introduce all his important ideas. C. G. Jung loved the feminine all his life. The feminine is the pivotal fulcrum of both his work and his psyche. Yet Jung was certainly not a feminist in the sense of promoting women's participation in the world.

Chapters 3 and 4 look at the way post-Jungians have tried to respond to his complex attitudes to women, gender and the feminine. Thereafter, I use the critical tools honed in feminist analysis, historical research, deconstruction, post-Freudian feminism and postmodernism to produce two new chapters of feminist revision of Jung.

To its own detriment feminism has neglected Jung. The reasons for this neglect range from the centrality of Freud to feminist thinking and the subsequent overemphasis of the reasons for his split from Jung, to the curious absence of critical analysis of Jung's writing that would enable feminism to get beyond his undoubted misogyny.

Of course, it would not be correct to argue that no feminists have tried to construct theories of gender and culture out of Jungian ideas. As well as the body of feminist-oriented thinking within Jungian therapy, a tradition of Jungian feminism that I call here 'goddess feminism' (see chapter 3) already represents the Jungian legacy on gender to the wider culture. 'Goddess feminism', a valuable and sometimes sophisticated body of works, has had the unfortunate effect of labelling Jung to non-Jungians as irredeemably religious and so cut off from gender as historically conditioned. This is an unnecessary oversimplification of his potential for feminist theory, as I shall show.

This book not only introduces Jung to those who have never before encountered his ideas; it applies the full range of feminist research to remedy the neglect. Therefore I explore not only what he wrote, but also, crucially, *how* he wrote it. I suggest that Jung's writings can be usefully characterized as haunted by two impulses. These I call 'personal myth', the generation of ideas out of his individual experience, and 'grand theory', the urge to present a comprehensive narrative of the human mind and culture.

Not confined to the therapeutic community, Jung's influence has been profound and enduring in contemporary culture. At last feminism has acquired the critical abilities both to explore the gender politics of his work and to offer a feminist revision that would look at his place in the gender politics of knowledge in the modern world. I aim in this book to introduce Jung to the feminism of the modern age.

Any feminist revision needs to respond to the problems encountered on first reading Jung. Conceptual complexities, the general shape of his psychology and its intellectual background need careful introduction. Thereafter I will show how the structuring of personal myth and grand theory arises out of complications of gender both personal and theoretical. Jung's work contains biased comments about women. He has a tendency to gender essentialism in assuming that a female body bestows an unproblematic feminine identity and vice versa. My use of the term 'gender' in this book is not essentialist. It assumes that gender styles and their representations cannot be isolated from the history and culture within which they are manifested.

Other feminist difficulties with Jung lie in his tendency to collapse gender difference within himself, his personal interior feminine (known as the 'anima'), into his biased statements about women in general. This crucial structure within Jung's writings can be connected to his fascination with Spiritualism and female mediums. I take these biographical elements as the basis for a historical feminist critique.

No analysis of Jung, feminist or otherwise, should ignore that his personal career has provoked accusations of anti-Semitism. Compounding such an accusation is the fact that he held a position in Nazi Germany in the 1930s, while remaining resident in Switzerland. While not the main subject of a feminist revision, Jung's disastrous excursion into politics and his anti-Semitic remarks are fully considered in chapter 1.

My purpose is not merely to subject Jung to up-to-date feminist criticism, using the resources available in postmodernity. A Jung liberated from his drive to essentialism, from complete confinement within the conventions of his culture, does have something to offer future feminisms. His persistent concern with the unknown, the unknowable and the inappropriable within the human mind could be the basis for progressive and radical thinking. There is a Jung recoverable for feminism in postmodernity just as there is a Jung who betrays all the limitations of Enlightenment thinking with its tendency to produce 'reason' out of a gendered suppression of irrationality as 'feminine'.

One way in which this book contributes to Jungian studies is by arguing that the post-Jungian field has now reached the point of offering Jungian feminisms rather than just Jungian feminism. This book is dedicated to exploring the new opportunities engendered by this expansion of feminist possibilities. In particular, I will suggest that Jung himself provokes such a development in his questioning of straightforward notions of authoritative theory. These impulses I will describe in chapter 2 as the drive to 'personal myth'.

Jung: A Feminist Revision provides a clear comprehensive introduction to Jung, to feminism and to a critical revision that aims to place this thinker *within* feminist research. The book therefore also gives an introduction to postmodernity. Jung is both Romantic and postmodern. This book shows that gender is the point of crisis within Jungian psychology in which issues of power, knowledge and identity collide. Not only does feminism revision Jung, but, also in this book, Jung offers a new light on feminism.

My acknowledgements must start with the invaluable support of Gerard Livingtone. I could not have written this book were it not for his unstinting encouragement and original insights. My family made their own contribution in their inimitable way. I would in particular thank my brother, Dr John Rowland, a mathematician, and my sister, Cathy Rowland, a music therapist, for their help.

I especially wish to thank Andrew Samuels. His perceptive comments on the very early stages of the book enabled me to find a structure to account for Jung's gender politics *within* his writing. Responsibility for the results and errors is, of course, wholly mine. Additionally, I would also like to thank Christopher Hauke, who both in his work and in person has provided encouragement to go beyond the habitual categories in which Jung is traditionally placed.

The University of Greenwich provided both financial support and a congenial environment in which to develop my ideas. Special mention must go to my colleagues Peter Humm, John Williams, Ann Battison, Nicole Bowyer, John Dunne and David Pattie for their calming influence. Students, notably Christine Ward, Sarah D'Cruz, Joanne Orrow and the 'Jung Postmodernism and Literature' class of 2001, have enormously stimulated and clarified my thinking. Friends, in particular Evan Davis, Edmund Cusick, Claire Dyson, Wendy Pank, Christine Saunders, Ailsa Camm, Juliet John and Val Gough, have provided consolation and cake at crucial moments. Thank you all.

How to use this book

New readers of Jung will find that the first two chapters introduce both the man and the work. Those more familiar with Jung, but not the post-Jungian developments, might like to read the sections on grand theory/personal myth and on women in chapter 2 before embarking on the map of gender in Jungian studies in chapters 3 and 4.

The new research in chapters 5 and 6 introduces important feminist contexts of deconstruction, psychoanalysis and postmodernism as well as providing new Jungian feminist thinking. Post-Freudian feminism of Luce Irigaray, Hélène Cixous and Julia Kristeva, deconstruction, the work of Judith Butler on the body, postmodernism, the Enlightenment, the sublime and the Gothic are all described for the new student. Chapters 5 and 6 suggest new Jungian feminisms that speak to the humanities in general as well as to new readers in particular.

I end the book with a return to Jung's ghostly feminine. Jung with his religious language represents something unspeakable and marginal to contemporary feminist theory. It is time that Jung, haunted by gender, and feminism, haunted by Jung, started to talk to each other.

Abbreviations

CW C. G. Jung, *The Collected Works of C. G. Jung,* vols 1–20, A and B, edited by Sir Herbert Read, Michael Fordham, MD, MRCP, Gerhard Adler, Ph.D., translated by R. F. C. Hull (London: Routledge & Kegan Paul, 1953–91); arabic numerals indicate volume numbers.

MDR C. G. Jung, *Memories, Dreams, Reflections,* recorded and edited by Aniela Jaffé, translated from the German by Richard and Clara Winston (London: Collins and Routledge & Kegan Paul, 1963; London: Flamingo, 1983).

Chronology

1875   Carl Gustav Jung born 26 July to Paul Jung, clergyman, and Emilie Preiswerk Jung.

1895   C. G. Jung starts medical studies at Basle University in April. Organizes first seances with cousin Hélène Preiswerk in June.

1896   Death of father.

1900   Starts work at Burghölzli Lunatic Asylum, Zurich.

1901   Reads paper to meeting about Sigmund Freud's *On Dreams*. Jung is put to work on word association tests.

1903   Jung marries Emma Rauschenbach.

1904   Sabina Spielrein arrives at the Burghölzli Lunatic Asylum as a patient. She is discharged 1905 but continues to see Jung.

1906   Freud writes to thank Jung for sending him a copy of his *Diagnostic Association Studies*. Their correspondence begins.

1907   Jung and Emma visit Freud in Vienna.

1908   At the Congress of the International Psychoanalytic Association in Salzburg, decision to publish yearbook with Jung as editor. Jung's intimate relation with Spielrein begins.

1909   Freud and Jung lecture in America on psychoanalysis. Jung starts to study mythology intensively.

1910   Antonia Wolff arrives as a patient at Burghölzli Lunatic Asylum.

1912   Spielrein marries and starts analysis with Freud. Jung's *Transformations and Symbols* published, which breaks with Freudian theories of libido as sexual energy.

1913   January. Freud breaks off correspondence with Jung, who then begins a prolonged mental breakdown. His fantasies from this period become important for the development of his psychology.

1916 The Psychological Club founded in Zurich. *Seven Sermons for the Dead* written.
1920 Jung travels to North Africa and England where he conducts a seminar in Cornwall.
1923 Starts his tower at Bollingen.
1928 Jung's study of alchemy begins in earnest.
1933 Jung becomes president of General Medical Society for Psychotherapy (based in Germany) and reorganizes it as the International General Medical Society for Psychotherapy with a category of individual membership.
1939 Jung offers to resign as President but stays on. Freud dies.
1940 Jung resigns Presidency. Lectures on psychological importance of Christian trinity.
1944 Jung seriously ill – has visions that are later described in the autobiography.
1945 Arrangements for co-publications of Jung's *Collected Works* finalized between Bollingen Press, USA, and Kegan Paul, UK.
1946 Opening of the C. G. Jung Institute in Zurich.
1947 Jung writes *Answer to Job*, an analysis of the God of the Bible.
1953 Toni Wolff dies. *Psychology and Alchemy* is the first volume of *Collected Works* to be published.
1955 Emma Jung dies.
1956 Aniela Jaffé starts work with Jung on *Memories, Dreams Reflections* (the autobiography).
1961 Jung dies on 6 June at Bollingen, Switzerland.

1

The Lives of
C. G. Jung

Ideas spring from a source that is not contained within one man's
personal life. We do not create them; they create us.

(Jung, *Modern Man in Search of a Soul*, 1933)

This opening chapter gives a biographical sketch of Jung's own history. I pay particular attention to moments of crisis in which the
cultural, the theoretical and the personal intersect in ways important
for Jungian theory. By concentrating upon the significant events in
Jung's life and career, it is possible to suggest how personal events
and preoccupations become implicated in the theoretical. Such an
approach forms a necessary prelude to the exploration of Jung's ideas
in chapter 2. The fundamental importance of the personal, I would
suggest, is a particular characteristic of Jung's work. It offers real and
hitherto neglected opportunities for feminism.

The chapter also aims to illustrate the important role of women in
Jung's life and work. As well as serving to situate his own theories
of gender, such attention also introduces the first women Jungian
theorists. The work of some of these women will be considered in
chapter 3.

Why start with a biography?

This book is designed to present the work of C. G. Jung to new
readers. I will then provide a feminist context for his profound and
influential psychological ideas. To this end, Jung and his theories
are introduced, followed by a guide to existing Jungian thinking on
gender. The final two chapters represent new research on Jung in the
light of feminist theory and postmodern feminism.

A life story is a helpful way of approaching any body of ideas for the first time. For Jung and feminism, biographical investigation provides even greater opportunities. Jung left his own autobiography, *Memories, Dreams, Reflections*, and subsequent biographies have necessarily been in a dialogue with this intriguing work. *Memories, Dreams, Reflections* reads as a legend of Jung's psychological growth. It illustrates his important ideas and shows that his intellectual career and interior history are indissolubly fused. Two key moments for both are the enthusiastic collaboration and the subsequent acrimonious break-up with Sigmund Freud,[1] followed by Jung's mental breakdown after this trauma.

Apart from Jung's parents, the autobiography records no other significant personal relationship, despite the very full emotional life we know from other sources. Indeed, *Memories, Dreams, Reflections* needs to be treated with caution if ascribed to the authorship of Jung. Published after his death, it was heavily edited by Aniela Jaffé,[2] and a chapter on Jung's important female colleague, Toni Wolff, was removed at the insistence of his family.

What no innocent reader of *Memories, Dreams, Reflections* would realize is the different directions Jung's work took at different stages in his life. This includes his tendency continually to revise his key publications, and the importance of his relationships with a number of women, many of whom were also writing about his psychology. Consequently, I am calling this chapter 'The Lives of C. G. Jung' to indicate not only the complexity of his history, but also the opportunity for feminist attention to it. After exploring a number of issues personal to Jung, the last section of this chapter, 'Biography and feminism', will use the historical knowledge to examine the gender politics at the genesis of Jungian theory.

Becoming Freudian

The child of myth

Jung dictated the early chapters on his childhood in *Memories, Dreams, Reflections*. In a very obvious sense there is no other possible witness to his psychological development at that time. However, the autobiography tends to fuse what may be childhood recollections of dreams and fantasies (suspiciously detailed) with later interpretations. For example, he records his first significant experience as a powerful dream aged 3 or 4, which involves his descending into an underground cavern and seeing a trunk of flesh on a throne. He hears his mother's voice naming the strange object as 'the man-eater'.[3] This dream was to haunt him all his life, he says, and he gives us his later interpretation of it as a ritual phallus.

It was also an early instance of his view of his mother as an uncanny presence. She possessed a conventional, everyday personality, behind which a ghostly, secondary, 'No. 2' identity had its being. Jung's mother, Emilie Preiswerk, was born into a family that regularly practised Spiritualism. She was the daughter of the second wife of a man who held weekly seances with his dead first wife. Her remarkable medium parent instructed young Emilie to stand behind his chair to discourage ghosts.[4] Perhaps unsurprisingly, Jung recalls that his mother spent a period in a mental hospital in his early childhood, which left him with a lifelong distrust of the linking of 'women' and 'love'.[5]

Jung's father, Paul, was a clergyman, seen by his son as ineffectual and as having lost any real contact with his faith. Biographers such as Ronald Hayman in his recent impressive study[6] have pointed out that Jung's career and psychology enact a lifelong struggle to combine the uncanny experiences of his mother (also suffered by her son) with the theological framework of his father. Jung's work was driven by the need to come to terms with religion, if not the conventional Christianity of his time. It was this very point that precipitated his later quarrel with Freud.

As a small child, Jung recorded regarding 'Lord Jesus' as sinister, since he seemed to have a lot to do with funerals and his father's growing unhappiness. Oppressed by the home atmosphere, Jung carved a human figure, a manikin, from a ruler and made him a bed in a pencil case together with a special stone. Hiding this cache in a forbidden part of the house brought the child a sense of relief.

Later, as a schoolboy, he became consumed by the sense of a terrible sin approaching him. He struggled for several days against the sense that he was being forced to commit an unforgivable act. At last he embarked on some individual theology and decided that, since God created Adam and Eve as they were, He must have intended them to sin. So he allowed the sinful thought into his mind: visualizing the cathedral, he saw God let fall a huge turd, which smashed it.[7]

This story, like the phallus dream, is given prominence in the autobiography. In describing it as a wrestling with God, Jung presented it as Jung's first experience of the divine as irrational. At the time, it allowed him to pity his discontented father, who was said to be suffering from the lack of personal contact with his religion. For Jung's later ideas, not only does this dream anticipate Jung's startling interventions into Christian theology; it also conforms to the basic structure underpinning all his later thinking. It is a demonstration of the *superior* power of the 'other' to which the ego *should* submit.

Given the significance of these experiences, it was not surprising that the young Jung decided that, like his mother, he too was a split being with an everyday self and a No. 2 personality. He did not find it easy to adjust to life as a schoolboy and allowed an episode of bullying to develop into an illness that kept him at home for many months. It was only his overhearing of his father express money troubles and despair over his dreamy son that made Jung decide to get better.

When Jung was a small child, the hidden manikin had expressed his split self and granted him a sense of security; the adolescent realized that he had to prioritize his conventional No. 1 self and be effective in the world. However, the sense of being split recurred upon choosing what to read at the University. His daylight self preferred science, while the No. 2 side remained fascinated by comparative religion. Typically, the decision to read medicine is said to be influenced by dreams directing Jung to seek knowledge of nature.

Jung's sense of being a split self, of course, became a key ingredient of his psychology. It is interesting that, in later life, he did not dispute the diagnosis of his junior colleague, Michael Fordham, that he had been subject to schizophrenic episodes in childhood.[8] The older Jung would not be disconcerted by this medical term because he believed that powerful psychological fantasies were not necessarily pathological. They need not be dismissed as merely signs of illness. Instead, overwhelming visions and dreams should be regarded as more like messages from a superior aspect of the human mind.

Before Jung made the decision to specialize in the despised branch of psychiatry, his divided self was again torn two ways. The death of his father resulted in financial hardship for the family. Just before this event, however, Jung and his mother embarked on a series of spiritualistic seances with his Preiswerk girl cousins. These would prove a key influence on his future work.

The spiritualist, the doctor and the married man

In *Memories, Dreams, Reflections*, Jung presents his attendance at seances as a continuum in a series of uncanny events focused upon his own household. Joining the regular seances is justified by his speculating upon possible connections between the young medium and these unexplained disturbances.[9] Jung later wrote an account of the seances as the core of his doctoral thesis and it now opens his *Collected Works* in Volume 1.[10]

In this document, Jung concludes that the ghostly voices emanating from the medium (disguised as Miss S. W.) are the product of a mental illness. He diagnoses hysteria in inducing dreamlike states of dissociation from reality. Footnotes link his suggestion that sexuality is at the root of the medium's storytelling or 'romances' to his recent reading of the work of Sigmund Freud on sexual repression and dreams.[11] However, later research has revealed how much the doctoral thesis conceals and distorts.[12] For example, it does not admit that Jung organized the seances himself, inducing the medium's trances by hypnosis. The medium, his cousin Hélène Preiswerk, was only 13½ when they began, not the 15½ of the thesis.

Therefore, when Preiswerk contacts 'grandfather', she is citing a mutual relation of herself and the fascinated medical student who was coordinating events. This tends to bear out later testimony by her family that she was in love with Jung and that the emotions were not wholly one-sided.[13] The 'objective' investigator himself gave the medium a book about a clairvoyant, which in turn bears a significant resemblance to some of her later material.

Most interesting for Jung's future work, though, was the medium's contact with the creative and superior spirit, called Ivenes. This phantom claimed to be a Jewish woman who had lived many times and who had been intimately involved with Jung in previous incarnations. The fantastic stories generated through Ivenes are given gravity by the impressive nature of her personality entirely manifested through the body of Hélène.

The doctoral thesis anticipates Jung's later theories through the description of Ivenes. The flamboyant spirit is said to signify both something autonomous in Hélène's psyche and a possible future personality (see chapter 2 on archetypes and the self). Apart from the misrepresentation of Jung's active and controlling participation in the seances, what is never hinted in the thesis is his willingness to take Spiritualism seriously at this formative stage in his life.

In fact, wrestling with the phenomena produced by mediums became a core pattern in Jung's career. As F. X. Charet has shown, a spiritualist narrative forms an intimate thread within Jung's activities and his *Collected Works*.[14] In terms of his intellectual development, Jung's early experiences with Hélène Preiswerk suggest a credence of Spiritualism as possible evidence of the supernatural. Then, although the doctoral thesis starts to assimilate the psychic 'evidence' to the theories of Freud, it also contains the germ of Jung's distinct theories by suggesting that spirits are psychic phenomena. This idea about spirits indicates that parts of the unconscious mind work independently of the ego.

In late publications and not least in *Memories, Dreams, Reflections*, Jung seems to suggest that these autonomous parts of the mind could also be regarded as metaphysical. Spirits again seem to surface in his writing as supernatural beings in an ambiguous embrace of religion and life after death. Jung justifies this continuum between psychology and religion in his references to himself as following in the intellectual tradition of Immanuel Kant.

The philosopher Kant introduced a crucial distinction between phenomena and noumena: phenomena are those objects existing in time and space, while noumena can only be objects of belief – religious realities can only be noumena.[15] Jung claimed that he took dream images to be phenomena and the power that forms them to be noumena. If noumena can only be deduced by reason and require faith, then autonomous creative parts of the mind can, by faith, be regarded as divine or the communication of spirits.

The problem with this position is that, first, many Kantians would dispute the designation of dream images to be phenomena or 'empirical' (as Jung frequently insists). Dreams, after all, are not objectively verifiable. Secondly, Jung frequently collapses his phenomena/noumena distinction when regarding the unconscious image as identical with the originary numinous mental power (see chapter 2 on archetypes and archetypal images). A further and feminist argument about Spiritualism in Jungian psychology will be considered in the last section of this chapter.

Jung completed his doctoral thesis while working as an assistant doctor at the Burghölzli Lunatic Asylum in Zurich. He was employed by a particularly enlightened psychiatrist, Eugen Bleuler, who pioneered the idea that the fantasies of schizophrenia were not useless babble. Bleuler encouraged his doctors to listen attentively to the visions of the mentally ill. It was Bleuler who introduced Jung to Freud's work by getting him to review Freud's most important early publication, *On Dreams*, for general discussion. Also it was Bleuler who asked Jung and another colleague to study word association.[16] This involved testing patients' reactions to stimulus words. Results seemed to point to the existence of repressed unconscious complexes, often to do with sexuality. Jung was working parallel to Freud here, although by now aware of his psychoanalytic theories of sexual repression.

In 1903 Jung married a wealthy young woman, Emma Rauschenbach, and they took up residence at the Burghölzli Lunatic Asylum. Their first child, Agathe, was born the following year. Before the birth, Jung started treating a new patient, a disturbed, intelligent young Jewish woman called Sabina Spielrein.

Freudian relations

Although Jung read Freud's *On Dreams* in 1900, it took several years for him to become engrossed by the ideas. His fascinating and quite startling correspondence with the older man began in 1906, when Jung sent Freud a copy of his work on word association.[17] Jung's text appears to confirm the core psychoanalytic idea of an unconscious dominated by sexual repression.

The emotional Freud–Jung alliance dominated the history of the psychoanalytic movement, until relations were finally severed early in 1913. If you read the published correspondence today, it is impossible to distinguish issues of passionate friendship, professional rivalry and theoretical conflict in their relationship. Freud was explicitly looking for a son and heir for the psychoanalytic movement. Jung seemed both to be seeking a father figure for his psychic security and yet also to be interested in power for himself. Ultimately he was unable to take up the mantle of another if it meant restrictions on his theoretical interests.

Both men reveal deep emotional investments in core ideas. These were the supreme importance of sexuality and Oedipal theory for Freud (see chapter 2). For Jung there was the need to account for religion and myth in ways that will not define it as *wholly* secondary and derived from infantile sexuality. Even early in the collaboration, Jung recorded reservations about Freud's exclusive notions of sexual repression and infantile desires.[18]

A fundamental divergence in the works of Jung and Freud remains deeply implicit in their distinct psychologies today. Jung is a theorist of the image; Freud of the word. For Jung, the unconscious image was primary; it was reality. The application of 'theory' to the unconscious image risked corrupting its purpose and function. Images are the way the unconscious thinks and speaks.

For Freud, thinking was a matter of words alone: the image was a *product* of a primary process of sexual repression. Given this fundamental dichotomy, it was possible to understand why Jung insisted on treating religious fantasies as important objects of study in themselves. Freud regarded such activity as, in the first place, an error, and, secondarily, as a betrayal of his work. In the end, Jung's theoretical deviance came to seem like a betrayal of Freud himself. Jung's publication of a study of mythical imagery and religious fantasies precipitated the final break-up.[19] In regarding the images as primary, Jung redefined Freud's concept of the libido as neutral energy, not exclusively sexuality. Chapter 2 will look further at the theoretical differences in the legacy of both Jung and Freud.

Although relations with Freud dominate Jung's psychological work at this time, his sexual life was beginning a more sustained pattern. Outside his marriage, Jung would find work and romance existing in a continuum. Sabina Spielrein was the first in the later Jungian pattern of a female patient, analysed by Jung, who then either stayed in Zurich as a fellow analyst or became a theorist and promoter of his work elsewhere. For Spielrein and the later Toni Wolff, the transition from patient to colleague was complicated and deepened by a romantic relationship. I am not suggesting that this is the case with other former women patients who became Jungian analysts and writers.

Toni Wolff remained Jung's partner and collaborator in his writing for over thirty years. By contrast, Sabina Spielrein, deeply in love with Jung at the time he was involved with Freud, moved away from Jung's influence to work in Freud's circle in Vienna. Originally analysed by Jung in the Burghölzli Lunatic Asylum, she entered analysis with Freud in 1912, just as the male collaboration was collapsing with distrust and acrimony. At the Vienna circle, Spielrein read her key psychoanalytic paper entitled 'Destruction as a Cause of Coming into Being'.[20]

John Kerr, using the newly available evidence of Spielrein's papers, has documented the extraordinary story of the theoretical and erotic interactions between Spielrein, Jung and Freud.[21] Her work actually anticipated much of Freud's later work on the death drive, but offered an alternative view of the interrelation of sexuality and destruction. Neither Jung nor Freud seemed to take Spielrein's theorizing seriously. She married unhappily and was later killed by the Nazis in Russia.

As Kerr shows, personal relations overlapped what were supposed to be professional alliances. Spielrein and Emma Jung both wrote to Freud about Jung. Jung and Spielrein also shared an extensive fantasy life centring on the myth of the Germanic hero, Siegfried. In this medical–erotic chaos, Spielrein, perilously, was both patient, lover and fellow theorist of the unconscious. Such a dissolution of boundaries prefigured Jung's own breakdown after the final break with Freud.

Freud and Freudian analysis continued to preoccupy Jung for the rest of his life. Both are frequently mentioned in his writings. For example, Jung first wrote the key essay 'The Psychology of the

Unconscious' in 1916, but revised it in 1918, 1926 and 1943.[22] It was only after Freud's death in 1939 that Jung was able to reintegrate aspects of Freudian theory to concede that the Oedipus complex was important for some patients. He acknowledges that a 'personal unconscious' of sexual repression is relevant in addition to his 'collective unconscious' (see chapter 2 for an explanation of these terms).

Becoming Jungian

A theoretical madness

In later years, Jung liked to claim that all his most important insights stemmed from his unconscious fantasies in the years 1913–18 during his illness after the break with Freud. *Memories, Dreams, Reflections* presents these events as a heroic 'confrontation with the unconscious' suffered on behalf of humanity.[23] Certainly, at this point, his former patient Toni Wolff became necessary to him. Emma Jung did not meekly accept the presence of Toni, by now in the role of lover as well as the medium-cum-analyst for Jung's fantasies. There was talk of divorce, but eventually Toni Wolff became the established mistress and important collaborator.

Feeling himself losing control in 1913, Jung was plagued by visions of blood in the prelude to the First World War. He typically explained these later as collective premonitions. The need to find mental images to embody his raging emotions was paramount – a desperation signalled by keeping a loaded revolver by his bed. *Memories, Dreams, Reflections* tells that on 12 December 1913 he allowed himself to plummet down to the unconscious.[24]

There he had a vision of a cave with a dwarf and a glowing crystal. Upon removing the crystal, he saw an underground river with a blond male corpse, a scarab, a red new sun and a flow of blood. Later, he dreamt of meeting a brown-skinned man who told him they were to kill the hero, Siegfried. Next came the fantasy figures of Elijah accompanied by a young girl, Salome. These creatures of his inner world, he later believed, taught him the autonomy of the unconscious.

From Elijah there evolved a more mythical figure, Philemon, a pagan with kingfisher wings. There was then a further male being whom Jung named Ka. A number of studies have noticed what Jung appeared not to, that, in Elijah and Salome, he had versions of the two important people he had just lost, Freud and Sabina Spielrein.[25] For Jung it was more important to see these figures from the unconscious as independent of his personal history (of emotional failure, perhaps). This conception crucially influenced his theoretical development.

At one point, a female voice intruded into his mind to inform him that he was engaged in art, not science. Once Jung learned to negotiate with this figure, she became the prototype of his seminal concept of the feminine, the anima (see more on this in chapter 2).

The spiritualist narrative in Jung's personal life reached a climax in 1916 when he became convinced that his house was crammed with spirits.[26] Even his children seemed to be sensing the presence of ghosts and on a Sunday afternoon the doorbell rang wildly of its own accord. Jung could alleviate the oppressive sense of haunting only by taking up a pen in the typically medium activity of 'spirit'-directed writing. What he produced was eventually published as *Seven Sermons to the Dead*.[27]

Although Jung adopted a medium's role in writing the text, the usual positions of master and pupil were reversed. Instead of dead spirits communicating their lore to the living, the authoritative Jung figure (in mythical guise as Basilides of Alexandria) is himself the *teacher* of the unhappy dead. These exhausted spirits have begged for his help in desperation because 'We have come back from Jerusalem where we found not what we sought'.[28]

Seven Sermons for the Dead is a crucial document because it anticipates Jung's later core theories of archetype and individuation. It bears out Jung's assertion that his breakdown was ultimately a creative illness. This piece of writing enabled him to focus his intuitions about the psyche and, significantly, he was able to break with the legacy of Freud. Throughout this time, Toni Wolff supported Jung as he underwent his own medium-like initiation. She was a woman frequently said to resemble a medium by her contemporaries. In her career, Wolff had the reputation of being a stunningly successful analyst in helping patients to get in touch with their unconscious fantasies.

The Jungian

In 1919 Jung produced the definitive term 'archetypes' for what he regarded as creative and numinous aspects of the unconscious.[29] From this period Jung recovered his mental equilibrium. He began to disseminate his ideas by travel and by expanding his activities at home. In the early 1920s he gave seminars in England and consolidated his reputation in America by cultivating contacts made earlier when working with Freud.

A key influence on later work was his growing fascination with alchemy. Jung's researches into the obscure writings and fantastic symbols of alchemy were stimulated by being sent a Chinese alchemical work, *The Secret of the Golden Flower* by Richard Wilhelm, in 1928.[30] Jung wrote a commentary upon it and later was to produce several volumes of his *Collected Works* devoted to the parallels he discerned between alchemy and his psychology. Jung's theory was now named 'Analytical Psychology' to distinguish it from the Freudian 'Psychoanalysis'.

Jung also bought land at Bollingen outside the city in order to build his own retreat, known as the Bollingen Tower. Here he invited a few favoured souls, but rarely his family. Toni Wolff spent a lot of time with him there. This very material structuring of his personal life was enhanced by travel. On visits to Africa and the Americas, he was particularly struck by the psychology of 'primitives'.

On the one hand, Jung recorded his realization of the cruelty of white colonization and his sense that other cultures may possess far better psychological attitudes than the Western nations. On the other hand, his free use of the term 'primitive' for African and Native American peoples demonstrated a classic colonial mentality in assuming that these cultures are merely far 'behind' in the Western narrative of 'progress'. Such an attitude to other cultures and ethnicities was about to get him into a lot of trouble.

Jung and the Nazis

From 1933 until 1940 Jung was President of the International General Medical Society for Psychotherapy and editor of its influential journal, *Zentralblatt für Psychotherapie*. This organization was based in Germany and heavily dominated by German membership. Consequently, it was subject to Nazi interference after their assumption of political power in 1933. That Jung was aware of the issues was clear from the fact that his Presidency inaugurated a reorganization of the Society.[31]

National sections were reformed to allow a category of individual membership so that Jews, by then universally banned, could remain members. The dominant section of the Society remained the German. It was supposed to have its own edition of the *Zentralblatt für Psychotherapie*, yet this did not materialize. Instead, the German-produced *Zentralblatt für Psychotherapie* came out with Jung's name as editor. It contained the recommendation of the German section leader, Matthias Goring, of *Mein Kampf*.

Jung refused unequivocally to condemn the Nazis until the out-
break of the Second World War, when his psychology became pro-
scribed in Germany. The nearest he came to criticizing the Nazis in
the 1930s was his 1936 essay 'Wotan', when he suggests that the
pagan god of storm and frenzy explains events in Germany more than
politics or history.[32]

Describing Hitler and the Germans as 'possessed', Jung argues that
they are possessed by Wotan as an archetype. He refused wholly to
condemn this condition, because archetypes are numinous powers for
good or evil: the Nazi phenomena, now (in 1936) so ominous, could
still have a positive potential. Such an attitude demonstrates Jung's
fundamental weakness in regarding himself as above politics. It illustrates the dangers of assuming that his psychology can adequately
account for all extremes of history, culture or power. This episode
illustrates the danger of what I call Jung's tendency to 'grand theory'
in chapter 2.

Moreover, it was in the controversial and horrifying arena of anti-
Semitism that Jung's association with the Nazis particularly demonstrates a moral flaw. Jung's articles in *Zentralblatt für Psychotherapie*
include the suggestions that Aryans possess 'higher potential' than
Jews,[33] that Jews are like women in being 'physically weaker',[34] and,
worst of all, that their culture requires a civilized nation to act as a
'host'.[35] Elsewhere in 1934 Jung wrote: 'To accept the conclusions
of a Jewish psychology as generally valid is quite an unforgivable
mistake . . .'.[36]

My conclusions about these unpleasant aspects of Jung's work and
career are that there is evidence of culpable anti-Semitism and a
morally flawed participation in Nazi culture. I do not believe that
Jung was 'a Nazi', a term that indicates unambiguous support for
their policies. I take the view of the eminent Jungian theorist Andrew
Samuels, who has written extensively on this aspect of Jung and
who concludes that, although Jungian psychology has reparations to
make, it should then be able to move on. What is important is to
remain mortally aware of sensitive issues of psychology, race and
culture.

To justify such a stand it is necessary to look further at Jung's
remarks on Jews and 'Jewish psychology'. As Samuels has pointed
out, in adopting as key distinctions 'Jewish' and 'Aryan', Jung was
engaging in a mindset that includes that of Sigmund Freud.[37] In
addition, Jung's lifelong struggle against the influence of Freud was,
tragically, behind a good part of his offensive comments on Jews.
One aspect of Jung's lapse into anti-Semitism was his fatal decision
to play out the struggle for power with Freud under the heading

'Jewish psychology'. Jung played on the ambiguity of the phrase to indicate both the idea of the different psychological make-up of Jews and the psychological theory that was made by a Jew, Freudian Psychoanalysis.

In retrospect it becomes clear that Jung was willing to engage with the cruelly pervasive anti-Semitism of the 1930s in order to gain the upper hand for *his* theory. This does not mean that there is any evidence of his sanctioning actual oppression. Indeed, he created the individual category of membership of the General Medical Society, specifically to aid Jews. However, a refusal to speak out against Nazi oppression, coupled with his disastrous excursions into 'Jewish Psychology', did lead him into anti-Semitic territory.

What about the other dimension of 'Jewish Psychology'? Did Jung believe in psychological differences based upon race? If so, how could he justify this? In fact, despite the core theory of a collective unconscious common to all peoples, Jung had developed a notion of psychic 'layers', corresponding to racial or national groups.[38] Below these layers is the overwhelming potential of unconscious archetypes. What forms these ethnic deposits in the mind is a bond between a people and their ancestral land.

Jung told a curious story of travelling amongst white Americans and believing that the people around him were taking on the characteristics of Native Americans because of their growing affinity with their landscape.[39] This was a suggestively non-racial racial belief, for any race can adopt the psyche of another homeland after sufficient generations. As a variety of nationalism, it affords no justification of aggression or expansion.

Unfortunately, such a concept fatally distinguishes Jews from non-Jews, for in the 1930s Jews remained the famously wandering people, bereft of a homeland. In conjunction with the tale of the ethnic transition of white Americans, Jung described Jews as lacking the rooted quality gained from a 'chthonic' connection to ancestral soil.[40] The racial-layers hypothesis was never integrated into Jung's total picture of the psyche. The idea was not taken up by Jungian analysts or included in the *Collected Works*. Therefore, the notion is not part of the Jungian analytic legacy.

Nevertheless, harping on Jewish difference in the 1930s, particularly in an organ published in Nazi Germany, cannot be regarded as innocently divided from the Jewish persecution of which Jung was well aware. In 1916, Jung sanctioned the founding of a Psychological Club in Zurich for his patients and fellow analysts (often very fluid categories). In 1944, the Club imposed a quota on Jewish members of 10 per cent with a 25 per cent guest membership. Likely to have been initiated by Toni Wolff and Linda Fierz-David, this anti-Semitic move must have had Jung's sanction.[41]

Jung was not a Nazi. He did not support Nazi politics or persecution. He did, in my opinion, engage in anti-Semitism and was a voluntary participant in Nazi culture. Attacked at the time for his actions, he never later expressed unequivocal contrition.[42] Consequently, the controversy has dogged his reputation to this day. A feminist revision of Jung needs this historical context. Historical perspectives on Jung's career enable his writings to be situated within the web of personal and cultural narratives of his time. Such a move can be a feminist act in challenging the notion of Jung's ideas as unambiguously authoritative *because* wholly detached from historical constructions of gender and ethnicity (see the last section of this chapter).

The wise old analyst and critic

By 1940 Jung was in his sixty-fifth year and war in Europe had broken out. After the Second World War he never again engaged in international psychological politics. Instead, his career was characterized by studies of Judaeo-Christian and alchemical writings. He produced what amounted to an analysis of God in the Bible in *Answer to Job*, and his last major work was his most considered book on alchemy: *Mysterium Conjunctionis*.[43] Marie-Louise Von Franz was a major collaborator on the latter and wrote the third volume. A major development in establishing the continuity of Jung's psychology was the opening of the C. G. Jung Institute in Zurich in 1948. It was formed to train future analysts and to promote Jungian research.

Jung had not ceased to be an involuntary explorer of the unconscious when ill. In 1944 he was dangerously close to death after a fall and a heart attack. His visionary experiences of leaving the earth and being about to enter another dimension stimulated much later speculations on the meaning of death and the possibility of a further psychic existence.[44] Such interests were naturally compounded by the deaths of the two women who formed his most sustained and intimate relationships: Toni Wolff died rather suddenly of heart problems in 1953 and Emma Jung of cancer in 1955. The relationship with Toni had cooled since Jung's 1944 illness, yet Jung marked her passing by carving a stone for her at Bollingen. It reads 'Toni Wolff. Lotus. Nun. Mysterious'.

Far more obviously devastated by Emma's death, Jung asked a family friend, Ruth Bailey, to take care of him. This she did until his

death in 1961. During his last years, *Memories, Dre* 16
was conceived and completed. This work was origi
be the work of Jung's secretary, Aniela Jaffé, with
tion, but Jung gradually became more engrossed in
Eventually, he wrote the account of his early year:
the text of the rest of the volume. However, it is v
ing that considerable editing took place after Jung's death, including
the removal of a chapter on Toni Wolff at the insistence of Jung's
heirs.

Women in life and theory

Although the only prominent woman in *Memories, Dreams, Reflections* is Jung's mother, Emilie Preiswerk Jung, later research suggests that five key women played an important role in Jung's life and the generation of his theory. They are, in chronological order, Jung's mother (who first suggested a secondary part of the self), his medium cousin Hélène Preiswerk (the first patient), Sabina Spielrein (the first patient in analysis), Emma Jung (his wife) and his long-time collaborator, Toni Wolff.[45]

There was then a second circle of women analysts and writers who usually began as patients. Their books were often given Jung's stamp of approval by his providing a preface. These women, Jolande Jacobi, Barbara Hannah, Marie Louise Von Franz, Esther Harding and Linda Fierz-David, together with Emma Jung and Toni Wolff, were the first female Jungian theorists. Some of their works mark the start of traditional Jungian feminism. Chapter 3 will consider their influence, while this section of chapter 1 will establish these important women in relation to Jung's career.

Medium women

Emilie Preiswerk Jung, Hélène Preiswerk, Sabina Spielrein and Toni Wolff form a chain of medium-like women deeply embedded in Jung's emotional life, and then realized in his theory. *Memories, Dreams, Reflections* testifies only to the role of Jung's mother in shaping his ideas. Despite Jung's revisions, the psychic impact of all these women can be discerned in the *Collected Works*. These women seem to have impressed on Jung the reality and validity of unconscious fantasy as something largely independent of the conscious ego. This was achieved through the revelation of their wn psyches (Sabina and Toni began as patients), but also and significantly, these four women inspired Jung's own capacity for unconscious fantasy.

What crucially distinguishes Jung from much of the psychiatric practice surrounding him (Freud included) was his refusal to regard spontaneous unconscious fantasies as definitively pathological. His unconscious was a meaningful, healing place. Schizophrenia was not necessarily a pejorative label to Jung and, indeed, there is no reason why a sufferer from a mental illness should not also be an important theorist of the mind. The medium women in Jung's theoretical world functioned as means to contact his own unconscious.

In particular, Toni Wolff became the 'medium' for Jung's unconscious fantasies after his break-up with Freud. Hélène Preiswerk was the prototype, succeeded by Sabina Spielrein, of a medium woman, engaging Jung's erotic interest and, in turn, stimulating his own unconscious fantasy. Jung's history suggests a significant sliding between Jung's desire *for* a female medium and his need to *become* his own medium in accessing and releasing the creative voices within *himself*. This biographical narrative became structured into his theory in the notion of the anima and the contrasexuality of the unconscious – see chapter 2.

The three medium women in Jung's romantic life outside his marriage met widely differing fates. Despite some attempts to disguise Hélène Preiswerk in Jung's doctoral thesis as 'Miss S. W.', she was recognized, and thereafter regarded as strange and unmarriageable in her home town. Eventually she was sent to learn dressmaking in Paris and died at the age of 35 from tuberculosis. Jung's claim in the doctorate that Preiswerk became mentally deficient seems wholly unjustified from the available evidence. Sabina Spielrein became a Freudian theorist and analyst, while Toni Wolff remained loyal to Jung and his creed for the rest of her life. Her important work on Jungian female psychology will be considered in chapter 3. Now to examine the careers of Jung's other female colleagues.

Women analysts and writers

Jolande Jacobi (1890–1973)   Born in Budapest to wealthy parents of Jewish origin, but Catholic in religion, Jacobi married, had children and became prominent in Austrian cultural circles.[46] She arranged lectures including Jung in 1927 and then asked him to train her as an analyst. He rather unkindly insisted that she got a doctorate (other students had not), so she studied at the University of Vienna. Forced to complete her degree in disguise because of Nazi persecution of Jews, Jacobi arrived in Zurich in 1938 and was allowed to join Jung's circle. During the Second World War she lost her husband and parents to the Nazis; her sons survived.

Jacobi was very much an extrovert (Jung's term) who grated on many of Jung's other colleagues and enjoyed an explosive relationship with the great man. Once, he threw her down a staircase. However, her introductory works on Jungian psychology were praised by him and it was Jacobi who drew up the original plan for the C. G. Jung Institute. When it finally opened in 1948, she was given a major role in liaising with visitors and establishing the reputation of the institution in the wider world.

Barbara Hannah (1891–1986)   The English daughter of a bishop, Hannah studied art in Paris and was inspired to go to Jung in Zurich by reading his 1928 essay 'Woman in Europe'.[47] Described as quite aggressive in the early days, she became a convinced adherent. Hannah became an analyst and Jungian writer, eventually teaching at the C. G. Jung Institute. Her biography of Jung is not quite as hero-worshipping as might have been expected, but it does treat the source material uncritically. She records of herself that Jung suggested that she took up residence with Marie-Louise Von Franz. They subsequently lived together until Hannah's death.

Marie-Louise Von Franz (1915–)   In recent times Von Franz has remained an authority at the C. G. Jung Institute as a measure of what the founder would or would not have wanted.[48] Such an attitude provides a key to the direction of her many published works, including her influential treatment of fairy tales and alchemy.

The daughter of an Austrian nobleman, Von Franz met Jung at 18, when she was taken on a visit with other young people to Bollingen. Much later she was to build her own tower at Bollingen with Jung's approval. After graduating with a doctorate in linguistics, Von Franz immediately became Jung's assistant. She was crucial to Jung's research on alchemy and a co-writer of *Mysterium Conjunctionis*. After the death of Emma Jung, Von Franz finished her book on the grail legend at Jung's request. Von Franz's work is characterized by her loyalty to Jung's writings and wishes.

Esther Harding   Esther Harding's books on female psychology in relation to myth are the most creative and most influential for later

Jungian feminism of all the women surrounding Jung (see chapter 3).[49] *Woman's Mysteries*, in particular, inspired the later feminist rethinking of women's spirituality, especially in the USA, where Harding conducted most of her career with her Jungian companion, Dr Eleanor Bertine.[50]

Born in rural England, Harding qualified as a doctor at the beginning of the twentieth century. She was one of a select group who attended Jung's first English seminar in Cornwall in 1920. Afterwards she followed him back to Zurich for three years' analysis and preparation to become an analyst. From then she was based in the USA, returning regularly to Zurich for contact and analysis with Jung. Together with Eleanor Bertine and Christine Mann, she founded the powerful New York C. G. Jung Institute.

For many years Harding dominated this institute as a formidable figure who was intimidating to many lecturers. Jung told her that she was like a priest of the mysteries and should strive for more humility. When she died at the age of 83, Harding left a million dollars to the New York Institute.

Linda Fierz-David (1891–1964)   As a citizen of Basle, Linda Fierz-David was the first woman permitted to enter the university, where she studied German linguistics and later married Hanz Fierz.[51] In the 1920s the Fierz family and the Jungs became friends. Jung travelled with the husband while analysing Linda on her unorthodox romantic situation: she was in love with both her husband and an Italian cousin.

Later, Fierz-David started work as an analyst and lectured on the Jungian interpretation of literature. As a result of Jung's suggesting that she work on some woodcuts, Fierz-David published a book on the search for the anima in 1938. She produced an even more significant work on the female psyche, *Women's Dionysian Initiation*, in 1955.[52] Nicknamed 'Sieglinde' by Jung, Fierz-David sought to remedy Jung's inattention to the feminine perspective.

Biography and feminism: From mediums to animas

If biography provides one way to approach a body of theory, then feminism offers tools for its critical examination.[53] One of the issues in any assessment of Jung is the construction of gender within his work. Later chapters of this book will take up this challenge. However, a biographical study of Jung not only allows me to suggest the less acknowledged (by him) role of gender in his life, but also to consider how his life experiences of the feminine become core structures within his theory.

Jung's involvement with the medium women Preiswerk, Spielrein and Wolff was not only evidence of his complex emotional life; they became for him the building blocks of his theories of the autonomy and creativity of the unconscious. In practice, Jung's relationships with medium-type women enabled him to get in touch with his own unconscious. If 'spirits' are redefined in psychology as unconscious fantasies, then the history of Spiritualism and Jungian psychology come together. Such a convergence occurs in Jung's first patient, medium Hélène Preiswerk, in Jung's shared fantasy life with Sabina Spielrein, and in the role of Toni Wolff, the medium midwife for Jung's most valuable creative fantasies. What a feminist critic can demonstrate here is the gender politics at work between Jung's encounter with the feminine as occult medium, redefined as patient, and his own later assumption of the 'medium' position for masculine subjectivity.

What I mean by this is that Jung was not only attracted to these medium women (and we must not forget his mother here); he wanted to *become* a medium. In truth, he did so, especially in the spiritualist writing of *Seven Sermons to the Dead*, which anticipated crucial aspects of his later psychology. Then, the theoretical formation of the concept of the anima is described in the autobiography as generated from a mediumistic contact with a feminine voice within his own mind. At this point in the building of a psychology, 'women', or, more precisely, 'the feminine', are displaced from medium to anima.

Of course, I am not arguing that Jung believed real historical women to be animas, who are feminine images in the psyche of a male. Yet, as chapter 2 will show, Jung seemed to model many of his pronouncements on women and femininity upon his notion of his own unconscious anima. 'She' first appeared in his 'medium' experiences of 'other' voices during his mental breakdown after the split with Freud. Here it was Toni Wolff who became so important in helping him realize his visions. Without actually regarding real women as fantasy animas, Jung assumes in his writings the medium position for masculine subjectivity and prefer to deal with the feminine in anima form.

I shall show how Jungian psychology contains a gender politics in a drive to displace the feminine into the position of 'other' (anima) to the masculine psyche. This drive can be traced to Jung's biographical involvement with medium women. His sexuality becomes theoretically complicit as it enables him to assume the medium position for himself and, from thence, for the masculine subject. An unanswerable question is: was Jung attracted to medium women because he was desperately seeking ways to express his tumultuous fantasy life? Or, conversely, did that fantasy world result from ungovernable sexual urges? Which is more fundamental: sexuality or unconscious fantasies (as not reducible to sexuality)? Freud had one answer, Jung another (see chapter 2).

Feminist criticism can expand the transition from medium to anima in Jung's life and writing and situate it in a larger historical context of gender, the occult and medicine. The Jung and Preiswerk families' preoccupation with Spiritualism in the late nineteenth century can be seen as part of the enormous vogue for seances and mediums throughout Europe and America.[54] What particularly distinguishes the Spiritualism of the second half of that century is the preponderance of female mediums, many of whom made a lucrative career of public or well-paid private 'performances'.

In fact, the short-lived career of Hélène Preiswerk illustrates perfectly the trajectory of female mediumship by the end of the nineteenth century. Once regarded as 'evidence' from beyond the grave, the medium's spirit 'voices' were at first seriously regarded as supernatural. Then women mediums suffered redefinition as mentally ill with the hysteria that Jung ascribes to his young cousin in his doctorate. The female medium moved from public platform to analyst's couch. What might be perceived by the culture as dangerously unlicensed female 'speech' and 'irresponsible' (literally) automatic writing came firmly under medical (masculine) control.

Therefore we can see in the genesis of Jungian theory a gender politics that was both personal to this theorist in his intimate relationships and ambitions, and also part of a larger historical movement. From the point of view of the culture, the medium could be seen as a 'feminine' position. The feminine is first of all 'other' to social norms in the medium as occult. She, the medium, then becomes pathologized into a patient. And for Jung, in the writing of a male-authored theory, the unreliable woman was given the position of the 'other' again, in the role of the anima, the 'other' of masculine subjectivity.

A feminist approach to Jung's biography traces a gender politics both historical and individual in the structuring of his psychology. The following chapter will introduce the theory. As I have argued, it will not be possible wholly to separate out Jung's ideas from his personal experience, at least in part because *Memories, Dreams, Reflections* offers succeeding generations a life story assimilated into a metaphysical framework. It is important to consider very carefully what Jung meant by describing both his theory and his autobiography as his 'personal myth'.

Concluding summary

Jung's life story is not a smooth history of career and intellectual development. On the contrary, it is punctuated by overwhelming psychic experiences, a traumatic relationship with Sigmund Freud and a deeply controversial involvement with Nazi Germany. Biographical accounts of Jung do need to engage with the autobiographical *Memories, Dreams, Reflections*. However this is a problematic work, in part because portions were removed after Jung's death. Also it is a legend of inner development and omits many outer, more political aspects of the life.

An analysis of gender politics within Jung's personal history suggests that crucial structures of gender within his writings need to be seen in both personal and cultural contexts (mediums become displaced into animas). It remains to be seen how far deeply personal formations of gender extend into the writings of his very influential psychology.

FURTHER READING

Anthony, Maggy, *The Valkyries: The Women around Jung* (Shaftesbury: Element Books, 1990).
A sympathetic and short account of the women in Jung's life and theory by one who managed to interview some of them. It is readable and useful, but shows the need for proper biographies of these women.

Charet, F. X., *Spiritualism and the Foundations of C. G. Jung's Psychology* (New York: State University of New York Press, 1993).
A very thorough and persuasive study of the role of Spiritualism in Jung's theory, especially in relation to his doctorate and autobiography.

Hannah, Barbara, *Jung: His Life and Work: A Biographical Memoir* (London: Michael Joseph, 1977).
Despite the heroic tone, this biography by one who knew Jung well is a wealth of helpful material and illuminating anecdote.

Hayman, Ronald, *A Life of Jung* (London: Bloomsbury, 1999).
An excellent detailed biography uniting recent research with an ability to give an open-minded account of his intellectual development.

Homans, Peter, *Jung in Context: Modernity and the Making of a Psychology* (Chicago: University of Chicago Press, 1979).
Useful for a wider intellectual introduction to Jung in cultural context, it works well with Von Franz – see below.

Roberts, Michèle, *In the Red Kitchen* (London: Methuen, 1990).
This stunning feminist novel precisely addresses the transition from medium to psychiatric patient in the late nineteenth century. Roberts informed me that Jung's doctorate was part of her source material.

Samuels, Andrew, *The Political Psyche* (London: Routledge, 1993).
This contains indispensable reading on Jung and the Nazis.

Von Franz, Marie-Louise, *C. G. Jung: His Myth in our Time*, translated from the German by William H. Kennedy (New York: C. G. Jung Foundation for Analytical Psychology, 1975).
A partisan and highly readable argument for the importance of Jung's theories.

2

Introducing Jungian Theory

I have no theory about dreams; I do not know how dreams arise. I am altogether in doubt as to whether my way of handling dreams even deserves the name of 'method'.

(Jung, *Modern Man in Search of a Soul*, 1933)

This second chapter introduces Jungian psychology to the beginner. The first section looks at the way Jung wrote and how he built up his concepts into a unique psychology. It introduces and explains the difficulties that many people encounter in reading Jung for the first time. I aim to show that Jung's writings do not resemble 'theory' in the conventional sense, because they also contain elements of fantasy and myth.

A second section describes all Jung's key ideas, showing how they connect to each other to give a 'Jungian' picture of the world. Thereafter theoretical disputes with Freud are clarified to show the distinct nature of the 'Jungian' position. The differences with Freudian psychoanalysis will be revisited in the feminist arguments of later chapters. Lastly, I look at what Jung actually wrote about women and gender. It is followed by a consideration of some of the implications for later Jungian and non-Jungian notions of the feminine.

Did Jung write theory?

Problems with psychology as theory

The expression 'Jungian theory' suggests that somewhere in the *Collected Works* we are going to find a neat explanation of all Jung's key ideas. Whatever is important to the understanding of Jungian psychology will be described without ambiguity. The text will offer subsequent generations a coherent, verifiable and above all *reliable* map of the mind.

Many first-time readers experience a sense of frustration with Jung when they discover that he did not provide such a work, and moreover that his own writing style almost seems to be a barrier to such a way of understanding. Jung writes about the psyche (a term taken to include all mental contents, conscious and unconscious), allusively. His sentences dip in and out of his own concepts, often embedding them in the fantasies of his patients or even his own.

Worse still for some readers, Jung draws extensively upon unorthodox religious writings such as the strange mystical texts of alchemy. He uses mythological parallels from many cultures. Every so often, he will even make statements that imply a deep-rooted resistance to the whole notion of 'theory' with its connotations of objectivity, rationality and scientific validity. One such example is when he suggests that ideas 'create' the person rather than the other way round.[1]

So does Jung provide a theory at all? And, if he did not write 'theory' in the conventional sense, what does this mean for the kind of psychology he produced? How is it possible to account for his profound influence on later culture, including a contribution to feminism?

The first part of this chapter will investigate the *texture* of Jungian writings before introducing the basic ideas. I will then give an outline of the conceptual relationship with Freudian psychoanalysis as well as looking at what Jung actually wrote about women and gender. Finally, the chapter will suggest some of the feminist potential in Jung's works as a prelude to the discussion of the directions taken by what I will call 'traditional Jungian feminism' in chapter 3.

To start by looking at the way Jung wrote, it is worth considering what is at stake in trying to describe a psychology. 'Psyche–logos', or words about the psyche, is a uniquely subjective activity. After all, the human mind is the only instrument available with which to investigate the human mind. There is no non-mental place from which to observe the mind with total objectivity. An individual psychologist may claim to record the mental events of other people dispassionately, but he can never be sure that his own mental states do not interfere with his results.

The word 'theory' is derived from Greek, meaning to 'see' and then conceptualize. Therefore, since 'seeing' the human mind at work can never be wholly separated from the mind's own dynamics, psychological theory can never be 'scientific' in the normal objective sense. A body of ideas about the psyche can never be guaranteed free of subjective and personal biases.

Such a problem with the making of a psychology is even worse when an investigator wishes to explore notions of the unconscious. It is easy to forget that the unconscious is, by its very definition, *unthinkable*, not knowable, not securely mappable. The unconscious is always a mysterious and frequently terrifying power in the mind. If it cannot be *known*, then there is a sense that it cannot be adequately theorized.

Classic Freudian psychoanalysis deals with this realm of the irrational by trying to produce a narrative that structures the unconscious into the formation of the human subject. The unconscious is formed within the development of the mental life of a young child.

Jung's works are comfortable with issues of subjectivity invading the pure scientific halls of theory. His writings make a point of acknowledging that not only his own personality, but even his unconscious fantasies, may be a shaping influence upon his ideas: 'every psychology . . . [he wrote] has the character of a subjective confession.'[2] It is important to realize that this insight has a significant impact on the kinds of writings that Jung produced.

Fantasy in the theory

Given the above description, it becomes less surprising that one of the most coherent and easy-to-follow accounts of Jung's ideas lies not in the *Collected Works*, but in his separately published autobiography, *Memories, Dreams, Reflections*. This work is very much a 'subjective confession' in that he describes with great care and deliberation his own mental breakdown. He argues that the resulting powerful fantasies played a crucial role in the evolution of his psychology. In effect, his own unconscious fantasy is portrayed as *the* key ingredient of his theory.

On the one hand, this may seem like a shocking way to structure such a profoundly influential theory – using a base of the personal and irrational. On the other hand, as Jung continually said, delving into his own unconscious was the truest form of research. When looking at other minds, such as the fantasies of his patients (where, of course, he did claim to find additional verification of his personal insights), the investigator can never wholly banish his own subjectivity. The unconscious of the analyst may intervene and colour his perception of the minds of others. The only immediate mind to that of any theorist of psyche is his own. Here is Jung's presentation of the distillation of the important idea of the anima in the context of his own breakdown.

> Then I thought, 'perhaps my unconscious is forming a personality that is not me, but which is insisting on coming through to expression . . .'
>   My conclusion was that she must be the 'soul' . . . Later I came to see that this inner feminine figure plays a typical, or archetypal, role in the unconsciousness of a man, and I called her the 'anima'.[3]

Given that unconscious fantasy proves to be so central to Jung's approach, it is less surprising to find him describing his theory as his 'personal myth'. This phrase occurs at three key points in the text of *Memories, Dreams, Reflections*,[4] and comes to resonate with Jung's whole attitude to myth and mythologies. In turn, myths of all kinds are crucial to the writing of his theory.

In the prologue of the autobiography, 'personal myth' is used to express fidelity to his own experience, acknowledging its necessary subjectivity. 'Myth' stands here for a life story more personal and individual than those possible to the narratives of 'science'.

Much later in the autobiography, at a time of emotional and career crisis for Jung, 'personal myth' becomes what he is lacking. It stands for the absence of any deeply held belief by which to organize his existence. His life is empty because he realizes that the Christian myth can no longer energize life with passion and inner meaning. The depiction of the agonies of Jung's breakdown concludes with an account of a dream leading to a sense of peace and the beginning of 'my personal myth'.[5]

What seems to happen here is that 'myth' becomes a *bridging term* between 'life story' and 'theoretical framework'. Describing his theory as a personal myth enables Jung to retain a sense of its subjectivity. It is personal to him and it has an interior quality as an object of belief that structures his whole life, not just his professional practice. In this, the theory-as-personal myth behaves like Jung thought religion used to do. The religious nature of Jung's psychology will be returned to later in this chapter. Now I wish to look at other aspects of Jung's use of myth.

The expression 'personal myth' is also valuable to Jung because the religious connotations of 'myth' can stand for the essentially unknowable and overwhelming nature of the unconscious. It enables Jung to embed in his conceptual writings a scepticism about conventional notions of theory (the power to 'explain' everything), as well as providing a way to respect the radical *otherness* of the unconscious. This is the reason that he insisted that those prime artefacts of the unconscious, dreams, must not be reduced to a theory nor even 'understood' in the normal sense.

In addition, the term 'personal myth' is significant because it allows him to expand into the cultural territory of 'mythology'.

So far in what I have described in Jung's writings, one would expect its *texture* to be one of modesty. The emphasis on the subjectivity of any psychology should surely limit the ambitions of both his statements in writing and in practice. However, any reader of Jung's *Collected Works* is immediately struck by the contrary impression. Alongside the renunciation of comprehensive theorizing are claims to be able to diagnose the key elements of all human culture: personal myth mutates sinuously and frequently into 'grand theory'. By *grand* theory I mean one that has the ambition to account for a variety of manifestations of human behaviour and history. Such a theory implicitly claims a superior place as the framework able to explain not merely the problems of individual patients, but culture as a whole. How does Jung manage this?

Grand theory and personal myth

I call Jung's intellectual ambition for a comprehensive psychology the drive to grand theory. In order to create a grand theory out of personal myth, Jung needs to go further than merely to claim verification for his ideas, because evidence is drawn from the fantasies most immediate to him, his own. If every psychology has the character of a subjective confession, then could every subjective confession provide a psychology? Could there be as many psychologies as there are human beings? In fact, the whole notion of not theorizing dreams yet treating them as expressions of the unconscious is fundamental to Jungian clinical methods. It represents the subjectivity of 'theory' enshrined in analytical practice.

Nevertheless, Jung's writings upon culture, religion and, not the least, women make a bid for a grand theory far beyond just asserting the superiority of Jung's own fantasy projections. In order to extend his 'personal myth' into a claim for wider validation, Jung needed to establish a link between his fantasy life and a series of cultural narratives. *His* personal myth was specific not just to his own life, but to many or most people. Like Freud and Oedipus, Jung found his cultural narratives as mythologies, particularly those of established religions and of alchemy.

Therefore the formation of the personal myth not only allowed autobiography to become theorizing; it permitted the theory to expand by making the term 'myth' also a point of transition between the personal and the cultural.

'Myth' is used in a dual sense in Jung's writings: as evidence of the unknowable unconscious in individual personal myths *and* as evidence of the unconscious in cultures (mythologies, including Christianity). In denoting religious and supernatural stories, myths supply an atmosphere of the superior and unruly power of the unconscious. In the form of the established mythologies, myths are the repository of the unconscious in culture over time. Jung theorizes the myths he encounters to be the stories of the human subjection to unconscious forces. Such narratives and stories then provided the tools with which to structure his theory.

For example, the autobiography portrays the anima concept as arising out of his fantasy of an autonomous feminine figure that becomes fused with his knowledge of medieval Christian myth. Once mythologies have provided some of the narrative blocks for building a theory, common cross-cultural elements such as sun gods, incest and sacred marriages provide fertile ground for textual and cultural verification. So it is unsurprising that Jung's work seizes upon mankind's sacred myths in addition to clinical records from analysis.

It might be argued that, if crucial elements of the theory are drawn from myths in the first place, then using myths to justify the theory risks becoming a circular process. Jungian theory makes the human mind mythological. To put it another way, Jung accounts for repeated dream images or unconscious fantasies *as* mythological.

What is intrinsic to Jung's use of mythology is the use of mythical narratives as stories of being, of psychological structuring, that value the unconscious as superior. This is a point I will pursue in the next section. What also needs to be stated is that Jungian psychology is also about Jung's practice as an analyst, and not only upon himself! Jungian theory is a theory of psyche and culture, *and* a therapeutic methodology.

Here I borrow from the following section of this chapter and speak of a bipolar tendency in Jung's writing style, as well as within the concepts. Just as his core ideas are based upon a tension between opposites, so do his writings possess conflicting yet interrelated impulses. In one moment Jung refutes a narrow sense of 'theory' as unproblematically reducing mental phenomena to some kind of all-encompassing 'code'. Yet, almost simultaneously, Jung provides grand narratives of culture and religion.

What is particularly indicative for Jung and feminism, I would suggest, is the literary quality of his theorizing, splicing, as it does, personal myth onto grand theory by means of mythological narra-

tives. Now I will take a closer look at just what his literary endeav-
ours produced.

Basic concepts in Jungian psychology

A good place to start is with the fundamental Jungian notion of
'psychic reality'. To Jung, all reality, all that the human being experiences, feels, learns, encounters, both inside and outside the mind, is
psychic. This is because we can know nothing that has not already
been filtered through our psyche. Here it is important to remember
that 'psyche' stands for all mental contents and operations; it includes
both conscious and unconscious effects upon the perceiving mind.
Whatever the person considers to be 'real' is also, by definition,
psychic.

Consequently, the definition of the Jungian unconscious stresses
that it is immediate and crucial to everyday experience. Jungian ideas
differ significantly from Freudian psychoanalysis in seeking to honour
the unconscious rather than fearing it. The Jungian unconscious is
conceptually far superior to the ego: it is the *source* of meaning,
feeling and the possibility of finding value in human life. There is a
lesser aspect to the unconscious formed (like Freud's) upon the lines
of Oedipal repression via the person's own family relationships. Jung
calls this the 'personal unconscious' and it does not detract from the
enormous positive potential of the unconscious proper. So what does
it mean to say that the unconscious is a source of healing and value in
human life? How could this possibly work?

In the first place, the unconscious contains inherited potential
structures called archetypes. As a result, Jung's unconscious is collective because all people inherit more or less the same archetypes as
basic substances. I have referred to archetypes very carefully as
'potential structures' and 'substances', because there is a common
misconception that Jung's archetypes are inherited images. This is not
true. An archetype is an inborn *potential* for a certain sort of image.
What the actual mental image will look like will not only depend
upon the collective unconscious. Archetypal images also reflect the
conscious experiences of the person as a subject in history, culture and
time.

If we take an analogy with a vase, the general idea of a vase as a
container may be inherited. Yet when a vase appears in a dream, its
style, material, and specific contents will owe most to the dreamer's
historical and actual encounters with vases and what fantasies they
may arouse. Such archetype-inflected mental images are known as

archetypal images: they are the fusion of the shaping power of the archetype with the life experience and preoccupations of the ego.

Unfortunately for the crucial conceptual distinction between archetype and archetypal image, Jung quite often wrote as if he were collapsing the two. He is partially responsible for this general misunderstanding of his theory. This aspect of Jung's writing style goes back to the structural importance of myth in his theory and is a problem when dealing with his work on women.

However, when called upon to define archetypes, he was unequivocal: potential structures are inherited, images are not. He makes a useful and intriguingly scientific analogy with crystals in saturated solutions. Of the archetype, he says: 'Its form . . . might perhaps be compared to the axial system of a crystal . . . although it has no material existence of its own.'[6] The archetype as such, as a potential structure, contains numerous possibilities within itself. Jung refers to such individual archetypes as the feminine in man (the anima), the masculine in woman (the animus), the mother, the wise old man/woman, the trickster and rebirth. They are all plural and androgynous, meaning that they can have many shapes and can be equally in feminine or in masculine. Archetypes are bipolar in that they contain their own opposites, so that the mother archetype can be manifested as a caring female form, yet will also be able to produce a devouring monster mother image: it all depends what the ego needs at the time.

As well as encompassing both genders, archetypes can represent themselves as good or evil, animal or human, divine or demonic, high or low. Their bipolar nature reflects Jung's intuition that the tension of opposites underpins the psyche. He borrowed the Greek term, *enantiodromia*, to signify his view that everything eventually turns into its own opposite. If that is so, then archetypes must be continually re-imaging, or imagining the subjectivity of the conscious ego.

The process by which archetypes intervene in and educate the ego is known as individuation. The unconscious has a compensatory relationship to the ego, which gives Jung's psyche its intrinsically self-healing nature. If the ego is damaged by traumatic events, or has evolved in too fragile a manner, then the unconscious will compensate and provide positive energies. Conversely, an over-strong ego, too confident in its limited powers, will find itself facing tremendous and perhaps horrifying opposition from below. To Jung, psychic health means forming ever-closer bonds with the unconscious as the superior and better guide.

Individuation is not only a matter for neurotics. The process is teleological, signifying that it is goal oriented, it has somewhere to go. Everyone needs to individuate. Jung believed that the first part of life required the building-up of ego strengths. In the second half of life the ego needs to develop an ever-deeper relationship with the mythical, numinous forces of the unconscious in order to make it a journey of meaning and value.

The collective unconscious actively promotes individuation as the ongoing dialogue between itself and the ego. Through the activity of archetypes the unconscious will compensate for ego one-sidedness. It structures its creative energies as opposite and overpowering if that is what is required to counteract the ego inflating itself as all sufficient and all knowing. At such moments, when the ego gets out of balance, individuation may require the aid of analysis.

If a person is experiencing the unconscious as particularly threatening, then Jung regarded the immediate problem as one of persona and shadow. The ego is the centre of consciousness, but it is inadequate and incomplete without developing an intimacy with the mythical unconscious. In everyday life in the world, the ego presents itself through the mask of the persona. The persona is a kind of surface 'personality', created to deal with the world in the form of strangers. It is the psychological 'face' shown in one's professional job, and perhaps even to the immediate family if the unconscious has been pushed (unhealthily) out of relationships.

Over-reliance upon the conscious persona provokes a dynamically opposite reaction from the unconscious in the form of the shadow. The shadow is literally the image of the thing the person has no wish to be. All the ideals, qualities, habits that the ego represses or denies go into the make-up of the shadow, which then manifests itself in dreams and unconscious symptoms. It is often pictorially represented as an evil person of the same sex. The more virtuous people believe themselves, the blacker their shadow. It can even take on a demonic guise.

Analysis, by definition, aims to facilitate individuation as the psyche's self-healing, compensatory mechanism. An early task is to help the patient come to terms with the shadow, usually by recognizing and 'owning' some of the darker qualities 'he' displays. Of course, that does not mean that a scrupulous person with a shadow 'criminal' in her dreams should take up a new career as a thief! Rather, instead of being terrorized by the criminal in dreams, she should accept the fact that she does, in fact, have criminal desires. It will then be possible to accept such fantasies and not become overwhelmed by them. Once the ego stops being so one-sided in claiming for itself all whiteness and virtue, the shadow is drained of its terrifying powers and the psychic ground is cleared for less horrific archetypal figures.

After the kind of horror movie or Gothic encounter with the shadow, the individuating being (in analysis or not) typically moves into romance: the archetypal figure of the other gender emerges. Jung names these figures as the anima, a male's archetypal feminine, and the animus, the corresponding masculine figure in the psyche of a woman. I am going to examine these creatures further in the final section of this chapter on Jung, gender and women, because the texture of his writing on the anima, in particular, is highly pertinent to a feminist re-vision.

Suffice to say here that Jung tended to collapse gender identity into bodily sex. He believed that a body shape bestowed a straightforward gender identity on women and men. Such an attitude leads to essentialist views of innate femininity or masculinity.

However, this bodily essentialism is tempered significantly by the implications of the theory of anima and animus (not sufficiently pursued by Jung), and by his explorations of the cultural shaping of the feminine in literature and religion. To put it at its most basic, the compensatory drive of the Jungian unconscious does not allow him to be as essentialist as he seems to wish.

What will be fruitful for later discussions of Jung and feminism is the religious nature of the Jungian unconscious. I pointed out earlier that Jung's theorizing of mythologies characterizes them as narratives of the unconscious acting in specific cultures. A myth, to Jung, is a story of a human subject because it enacts the ego's subjection to the greater, more meaningful and archetypal energies of the unconscious. In such stories the unconscious can appear as infused with divine power or as personified into divinities such as in the Greek and Roman myths.

The Jungian unconscious is fundamentally religious for two related reasons: one is that religious myths are a necessary narrative resource for the unknowable and uncontrollable dimensions of the unconscious as well as the fact that the unconscious is the ego's source and future fate (in individuation). In a sense that is hardly metaphorical; Jung's archetypes *are* gods and goddesses because they are the most active powers in the formation of the human subject who constantly affect her encounters with the outer world. Like gods (or goddesses), archetypes *make* the person by representing themselves in the person's life (through mental images).

The second reason for Jung's unconscious as religious goes back to his most basic proposition: that all reality is psychic. Therefore, when anyone has a religious experience of any kind, he or she is in the first place encountering numinous activity in the psyche. Jung would define this as meeting the creative powers of the archetype. What prevents this psychological definition of religious feeling from collapsing into a traditional religion is that Jung's religious unconscious does not require an external God or gods. Nor does it deny them.

Religious experience in Jungian ideas (in total contrast to Freudian theory – see next section) is genuine and authentic. Yet its authenticity is that of the archetype, not of somehow 'proving' an official religious doctrine. The sense of the divine is always archetypal, of the collective unconscious. It may be a manifestation of an exterior and transcendent god working through the unconscious (because all reality is psychic), or it may merely be the unconscious representing itself. There is no way to tell the difference.

A believer in a transcendent religion such as Christianity can accept Jungian theory, but so also can the atheist. God or gods may or may not be deemed to function within the theory. This aspect of Jung's work demonstrates one reason for his potency in contemporary culture. He enables a rediscovery of religious authenticity without the need to subscribe to a traditional doctrine.

As the goal of individuation, Jung placed a supreme, potentially governing archetype he called the 'self'. It is very important to stress here that, for Jung, the word 'self' has a totally different meaning from the conventional 'personality'. The Jungian self is the *not known*. It is the numinous, potential, unconscious nature of every person. Knowledge of the self, in its peculiar Jungian sense, is the purpose of individuation. The self is paradoxically defined as the totality of all a person's psychic processes, and is simultaneously the archetype of wholeness and meaning, necessarily religious in nature. The paradox becomes easier to live with if the self is regarded as the deepest centring principle of the psyche.

Individuation's goal is self-realization, not in the conventional sense of the self being identified with the ego, but by making the unconscious archetype of the self the core of one's being. The ego's most fulfilling role is to be the realized self's satellite, orbiting around it as inferior, and yet energized by its starlike powers.

Living with the numinous unconscious at the centre of being through establishing a profound relationship to the self is to live a life of religious feeling. Jung believed that a person should live within a religious myth as a way of comprehending and permitting the expansion of the unconscious as superior and meaningful. This is what he meant by his personal myth in the sense of a *belief* and is how it becomes indivisible from his psychology. Personal myth is necessarily religious; it is not necessarily metaphysical in the sense of entailing an exterior divinity.

What Jung seems to have wanted is for his 'theory' to be the offspring of both his conscious and unconscious creative powers. 'Myth' is the cultural form he uses to express this. Therefore, it is unsurprising that Jung's self is often known as the god-image in the psyche, or even that Jung wrote of Jesus Christ as providing a self-image for Christians. Since archetypes are androgynous and plural, the association of Christ with the self entails a radical reading of Christian tradition with Christ as potentially female and even demonic. The possibilities of such a revisionary attitude to religion and gender will be explored in subsequent chapters.

Some of the implications of Jung's unconscious can be summarized in his phrase 'the objective psyche', or, in today's terms, 'the autonomous psyche'. Consequently, dreams are not disguised wishes to be decoded, as in Freudian theory, but are themselves creative texts to be respected as meaningful.

Jung believed that dreams are direct communications from the unconscious.[7] They are the psyche speaking to the ego in the unconscious's own language. The ego should attend to the matter of the dream and not try to reduce it to words or concepts. So-called rational theorizing is the ego's way of illegitimately appropriating the power of the dream by translating it into its own terms.

Of course, it is not possible wholly to remove 'theory' or 'interpretation' from dream analysis, because even the principle of respecting the authenticity of the dream is itself a theoretical notion. Nevertheless, for Jungians any deciphering must be in the service of getting to know the creative unconscious, not shoring up the ego.

In order to get closer to unconscious fantasy, Jung used a therapeutic technique, which he called 'active imagination'. The person would be asked to meditate upon an image from her dream or from an external cultural (often mythical) text. Out of the initial image creative fantasies would flow. The aim was to release conscious controls in the mind to allow unconscious material to reach the surface. In active imagination, the fantasies appear to be spontaneous because the 'other', the unconscious, is directing them.

Almost in a reverse direction was the Jungian method called 'amplification'. Analysts and patients were encouraged to draw parallels between dream stories and cultural mythologies. Amplification means linking individual psychic events to mythology, fairy tales or religious narratives. It is a way of making a dream less wholly *personal*, so less ego oriented. However, it could result in underemphasizing the particular historical situation of the dreamer.

Also important in individuation is what Jung named the 'transcendent function'. This is the aspect of the psyche that mediates between opposites, particularly where conflicts and difficulties may be occurring. Usually the transcendent function works by forming symbols resonant enough to hold the tension of opposing forces. Such symbols are often numinous or explicitly religious. Jung believed that many of the images he saw in alchemy texts were examples of the transcendent function.

Popularly held to be a method of conning the gullible by falsely claiming to turn lead into gold, alchemy was a philosophy taken seriously by many early scientists as well as theologians. Jung believed that alchemists were primarily practising individuation by projecting their unconscious creativity onto their complex chemical experiments. Their activities were an early form of Jungian analysis. The quest for gold was the material shadow of the true gold or philosopher's stone, the divine powers of the self.

Such a view of alchemy provides a clue to Jung's aims in extending his ideas of psychic reality to social and material existence. In later works he produced the notion of synchronicity to describe those significant coincidences in human life where events are meaningfully, but not causally, connected. Synchronicity occurs when outer and inner reality meet, such as when an inner need is suddenly met by a complete stranger.

Lastly, I want to consider the Jungian body. The stress on spirit, religion and the autonomous supremacy of the Jungian unconscious could give the impression that Jung discounts the role of the body. This is far from the truth. For Jung, the body is both a phenomenon with its own needs and indissolubly bonded to the psyche. Archetypes are psychosomatic, meaning that they are also of the body. Having deep roots in the body in the form of instincts, archetypes extend also 'up' into spirit in another bipolar dimension. Body is, therefore, connected to spirit through archetypes. In effect, archetypes make the body psychological by representing it through archetypal images.

Contrariwise, the body expresses the physical aspect of the psyche: bodily experiences and needs can reflect psychological experiences and needs. This is what is meant by the Jungian body being a 'subtle body', experienced as psychological and archetypal. Sexuality, as a particular kind of bodily instinct and experience, can be archetypal as well as physical. In turn, this leads to Jung's valuable contention (for feminism) that sexuality can be connected to religious experience (through the archetypes in spiritual mode). Therefore sexuality should not be regarded as intrinsically 'other' to the divine.

Now that we have looked at Jung's key ideas, it is important for feminism to consider his major differences with Freudian psychoanalysis.

Differences with Freudian psychoanalysis

Conceptual disputes

Freud and Jung fell out, at least in part, because they could not agree about the nature of psychic energy. To Freud, the dynamics of the psyche were grounded in sexuality. His concept of the libido as a foundational sexual drive was his signature upon this principle. Jung rejected the idea of the libido in the predominately sexual sense. He preferred the more neutral term 'energy', which could be manifested as sexuality, or equally, not.

An even more significant disagreement concerns the characterization of the unconscious. Freudian psychoanalysis regards the unconscious as structured into the nature of the human subject through sexual repression. The Oedipus complex is the principal means of such repression. As the boy child discovers that exclusive sexual bonding with the mother is forcibly discontinued by the powerful role of the father, the passions thereby aroused, and the subsequent repression of forbidden desires, structures the Freudian unconscious.

Only fear of castration at the hands of the terrifying father interrupts the boy's incestuous passion. His individual self, his gender and his repressed sexual unconscious simultaneously come into being. The girl child has a more perilous passage to femininity. She has to recognize that she has already been castrated. Turning in disappointment from the parent like herself, the mother, she shifts her love object to the father. Only by this tortuous move can she achieve what Freud regarded as natural, heterosexual orientation.

Since the Oedipus complex is so central to this developmental narrative, traces of its traumas frequently surface in neuroses. Dream analysis in classic Freudian practice means decoding the disguised sexual wishes buried in these texts of the unconscious.

As is apparent from this brief summary, Jungian theory departs from Freud not only on the nature of the unconscious, but also on the Oedipus complex and dreams. To take Oedipality first of all, Jung concluded that Oedipal agonies were a useful way of understanding the structure of the personal unconscious in the development of a child. The Oedipus complex did exist, but was significant only for some, not all, patients. Far from being central to his notion of the unconscious, the Oedipus complex is marginal compared to the overwhelming influence of inherited factors in the collective unconscious of archetypes.

The resulting principle in Jungian theory is the need to respond positively to the unconscious. Dreams must be respected for what they have to impart of the unconscious in itself. Very emphatically, they must not be automatically referred to Oedipal stories of the subject: they are messages from a superior 'other'. To try to decode or translate dreams is to damage their authenticity as the spontaneous products of archetypes. In a very real sense, to do so would be to betray the dreamer because her true 'self' lies in the unconscious, never in the ego.

This very different approach to the unconscious and dreams accounts for further disputes with Freudian psychoanalysis over symbols and religious experience. Jung believed that Freud read dream symbols merely as signs or as symptoms of unconscious repression. Such a treatment of dream symbols is a necessary accompaniment to the Freudian practice of decoding dreams, often in ways that lead back to the Oedipal make-up of the person.

To Jung, a symbol was a means of unconscious archetypal representation. Although Jung (like Freud) conceded that many dreams did reflect ego trivialities, powerful symbols in dreams signified the activity of a collective archetype. Symbols as archetypal images refer to the ungraspable world of unconscious creativity. They must be read as pointing to the unknowable and therefore to the un-theorizable. Symbols also point forwards, to a person's future development in growing intimacies with unconscious forces, not back to the archaeology of the Oedipal child.

Equally, a Jungian symbol may be so powerful in impact that it carries a sense of the sacred. Whereas Freud regarded religious experience as a mystification of the fundamental truths of psychic sexuality, Jung held religious feeling to be authentic expressions of the collective psyche. This is what he meant in describing the psyche as essentially religious. His psychology does not require belief in an exterior transcendent god, although it does not exclude it.

Since sexuality can also be archetypal, can be connected to the numinous, it is possible for Jungian ideas to go some way with Freudian practice and see a religious dream image as *additionally* a representation of a sexual issue. It will be equally likely in a Jungian analysis for a sexual image in a dream to be explored for its divine connotations. This is because sexuality is part of the continuum of unconscious communication that includes the spirit – Freud did not approve.

Such a flexibility in Jungian practice stems directly from his integration of his notion of the collective unconscious as a potent, superior, 'other'. A similar flexibility can be seen in Jung's lesser-known version of the early developmental story of the child. Jung did not ignore childhood development, despite disagreeing with Freud over the centrality of Oedipal configurations. He was one of the early thinkers to stress the pre-Oedipal, mother–baby bond.

The mother is the bearer of the child's first images of the unconscious. Just as the bodily mother has given birth to the body of the child who is not yet psychically a separate person, so the active unconscious starts the process of giving birth to the child as an individual human subject. In order to accomplish this major task, the child's nascent unconscious will use the child's psychic bonding to the mother.

For Jung, the Oedipus complex will assist the development of the child by working as a *partner* with the proactive unconscious. In his reassessment of his relation to Freudian theory in the revised edition of *Two Essays on Analytical Psychology* (significantly after Freud's death),[8] Jung deliberately conceded that Freudian Oedipality could have a defining role for some patients. However, he retained his earlier notion that incest fantasies could also be read *metaphorically* as symbols for something not exclusively or not predominantly sexual.

Describing conceptual differences with Freudian theory has necessarily suggested variations in clinical application. Analysis with Jungian- or Freudian-trained therapists will *feel* different as well as *be* theoretically different. I want to finish this section with a word about analysis and the current field of Jungian practice.

Differences in analysis and the emergence of post-Jungian schools

Jungian analysis varies some of the practices of Freud and his successors. Variations include being oriented towards the future direction of the analysand by regarding psychic processes as leading the ego into deeper relationship with the unconscious self. A Jungian analyst may also aim to resist the temptation to decode dreams. He or she may look to the unconscious to form compensatory structures to ego concerns, and often will seek out the religious as inherently healing.

Jung was also the first practitioner to describe the importance of counter-transference in the analytic encounter. Freudian psychoanalysis early developed the concept of transference as crucial to 'the talking cure'. This means that, in working on dreams, feelings and unconscious symptoms, the analyst should function as a screen upon which significant parts of the patient's psyche are projected. By using this unconscious transference, Freud hoped to alleviate some of the patient's pain. Counter-transference goes one stage further in bringing an awareness of the analyst's own projections into the arena: the ways in which her or his psyche unconsciously conceives the patient. In contemporary practice both Jungian and Freudian analysts take counter-transference seriously, and this is not the only point where the psychologies have developed analytic parallels.

Now I will look briefly at the three acknowledged schools of post-Jungian analysis, one of which is more attuned to the Freudian legacy.

Andrew Samuels's book *Jung and the Post-Jungians*[9] has become the standard work in setting out the post-Jungian schools. These consist of three: the 'classical', those analysts who aim to follow Jung's own therapeutic practice most closely, the 'archetypal', formulated in the USA, and the 'developmental'. This last is the most co-herent with post-Freudian theorizing, particularly in the role of the pre-Oedipal mother.

Like the developmental school, the archetypal school, calling itself archetypal psychology, moves away from the notion of fidelity both to Jung's *Collected Works* and to his known clinical methods. Archetypal psychologists look to new avenues of theory in a conscious alignment with poststructuralism. Chapter 4 will evaluate the contribution of archetypal psychology to a feminist revision of Jung. This chapter needs to turn to Jung's own views of women and gender, which have contributed largely to what I will call 'traditional Jungian feminism', the subject of chapter 3.

Jung on women and gender

The grand theory and the personal myth on women

My use of the term 'feminine' in this book is non-essentialist. It refers to the cultural construction of feminine characteristics as 'other' as historically conditioned, and not necessarily located in those with female bodies. This needs to be restated in the context of Jung's use of the word 'feminine', which frequently collapses bodily sex into psychic gender. Such a move places Jung as an essentialist on gender, although key areas of his psychology combat such a straightforward definition.

As in all of Jung's concepts, his pronouncements on women and gender need to be seen in relation to the writings structured upon the premises of grand theory and personal myth. Both the ambitions of the grand theory and the assertions of the value of fantasy in the personal myth have to make a vital concession about the non-objectivity of his *Collective Works* on women: 'most of what men say about . . . the emotional life of women is derived from their own anima projections and distorted accordingly.'[10]

The grand theory that makes all reality fundamentally psychic backs up Jung's description of how his knowledge of women is crucially coloured by his own unconscious archetype of the feminine, the anima. Men, therefore, cannot be objective about women in a scientific non-personal sense. This pleasing admission from the point of view of feminism is somewhat marred by the contrasting language in which Jung makes the reciprocal point: women cannot be objective about men because their unconscious masculine archetype will similarly intervene: 'the astonishing assumptions and fantasies that women make about men come from the activity of the animus, who produces an inexhaustible supply of illogical arguments and false explanations.'[11]

Before accusing Jung simply of sexist essentialism, we need to remember that unconscious archetypes are all androgynous and plural. If Jung collapses gender into bodily sex, which his writings here (as often) seem to do, then readers have his own word for it that it may be his unconscious fantasies at work (anima distortions). Body cannot simply equal psychological gender if the psyche is itself gender fluid. Jung cannot be a simple essentialist in believing that a female body equals an innate (or even a deep-down innate after cultural distortions are eradicated) femininity of the mind.

Androgynous archetypes are multiple and have a compensatory role to ego experiences. The mind can never be of one fixed gender and archetypes will *work with* and produce *contrasting notions* of the femininity and masculinity witnessed in material culture. There cannot be an innate and stable gender identity, because once such a state was realized then one prime method of the archetypes in weaning the ego onto the better nourishment of the unknowable, unfixable unconscious would cease. Gender *has* to be a process. So how is Jung able to write so often as if he is collapsing gender identity into bodily sex?

Jung's dismissive language of the animus and the intellectual capacities of women cannot be attributed solely to the eruption of cultural prejudice into grand theory. In another oppositional pair of concepts, Eros and Logos, Jung comes closest to providing a theoretical framework for his essentialist language.

Eros and Logos are archetypal principles of mental functioning. Eros denotes connective qualities of feeling and relationship, while Logos covers rationality, spirit and intellect. No surprises lurk in the genders usually bestowed on these dispositions: Eros is feminine and Logos masculine. Nevertheless, these principles do not represent a straightforward essentialism: Eros and Logos exist within a person of either bodily sex.

However, whereas contemporary analytic practice regards these qualities as equally available to both genders,[12] Jung's language on Eros and Logos betrays his own drive towards essentialist assumptions about women. Believing that males are likely to be dominated by Logos and females by Eros, he wrote: 'In women, on the other hand, Eros is an expression of their true nature, while their Logos is often only a regrettable accident.'[13] What is the justification for this assertion that the true nature of women is the function of relationship and that their rational thinking is somehow a mistake? Given the compensating and androgynous nature of the archetypal unconscious, such an opinion seems to be a prime example of a misogynist distortion. Jung's underlying psychology remains coherent if such a crude essentialism is discarded. Before we do so, it is worth remembering the distinctive texture of Jung's writing as grand theory and personal myth.

The dual approach to the writing of theory means writing out of the rational ego *and* the irrational fantasizing other in the unconscious. Seeing grand theory as entwined with personal myth reveals unsustainable cultural prejudices within Jungian writing as the distorting artistry of Jung's own anima. What I mean by this is that the qualities of Eros that Jung airily and dismissively applies to women are most immediately *psychically experienced* by him as the property of his own anima.

In *Memories, Dreams, Reflections* we are shown Jung's anima as devious, erotic, artful and connective. Jung makes assumptions about the feminine from the evidence of his own anima, and uses them to colour and even at times to take over his thinking about women's psychology. Here we see personal myth very precisely at work in the collapsing of 'anima' into 'women'. It is an aspect of his myth that finds a very forceful realization in his writings. This 'women-into-animas' drive cannot be wholly separated from his grand theory because Jung's anima is, in his own conceptual terms, the most immediately 'real' form of the feminine available to him. After all, if all reality and mental experience is in the first place psychic, then his own archetypal psyche is most intimate to his writing consciousness. It is necessary to look further at his language of anima and animus.

Animus, anima and women as animas

Animus and anima are archetypes of the other gender in a person's unconscious. In producing archetypal images of the opposite sex, they work by using a different anatomy as a metaphor for the otherness of the unconscious. Of course, as archetypes they are plural even in gender, so they are not restricted to manifesting themselves as one bodily image or in human form. For example, both can represent themselves equally well in animal or divine images.

Unfortunately, Jung's language of these terms seems to be energized by his personal investments in these archetypal configurations: he very much associates them with Eros and Logos potentialities. Where an anima typically has 'moods', the animus will have 'opinions'. In fact, linking the anima to Eros characteristics (the way he describes his own anima) is the only theoretical way he has of defining masculine consciousness as primarily Logos dominated. Resting upon the core Jungian principle of the tension of opposites, making the anima 'Erotic' in a male's unconscious, means that culturally valued Logos talents of rational argument can reside in the masculine conscious mind. Male intellect is dominated by rationality and discrimination, feminine thinking by 'diffusion' and a talent for relating, thanks to Logos and Eros as opposites.

Furthermore, the parallel taking of women's Logos powers into the usually superior unconscious by hooking them to the animus is far from empowering for women. The animus tendency to produce 'opinions' is unkindly expanded as a rigid 'intellectuality', 'the worst enemy of woman' and even provoking a 'demonic passion that exasperates and disgusts men'.[14] Women who cultivate their animus by taking up 'masculine' professions are liable to a masculinization resulting in frigidity or sexual aggression or homosexuality. Such women are going against their 'feminine nature'.[15]

No one, I hope, could take such gender hysteria seriously. Indeed, it is possible to situate such misogynist comments by Jung as a hysteria in the writings. The underlying and often fruitful tension between grand theory and personal myth here produces an *animated* incoherence at the point of gender. It is hysteria because the misogynist essentialism of these remarks cannot be validated through the core principles' archetypal unconscious. Gender bias against the feminine does not work with either the androgyny or the unknowability of the unconscious.

In particular, there can be no theoretical justification for suggesting the permanent assignment of Logos to male consciousness, Eros to women. Traditional cultures may do so in the historical influences upon gender development (not denied in Jungian theory owing to the structuring of archetypal images as also cultural), but the Jungian unconscious is a nexus of superior creative powers, not culturally derived. The unconscious should compensate for and combat cultural stereotyping.

Nor can Eros and Logos be stamped into position owing to bodily sex, again because the Jungian unconscious works against bodily essentialism. Even Jung's apparent warning to women against careers is not borne out by his practice of encouraging female 'Jungians' to work under his general direction.

Interestingly, he does, at one point, describe the animus rather as if it was a cultural absorption of patriarchy in comparing its operation to 'an assembly of fathers or dignitaries' whose portentous opinions prove just to be sayings half-remembered from childhood.[16]

It is worth recalling chapter 1's account of the transition of women from the role of mediums to animas in Jung's career. Now the slippage of woman-as-medium, then sliding inexorably into the anima, is apparent in the writing of the personal myth. If the historical root of the anima in Jung's life is the medium woman, then it is possible to trace the evolution of the personal myth from a therapeutic practice that combined medical research with occult spiritualism in a crucial gender politics.

Jungian psychology medicalizes (and thereby masculinizes in the male-dominated profession of the period) spiritualist practice. Prior to Jung's work Spiritualism was characterized in the nineteenth century by women mediums working outside official or conventional structures. Jung takes over the medium position for himself in the way he contacted his anima. His version of the medium then became the basic stance from which he composed his personal myth and thereby the masculine subject position within it. The personal myth becomes embedded in the grand theory so that some of Jung's subsequent adherents are enabled to solidify Jung's more *animated* pronouncements on women and gender prescriptions.

Having looked at the personal myth dimension on women and gender, what about the role of grand theory in which culture as a whole is encompassed by Jungian psychology?

Jung, the cultural critic of the feminine

Despite Jung's habitual collapse of gender into bodily sex, he did not reliably do so when such a move could have been helpful for female liberation. In fact, it is as a critic of culture that Jung tends to detach 'feminine nature' from biological women. A good example is his persistent criticism of Christian teaching for ignoring the gender plurality of the divine (because of the androgyny of archetypes), which must encompass a feminine element as well. His solution is not women priests (material and symbolic power for women). He prefers a cultural revaluation of femininity, especially in the form available to men through their unconscious animas.

Nevertheless, an onslaught upon such Christian repression of the 'other' does involve him in instancing witch hunts against women as a concrete form of a disastrous theological error.[17] In addition, his extensive theorizing of multiplicity in the divine and the sacred aspects of sexuality is potentially valuable to feminist approaches. Such initiatives paved the way for later Jungians to challenge male-dominated religion in the cause of feminism.

Usefully, Jung saw that cultural repression of the feminine had occurred over centuries, and he defined it as neurotic. Repressing the feminine is a source of psychic and cultural sickness. Jung's misogyny is suggestively clustered around his personal myth in the form of damaging language. Perhaps it penetrates the cultural dimensions of his writing in the way in which the necessary promotion of the feminine in culture becomes divided from the social advancement of women.

When essentialist, the personal myth colours the portrayal of women negatively; when non-essentialist about the feminine in culture, it seems to be designed in the interests of the masculine subject. What can this chapter finally suggest about Jung for feminist revision?

Jung for feminism?

A defining feature of Jung's treatment of gender is his placing of the feminine at the centre of his psychology while at the same time displacing women as social, material and historical beings. As a theorist of the feminine in culture, Jung provides a useful starting point, as long as the gender politics and the historical location of his authoritative texts are scrutinized.

In particular, the drive to subordinate women in anima garb needs a historical challenge in order to clarify a masculine bias in the writings. However, a consideration of Jung as a producer of grand theory entwined and mutually upheld by personal myth enables his anima texts to be described as a theory of 'Woman', firmly and *overtly* rooted in masculine fantasy. Anima theory can be situated *within* Jung's conceptions as quite distinct from the historical experience of women and the feminine.

Ultimately, the core theory of the collective unconscious as a superior, creative, meaning-producing function within all human subjects will prove important for feminist argument. Such a resource is not negated by the necessary criticism of the gender fantasies of the personal myth. Indeed, what this chapter has tried to show is that Jung's psychology of grand theory and personal myth *by its very nature* makes room for a feminist criticism that can work with Jungian ideas in both a critical and a positive spirit.

What will prove most significant about Jung is his privileging of the voice of the other, the unconscious represented through fantasy and myth, in the composition of theory. The next chapter will describe the development of traditional Jungian feminism in which Jung is largely responded to as a producer of grand theory. An alternative feminist approach to Jung will be suggested through new research later in this volume. This seeks a feminism that does not position itself in a hierarchy subordinate to a grand theory, which works with him as also a writer of a personal myth.

Concluding summary

Jung's description of his psychology is distinctive because it structures within the theory a sense of fantasy and myth. I describe this as Jung writing in the form of personal myth entwined with grand theory. The starting point for understanding Jung's ideas is that all reality is fundamentally psychic and the unconscious is primarily a function of superior creative powers called archetypes.

Jungian psychology differs from Freudian psychoanalysis theoretically in the definition of the unconscious, in sexuality and in the role of religion. It differs therapeutically in work on dreams, symbols and the prospective direction of analysis. A crucial aspect of Jung on the feminine is that he tends to collapse gender into bodily sex. Yet he cannot be described straightforwardly as a gender essentialist owing to the priority given to plurality and androgyny in the unconscious. Despite masculine bias in the writings, positive potentials for a number of feminist approaches exist. An example would be Jung's criticism of the persistent neglect of the feminine in culture.

FURTHER READING

http://cgjungpage.org/
The best Jungian web site with help for beginners, seminars, book reviews, articles and sophisticated links.

Fordham, Frieda, *An Introduction to Jung's Psychology* (Harmondsworth: Penguin, 1953).

A clear introduction to the key concepts with an intriguing foreword by Jung suggesting the difficulty of extracting 'theory' in the conventional sense from his works.

Jacobi, Jolande, *The Psychology of C. G. Jung: An Introduction with Illustrations* (London: Kegan, Paul, Trench, Trubner, 1942).
An early attempt to get to the heart of Jung's ideas by one who knew him. His foreword similarly refers to the difficulty of considering his works as conventional theory. Useful, but too detailed for the beginner.

Jung, C. G., *Modern Man in Search of a Soul* (London: Kegan, Paul, Trench, Trubner, 1933).
An early collection of Jung's essays in English containing accessible material on dreams, therapy, Freud and literature.

Jung, C. G., *Aspects of the Feminine* (Princeton: Princeton University Press, 1982; Ark Paperbacks; London: Routledge, 1982).
A representative selection of Jung's writings on women and the feminine from the *Collected Works*. Contains the important examples of *animated* language.

Samuels, Andrew, *Jung and the Post-Jungians* (London: Routledge, 1985).
The standard work on Jung's psychology in the context of developments by Post-Jungian analysts. Outlines the three post-Jungian schools. Indispensable for the serious student of Jung.

Samuels, Andrew, Shorter, Bani and Plaut, Fred, *A Critical Dictionary of Jungian Analysis* (London: Routledge, 1986).
Details Jung's ideas and many subsequent developments of them. A valuable reference work for those who have mastered the basics.

Storr, Anthony, *Jung* (Fontana Modern Masters; London: HarperCollins, 1973).
A witty introduction to Jung. Will whet the appetite.

3

The Goddess and the Feminine Principle

> We find that myths are not just delightful yet idle stories of gods and goddesses, heroes or demons from a forgotten time; they speak of living psychological material and art as a repository of truths appropriate to an individual's inner life, as well as to the life of the community.
>
> (Nancy Qualls-Corbett, *The Sacred Prostitute: Eternal Aspect of the Feminine*, 1988)

This chapter introduces what is known as 'Jungian feminism'. I will identify it as 'traditional Jungian feminism' to distinguish it from the different possibilities for more plural 'Jungian feminisms' suggested in later chapters. Traditional Jungian feminism takes a confident, grand-theory attitude to Jung. This means that it seeks a stable conception of gender and the feminine from Jung's own attempts at a comprehensive theory of psyche and of culture. The work of the key authors in Jungian feminism is explored in this context.

Jungian feminism works outward from Jung's writings via the techniques of extension, revision and the Jungian notion of amplification. Authors extend and revise the theories of animus and anima in response to a variety of new social conditions. Under amplification, Jung's problematic linking of Eros with 'the feminine' is developed. A response by one group of theorists is to define 'the feminine' as a metaphysical principle of gender available to both sexes and disastrously suppressed in Western culture.

A remarkable amplification of Jung's feminine within the numinous (in archetypes) is the rejection of masculine-dominated monotheistic culture in favour of a 'return' to the divine as a great mother. 'She' infuses and makes sacred the natural world. She is the divine within or immanent in the world, not apart and transcendent of it.

Here Jungian feminism becomes a most ambitious feminist myth of history, culture, religion, aesthetics and psyche.

The chapter concludes with an evaluation of the achievements of Jungian feminism (grand theory). It shows the attraction of the goddess myths for a psychological feminism, extending beyond the realms of theology. Then I suggest alternative, more postmodern ways of construing the preoccupation with 'goddesses'. Rather than an objective theory, it is possible to see 'Jungian goddess feminism' as a kind of experiment in the imagination. Goddess feminism may offer fictions of the self for a postmodern era.

Introducing grand theory and Jungian feminism

In the previous chapter I defined a dual impulse within Jungian psychology. The tendency to describe an authoritative all-embracing theory of psyche and culture I named 'grand theory', while the urge to limit such claims in the face of the unknowability of the unconscious in purely rational terms was called 'personal myth'. The notion of 'personal myth' follows Jung's own autobiographical account of the generation of his key ideas.

Work after Jung on gender and the feminine can be most usefully viewed as linked to these two directions in his thought. In the first place, this is because what might be loosely termed Jungian feminism (to indicate a specific, critical interest in his treatment of gender) stems not only from Jungian psychology as a therapeutic practice, but also from his attempt to construct a theory. Additionally, in picking up Jung's dual sense of the activity of theorizing, Jungian feminism simultaneously engages with wider concerns of feminism. Such issues range from conservative positions on innate 'feminine nature' to the consideration of gender as contextual and contested within specific cultural settings.

This chapter will look at gender and the feminine after Jung in terms of his desire for a grand theory of psyche and culture. The writers considered here are looking to Jung to provide material for a workable, authoritative theory of gender. Such a theory can then be put to use in the service of women and the feminine, however varied the feminism of such writers may be in the political spectrum. What follows from taking the Jungian line of grand theory is the belief that gender is a knowable and stable category. Far more so than their biased founder, some of these Jungians admit that gender is susceptible to social influence.

Three methods are employed in the working outwards from Jung's writings to more comprehensive works on gender and the feminine:

these are extension, revision and amplification. From early in the history of Jungian psychology, women writers in particular were emboldened to take issue with some of Jung's reductive pronounce-ments on women in areas such as the animus (see Linda Fierz-David in the section below). Such authors extend and revise Jung's own treatment of gender.

Amplification needs a little more explanation, since it refers to a method Jung developed in analysis as well as in his writing. In the dis-cussion of dreams, 'amplification' means to make the leap from the psychic image or narrative to the myth, which seems to depict the same archetypal event. Jung used mythology in the generation of grand theory. His own psychic imagery displayed in *Memories, Dreams, Reflections* forms his personal myth. Linking his own arche-typal figures to existing mythologies enabled Jung to structure a psy-chology with universal claims. So amplification is both a therapeutic practice and a structural device for constructing theory.

In terms of both Jung's works and those of the Jungian feminists of this chapter amplification moves in two directions in the writing of theory. Within the autobiography and in analysis, psychic imagery is theorized as archetypal and then linked to a myth. The myth is then written up as a further illustration of the theoretical argument. The psychology moves from psychic image to cultural myth. Jung justifies this direction, since it stems from actual psychic material. Myth then becomes the validation for shifting in the opposite direction: a mythology such as the myth of Persephone and Demeter is defined as containing archetypal material. So images and events corresponding to the Greek story are sought for in the dreams of individual patients and are written up into a psychological text.

Here is the Jungian premise for what I would call 'goddess femi-nism', which is usually designed to empower the insecure female psyche. An early and classic example of goddess feminism is *Woman's Mysteries* by M. Esther Harding.[1] This fascinating work amplifies Jung's identification of the female psyche with Eros, the function of relatedness, and with the signification of the moon in alchemy. *Woman's Mysteries* is a marvellous elaboration of moon goddesses as active authors of the feminine principle. Such femininity is regarded as native to women, but present in the psychology of men in the anima.

What is inspiring about the work is that it bestows upon women a metaphysical 'home' quite outside the restrictions of Christian monotheism. Less helpful is Harding's adherence to Jung's reductive notions of women's consciousness as more diffuse, more suited to relating to other people than to playing an active part in society. This example shows how Jungian feminism characterized by amplification can be radical in its philosophical or theological propositions, yet also conservative in its prescriptions for women's material lives.

The rest of this chapter will explore the implications of grand theory on gender and the feminine after Jung in its three main aspects: the extension and revision of animus and anima theory, the amplification of Eros and the feminine principle and the generation of goddess feminism. In each section, a brief account of the field will be followed by consideration of some key authors.

Extension and revision: animus and anima

Jung wrote little about the animus and most of it was negative. Of course, since he defined the animus as archetypal masculinity in a woman, there is some basis for regarding the animus as best elaborated by women writers. After Jung, the animus and anima have undergone considerable revision and elaboration. Both have been equally considered to possess positive and negative poles. These gender archetypes have been regarded as functioning actively or passively and have been described as changing in function as an individual matures and individuates. From Jung's depiction of the animus as plural and negative, women writers have produced a revised version of an animus capable of being unitary and positive.

Taking a different approach, some feminists have followed up Jung's *animosity* in his animus portrayal and have taken the negative animus to be a women's internalized psychic reception of patriarchy. Recent work has included greater consideration of cultural factors in the construction of archetypal images of both animus and anima.

Also, just as Jung implicitly counters his assimilation of bodily sex and gender by having the anima/mus as figures of gender otherness within, so some Jungian feminists have gone one stage further. They propose disconnecting the anima and animus from one gender by having them equally available to either. Therefore, men and women can participate equally in the archetypal figures of Logos-bearing animus and the Eros-entwined anima.

Key authors

Emma Jung Intriguingly, the wife of Jung[2] is obedient to his general principles while concerned to encourage women to resist their culture's conviction of female inferiority. Women must not languish, but 'lift themselves' to dismiss society's denigration.[3] In complete contrast to that of her husband, Emma Jung's idea of the animus can be very positive and his integration leads to 'active, energetic, brave and forceful women'.[4]

Continuing to define the animus as Logos, spiritual meaning and intellectuality, she proposes that the animus is progressively integrated via a series of stages in the forms of power, deed, word and meaning. By such methods a woman may absorb her Logos faculty and become capable of intellectual as well as Eros-related emotional activity. Emma Jung is clear that a woman needs to take firm control of the animus if she is ever to find her own authoritative self. Otherwise the masculine principle symbolized by the animus may become an inner tyrant. It may be projected onto a powerful man, resulting in an unbearable state of psychic dependence (a suggestive thought!).

While remaining fully within Jungian notions of the animus as the bearer of Logos for a woman, Emma Jung portrays a positive picture of a woman achieving emotional and intellectual independence. At the same time, she draws attention to the problems of women in a society that refuses to support their inner development.

Linda Fierz-David Two moments in Fierz-David's engaging account of women's individuation through initiatory myth point to later critical revisions of the animus. At one stage, she seems to be defining the animus as internalized patriarchy when describing women gaining spiritual instruction (the gift of the animus) through their fathers and other male authority figures. Secondly, she unpicks Jung's tendency to describe animus and anima as beings of fixed gender, contrary to the plural and androgynous processes of the unconscious. For Fierz-David, some of the spiritual potency of the animus takes on a maternal cast: 'The archetypal image of the animus as leader of souls . . . stands visible . . . as the Orphic Silenus, a mother-father and wise teacher, such as never exists in reality.'[5]

Irene Claremont de Castillejo Irene Claremont de Castillejo extends Jung's portrayal of the negative aspects of the animus. Yet her particular focus is to stress that it can be integrated as an energizing ingredient of women's diffuse consciousness. She revises Jung most decisively when she argues that thinking can be a normal woman's leading function without being equated with the animus.

Regarding negative manifestations of the animus as coloured by sociocultural determinants, in *Knowing Woman* (1973), she suggests that the voice of the negative animus is an internalization of male aggression against women.[6] Claremont de Castillejo starts to break with the gender binary in Jung's work of animus in women, anima in men, when she asserts that a woman's 'soul image' is feminine, not the masculine animus. However, in anima terms she is more conservative when she regards women as enabling male individuation by embodying his anima.

Hilde Binswanger Hilde Binswanger's attitude to gender combines the biological and cultural. In a 1963 article she differentiates between two aspects of masculinity in women: the animus consists of a woman's inner images of men, but a woman also has her own masculinity in biological terms.[7] This secondary masculinity extends to her understanding and consciousness linked to Jung's Eros (not Logos as consciousness, as he preferred). Negative versions of the animus are likely to be culturally induced. The goal of therapy is to reconcile a woman's own masculine side with the animus in ways that work towards feminine forms of vigour, action, word and meaning. Binswanger argues cogently that these qualities are called masculine only because men first named them in themselves. 'Could it not be that . . . as women also develop their minds . . . there might develop a specifically masculine and specifically feminine vigor, a masculine and feminine word, masculine and feminine action and masculine and feminine meaning?'[8] Binswanger has managed to preserve a sense of difference between genders while theorizing equal agency and intellectual capability for the feminine. Here, the animus becomes the means of individuating women by dealing psychologically with the power and privilege of the masculine in society.

Ann Ulanov A dedicated writer on Jung and the feminine, Ann Ulanov has produced a series of works, from her very influential *The Feminine in Jungian Psychology and in Christian Theology* (1971)[9] to, amongst her most recent, *Transforming Sexuality: The Archetypal World of Anima and Animus* with Barry Ulanov (1994).[10] She usefully insists that the anima is not to be equated literally with real women.

Faithful to Jungian conceptions of the roles of anima and animus, Ann Ulanov did not comment upon Jung's misogynistic language until an appendix of her 1971 work. By 1994, the Ulanovs also criticize 'Jung's own predilection to typographical reduction', stating: 'it is all but impossible with anima/animus theory to make clean, clear lists of "masculine" and "feminine" qualities, even categorized distinctions so long consecrated in Jungian usage as "Logos" skills for the male and "Eros" for the female.'[11] The extension of Jung's notions of animus and anima is revised towards a more complex notion of gender difference than the easy polarity assumed in Ann Ulanov's earliest writing.

Marion Woodman   Marion Woodman's work is particularly striking in her interest in the body and archetypal manifestations of gender. One aspect of this is her analysis of women with eating disorders. On the animus and anima theory, she takes a traditional line, extending it to argue that animus problems could account for some eating disorders. Books such as *Addiction to Perfection: The Still Unravished Bride* (1982)[12] and *The Owl was a Baker's Daughter: Obesity, Anorexia Nervosa and the Repressed Feminine* (1980)[13] describe the damaging results of fathers projecting their anima onto daughters. Eating disorders in women may occur through animus possession. A woman may be driven by an impossible perfectionism focused through her sense of her body.

Polly Young-Eisendrath   Polly Young-Eisendrath has consistently revised and extended Jung's portrayal of animus and anima in the cause of a feminist and empowering clinical practice. Her revisionary use of cultural myths and stories to attack sexism is an imaginative and influential feature of her work.

Female Authority: Empowering Women through Psychotherapy (1987), written with Florence Wiedemann, proposes a 'comprehensive Jungian psychology of women in which the female self reaches consciousness and power through the integration of the animus complex and reclamation of the authority women project on it'.[14] This is not so much a revision as a reinterpretation of classic Jungian theory of the animus in the cause of female empowerment. The method resembles Emma Jung's innovation of stages of therapeutic animus integration.

Young-Eisendrath and Wiedemann suggest a schematic vision, contacting the animus as the alien other, then as the father-god or patriarch. These stages are followed by the animus as a youth, a hero or a lover, then as the partner within. The woman should finish with the integrated animus revealed in his archetypal 'truth' and androgyny. An earlier work of Young-Eisendrath alone, *Hags and Heroes* (1984), emphatically criticizes Jung's portrayal of women as naturally passive. She describes how he opposes women's sense of competence in the notion of being 'animus-ridden'.[15]

Claire Douglas   An invaluable work on the entire field of Jungian psychology and gender is Claire Douglas's historical analysis *The*

Woman in the Mirror: Analytical Psychology and the Feminine (1990).[16] Her own views reinscribe the animus not as Logos and intellect, but as a mediator of a feeling function for women in imagery as an earth-father, nature spirit, gardener, nurturer or poet. She argues that the terms 'animus' and 'anima' must not be lifted straight from Jung's texts, lest the early twentieth-century gender roles encoded in their descriptions become prescriptive.

Douglas is part of a strongly argued tradition of Jungian women writers in characterizing the negative animus as the voice of patriarchy, damagingly internalized in a woman's psyche. She remains within the orbit of 'grand theory' by retaining conceptions of anima and animus as theories of the inner 'other'. Nevertheless, her work strengthens the valuable tendency to include social and cultural factors in the extending and revising of gender within Jungian psychology.

Amplification: Eros and the feminine principle

Traditional Jungian feminism of the feminine principle addresses two defining characteristics of Jung's writings on gender: the slippage of psychological gender into bodily sex (despite the androgyny of archetypes) and, more profoundly, his binary approach. Jung's descriptions of gender fall, over neatly, into two mutually defining and mutually exclusive modes: the anima collapses into woman, feeling, Eros, relating, the feminine, while the animus stresses thinking, Logos, spirit, creating and, hence, the masculine.

In the previous section of this chapter I have shown how the extension and revision of animus/anima theory have started to loosen the psychological gender binary, not least by the admission of social and cultural factors. However, a mainstream direction in Jungian feminism serves to accentuate the binary approach to gender while allowing for cultural influences in the lives of actual women and men.

These theorists amplify Jung's description of Eros-relatedness into something metaphysical called the 'the feminine principle' while simultaneously detaching it from bodily sex. The feminine principle exists in a dualistic relationship to a 'masculine principle'. Both are available unequally and variously to both human genders. Behind human cultures, histories and religions lie these two metaphysical gendering principles as active, solar, phallic masculinity and passive, receptive, lunar femininity.

> But why speak of masculine and feminine at all if we merely mean traits shared to varying degrees by males and females? . . . We must

stress again that male–female differentiation is neatly ingrained a-priori; it is an archetypally predetermined perception, patterned in the unconscious psyche. Opposition and complementariness of male and female belong among the most basic representations of the experience of dualism. They underlie the polarities of solar and lunar, light and dark, active and passive, spirit and matter, energy and substance, initiative and receptiveness, heaven and earth.[17]

Jung introduced Eros into his work as an archetypal mode of functioning concerned with feeling and relating. He believed that Eros would be the dominant mode of female consciousness, likely to be dormant in men and associated with the unconscious anima. Therefore Eros becomes the psychological feminine, the principle means by which Jung fuses sex and gender, and is amplified by him as lunar consciousness in his alchemy texts.

Later Jungian feminists evade the reductive nature of Jung's identification of sex and gender by claiming that the feminine and masculine principles are purely archetypal and available to both women and men. I would describe this amplification from Jung's work as 'metaphysical' because it takes the feminine and masculine principles as non-material pre-patterning in the unconscious. These 'principles' are deeply affected but not *determined* by social and historical factors because they operate through archetypal images. The feminine and masculine principles are transcendent of culture yet can only *appear* (via archetypal images) as immanent within it.

What drives these Jungian theorists as feminists is the perception that the feminine principle has been disastrously suppressed in culture and in individual psyches by centuries of patriarchal thinking. They therefore write and practise at both a sociocultural and an individual therapeutic level to heal the world of its wounded, angry feminine. Of course, there is a wide variety of feminist consciousness within the Jungian adherents to this feminine principle. A conservative attitude to society can find justification in arguing that the feminine principle of receptiveness and relating means that women are more suited to domestic duties.

Despite the theoretical severing of sex and gender from the archetypal principles, most writers see women as likely to be more attuned to the feminine principle, men to the masculine. On the other hand, embracing the binary approach of the feminine principle does allow for profound critiques of masculine-dominated corporate capitalist existence on a social level. It permits attacks upon the limitations of Christianity as over-masculine and predatory upon a nature defined as feminine. The further amplification of the feminine principle into 'goddess feminism' will be the subject of the next section.

Key authors

M. Esther Harding *Woman's Mysteries* (1935) is not Esther Harding's only work on Jungian thinking on gender, but it remains her most influential. Continuing Jung's gender dichotomy of Eros/ Logos enabled her work to be acceptable to him. Amplifying Eros as 'the feminine principle' enables her to cover a far greater and more powerful range of qualities than those envisaged by her mentor.

Crucially, Harding is able to invest a range of energies in the feminine principle by adopting the narratives of moon goddesses from pre-Christian periods: she looks to moon goddesses for accounts of 'the feminine principle [which] has not been adequately recognized or valued in our culture'.[18] The originality of the book lies in its development of ambivalent, potent and dark aspects of the feminine.

While still apparently following Jung in regarding women as more suited to relating and domesticity, Harding writes eloquently of the potentials for bias against women in a patriarchal society. She brings the feminine principle into analytic practice by linking women's initiation into Luna mysteries in a pagan past to the female experience of analysis in the contemporary world.

Harding's moon goddesses of the feminine principle have inspired a generation of Jungian feminists because they are virginal in the sense of standing alone, not dependent on any male. Such 'Jungian virgins' can be sexual and procreative. Their independence rests in a self-sufficiency generated by contact with the numinous unconscious.

Toni Wolff   Toni Wolff's most significant work on gender is 'A Few Thoughts on the Process of Individuation in Women' (1934).[19] Here, she helpfully proposes that Eros is by no means the leading mode of conscious functioning in all women. For her, many problems of modern women stem from the loss of the feminine principle in the lack of the feminine in Judaism and Protestant theology.

Thereafter, she goes on to discuss four types of feminine instinctive personality: the mother, the companion to men called the hetaira, the independent Amazon and the medium. In effect, Wolff is using the notion of conscious 'type' to extend the range of what might be denoted by 'the feminine principle' in women's psychology. Each of Wolff's types is not a uniform pattern of behaviour but a multitudinous range of possibilities.

The four types are creatively framed: for example, the mother is not limited to the biological bearer of children and includes various metaphors of nurture and maternity. The hetaira operates principally through sexually relating to men, while the Amazon, unsurprisingly, is identified with feminists.

Descriptions of the mediumistic type neatly demonstrate Wolff's tendency to define the feminine and female potential predominantly in relation to the male. The medium is a woman who aids a man to realize his unconscious ideas. Later Jungians have speculated that Wolff's own relation to Jung may have helped to shape her sense of 'medium' women.

Erich Neumann   Regarded by Jung as a second-generation Jungian and using much the same material as Esther Harding, Neumann writes in a grand authoritative style. A historian of culture, he proposes a grand narrative of stages in the development of human consciousness in his *The Origins and History of Consciousness* (1954).[20] Humanity begins in the uroboric stage close to unconscious non-differentiation. Then comes the rise of the matriarchal in the religions of the great mother.

These stages are succeeded (fortunately Neumann thinks) by patriarchal monotheism and the refining of Logos-oriented conscious thinking and discrimination. There is some indication of a possible higher stage to come when matriarchal goddess consciousness may reunite with the patriarchal masculine principle, but Neumann leaves this notion unexplored. It is taken up, particularly by E. C. Whitmont, in subsequent Jungian work on the great goddess, discussed later in this chapter.

No one could accuse Neumann of being a feminist in the usual sense. His feminine principle belongs to the matriarchal phase of human history, and, for him as for Jung, women's psychology is largely a matter of this binary conception of the feminine. Women are doomed to a 'more unconscious' type of mental functioning. Hence, for Neumann, the confusion of the feminine with matriarchy places women back into prehistory, with men further advanced in the culturally valuable qualities of thinking and reason.

Neumann seems to write with great underlying fear of the mother as both an archetypal and a biological being. His story of the evolution of consciousness is a form of Oedipal narrative – from unconscious undifferentiation, to bonding with an all-powerful maternal figure, to repression, splitting and identifying with the paternal function. This particular use of Oedipal patterning further historicizes and marginalizes the feminine principle. Later Jungians will take his evolutionary allegory and reinterpret it more productively for the feminine and feminism.

June Singer   In works such as *Boundaries of the Soul* (1972)[21] and *Androgyny: Toward a New Theory of Sexuality* (1976),[22] June Singer develops her acceptance of Jung's gender binary. On the way she acknowledges the lessons of 'the Women's Movement'. In disassociating the feminine and masculine principles from simple identification with biological women and men, she still asserts in *Androgyny* a belief that she feels to be at variance with contemporary feminism, that 'at some point a woman is basically different'.[23]

For Singer, the Jungian notion of potential archetypal 'androgyny' becomes a means of theorizing a goal of psychological wholeness. In tracing what she argues is a cultural history of this archetype, she suggests that contemporary women and men take the androgyne as a desirable cultural model. That way, individuals may evade the perils of polarized notions of gender. Archetypes are the residues of an ancient divine androgyny before the primordial 'fall' or splitting of consciousness. Singer wants to go beyond theorizing gender solely in binary structures. However, her androgyny still rests upon gender as a duality.

> The movement towards androgyny that is emerging today grows out of the tensions between the 'masculine' and 'feminine' elements in contemporary western society. It spirals back on itself to discover the older androgyny that is revealed in the mythology of that primordial time when the masculine and feminine were not yet separated in the godhead.[24]

Irene Claremont de Castillejo   Knowing Woman (1973) updates Irene Claremont de Castillejo's earlier work on the psychology of women. She expands Toni Wolff's four personality types in the context of traditional Jungian concepts of the feminine. There is a valuable separation of anatomical sex and gender: Eros does signify the feminine, but women are not restricted to its attributes. Similarly, thinking can be a primary function in women and need not be linked to reductive notions of the animus. The implicit rigidity of Wolff's four types is counteracted by emphasizing their role as a range of psychological possibilities within any one woman.

Most crucially, Castillejo's work challenges the identification of a diffuse ego in women by such thinkers as Wolff and Neumann. Instead, she advocates a woman developing a strong, focused ego – a very real possibility for her. Part of the process of Castillejo's individuation is a woman discovering her shadow as a cultural, as well as a psychological issue. Women are subjected to three forms of the shadow: one of nation, of personal psyche and of 'being a woman' in a male-oriented society. Individuation seems to grant a woman her personal authority by bringing to consciousness the shadow that society has foisted upon her gender. To discover the feminine within, for Castillejo, is to align with inner heroines and heroes to penetrate her 'inner rage' in a lucid phrase within the 'machine of civilization'.[25]

Finally, Castillejo stands for a progressive Jungian feminism of the 'feminine principle' in arguing that women and the feminine do not connote merely nature, body and earth. Whatever the binary notions of 'principles', women should not be seen just as the 'opposite' or 'other' to men.

Ann Ulanov   In her very influential early volume, *The Feminine in Jungian Psychology and in Christian Theology* (1971), Ulanov celebrates Jung's notion of the feminine as 'a distinct category of being and a mode of perception inherent in all men, all women, all culture'.[26] Such an adherence to Jung enables Ulanov to write a work of feminist theology, following his lead in criticizing the downplaying and sometimes demonizing of the feminine in Christian culture. This theological perspective underscores Ulanov's later work on gender in Jungian ideas.

The initial book also develops Wolff's four types in the psychology of women. Ulanov is careful to separate women from Jung's reductive language of the anima. As with most adherents to 'the feminine principle', Ulanov's severance of sex and gender is somewhat compromised by her working assumption that women have a closer relationship to the feminine. They should aim for integration of the feminine principle in analysis.

E. C. Whitmont   E. C. Whitmont pursues Neumann's myth of the three stages of human consciousness – uroboric (undifferentiated, largely unconscious), matriarchal and patriarchal – into the fourth, the reconciliation of matriarchal and patriarchal modes of thinking. To put it another way, Whitmont longs for the absorption of the feminine principle into a patriarchal, over-rationalistic culture that has repressed it for so long.

Of course, in separating these metaphysical principles of gender from bodily sex, Whitmont looks to myths outside, or on the margins of, patriarchal Christianity for narratives of feminine reincorporation. One such myth is of the search for the Holy Grail. A fragile and masculine-oriented society seeks for feminine symbols in order to achieve psychological resolution that is simultaneously spiritual and social. Another, highly potent source for myths of the feminine principle is to be found outside Christianity and monotheism in the

pursuit of pagan goddesses. Whitmont's work stands as a major progenitor of Jungian goddess feminism.

Amplification: in pursuit of goddesses

To understand both the appeal and the theoretical background of
goddess feminism I need to clarify a division within Jungian feminism
over gender and the role of Christian myth. Western feminist theory
has also been generated in the context of a post-Christian set of
assumptions about the roles of women and men, their psyches, the
way gender is constructed and manifested. Explicitly or implicitly,
writers and activists have to decide whether to revise Christian core
assumptions or to reject them utterly and look for new models. This
does not only apply to those feminists who have religious beliefs or
who take spirituality seriously. Rather, the framework of Christian
assumptions in contemporary culture also affects urgent political
issues such as the right to abortion.

The key issue is whether Christianity (and/or other monotheistic
systems) is entirely patriarchal or whether it has just become mani-
festly so in its collaboration with capitalist culture. Can Christianity
be feminist or must it be replaced? Jungian feminists such as Ann
Ulanov believe that Christianity can be reinvented along Jungian lines
to incorporate the feminine principle as life affirming and divine. The
feminine is no longer restricted to the dark, corporeal other.

A particular aspect of the debate about whether masculine
monotheism *can* be reformed is the relationship between Enlightenment forms of reason and the religious culture it appeared to be react-
ing against. On the one hand, the Enlightenment promotion of
reason, science, empiricism and Logos seems to be totally opposed to
established religion and the means of its decline. On the other hand,
feminists would argue that the suppression of the feminine within
Christianity *continues* with the suppression of the feminine *as irrationality* within the Enlightenment narratives of modernity.

Christianity's patriarchy, with its belief in the divine as masculine,
modulates into the privileging of masculine reason structured by its
separation from inferior irrationality. One way of separating the
unwanted qualities of irrationality from reason is to interpret the
reason/irrationality binary as a gendered structure where reason is
masculine, the irrational is feminine. Prior to the Enlightenment, masculinity is privileged by being associated with God. After the Enlightenment, masculinity is privileged by being associated with reason. See
chapter 6 for Jung in the Enlightenment and postmodernism.

Jung's writings on gender are conditioned by his attempt to address the Enlightenment's turn away from religion. His persistent returns to feminine figures in the Christian canon and his extensive work on alchemy are attempts to reform Christian thinking in ways that heal the Enlightenment's severing of reason and irrationality, or, in his terms, Logos and Eros. Some of his reductive misogyny comes down to his adopting of Enlightenment notions of polarity represented in gender terms. Nevertheless, Jung has feminist credentials in wanting to put the feminine and the irrational (unconscious) back into both religion and philosophy.

Some Jungian feminists follow Jung in trying to reform Christian or monotheistic structures. Others want an escape from Christianity altogether. These Jungian feminists collapse Christianity into patriarchy, so providing no basis for reform. If monotheism is not recoverable, then, to these feminists, what are needed are goddesses. Goddesses are required because, if gender is to be a stable category (*the* defining feature of traditional Jungian feminism), then some 'higher' narrative is required to ground it. If Christianity is rejected as too overwhelmingly patriarchal, then another metaphysical framework must be inferred.

Jungian goddess feminism results from an amplification of Jungian theory that goes beyond what Jung himself envisaged. Jung fashioned his psychology into monotheistic notions of subject-hood by prioritizing one archetype, the self, as the goal of individuation. Jungian goddess feminists reject the unifying energy posited in the self archetype and latch onto its plurality, including that of gender (see the next section on the great goddess). Alternatively, they may ignore a notion of the one self and draw upon the idea of many potential archetypes, capable of representation as feminine divine beings, playing important roles within a person's individuation.

In goddess feminism, the metaphysical feminine principle is mapped onto pre-Christian mythologies in order to seek out non-patriarchal narratives and ways of thinking. Such feminists remain *Jungian* when they stay within the Jungian paradigm of theory-into-myth: psychic imagery, theorized as archetypal, is identified with a traditional mythology and vice versa.

Jungian feminists of this creed are not advocating literal goddess worship. Their divine beings live in the human imagination in the unconscious. A transcendent existence of goddesses actually 'out there' is not considered. Instead, goddess feminism defines analysis and individuation as initiation into the realm of the divinities. 'Initiation' here is not a metaphor. What initiates did in ancient goddess cultures is regarded as a variety of guided or analytic individuation.

After all, in Jungian theory, primary reality is the psychic image and religious experience is, in the first place, authentic intimations of the unconscious. Any ideas of a transcendent realm of immortals are not knowable or provable.

Goddess feminism is not fashionable in today's capitalist, materialist, non-religious culture. It is additionally unacceptable to feminist theories stemming from Freudian psychoanalysis (see chapter 5). Nevertheless there may well be value in looking at the resources of narratives drawing from pre-Christian religious traditions. Can stories of goddesses aid the contemporary understanding of gender and women as tales of psychological possibilities? Can such legends of goddesses be at all relevant to social and material conditions today?

Ginette Paris's *The Sacrament of Abortion* (1992) demonstrates the feminist potential of using a non-Christian narrative to structure thinking on a deeply contentious personal, political and social issue.[27] After showing how the contemporary abortion debate is dependent upon patriarchal Christian myths, she uses legends of Artemis, a virgin goddess invoked by mothers in labour, to reimagine abortion. Through legends of the goddess, Paris considers abortion as a sacrifice of mothers who must control their reproductivity or be themselves sacrificed to patriarchal attitudes. 'In this context the return of the ancient goddess Artemis invites us to imagine a new allocation of life and death powers between men and women, an allocation that allows men to appreciate the cost of a life and women to make decisions based upon their mother-knowledge.'[28] Paris shows that the value of goddess feminism is the opportunity to 'think differently' about concerns of gender and the lives of women. Although this feminism may be primarily psychologically and therapeutically oriented, it may still contribute to a broader political and cultural criticism.

Key authors

Sylvia Brinton Perera   An influential work of therapeutic goddess feminism is Sylvia Brinton Perera's 1981 *Descent to the Goddess*.[29] Here she reads the Sumerian myth of the goddess Inanna's descent to the underworld of her shadow-sister Ereshkigal as a model for women to encounter the psychological and healing value of a dark, depressive archetype. In fact, this goddess myth of an underworld journey and return enables Perera to shape depressive mental states as potentially empowering women.

The goddess myth provides an alternative to viewing dark, repressed feminine pain as an abyss of inferiority. A culture whose religious archetypal images provide only the impossible lightness and bliss of the Virgin Mary or evil, sinful Eve is rethought in terms of a positive feminine darkness.

Christine Downing   As an academic in psychology and religion, Christine Downing published what she called an 'individuation autobiography' in 1984 as *The Goddess: Mythological Images of the Feminine.*[30] Downing understands her interior emotional history through associating her inner self with a succession of goddess myths. She is variously linked to Persephone, Ariadne, Hera, Athene, Gaia, Artemis and Aphrodite. In taking these mythological goddesses as stories, Downing shows the potential of pagan narratives to produce more plural and active forms of feminine imagery than Jung's apparently more static images.

Although Downing admits that some of these goddesses are available archetypally to men, she is close to an essentialist position of linking feminine divine forms mainly with the female psyche. Her work remains persuasive on the possibilities of goddess myths as the means of imagining women's psychological being in ever-more complex and dynamic terms. 'We are starved for images that recognize the sacredness of the feminine and the complexity, richness and nurturing power of female energy.'[31]

Marion Woodman   Woodman's *The Pregnant Virgin* (1985) models healing the feminine psyche back in the tradition of Esther Harding's pioneering departure from Jung's primarily Judaeo-Christian frame. Like the earlier woman, Woodman takes up the narrative resources of moon goddesses.[32] Expressing, in authentic Jungian 'personal-myth' mode, the difficulty of writing psychological theory in the rational language of the ego, Woodman goes further than Jung in pointing out that women theorists have an additional issue in that rational language has been traditionally assimilated to masculinity. Her 'pregnant virgin' is the despised feminine, cast out of culture, which encourages women to repress her in their own psyches.

> The word 'feminine', as I understand it, has very little to do with gender, nor is woman the custodian of femininity. Both men and women are searching for their pregnant virgin. She is the part of us who is outcast, the part who comes to consciousness through going into darkness, mining her leaden darkness, until we bring her silver out.[33]

Most significantly, this archetypal feminine is divorced from gender as well as bodily sex, moving away from the essentializing tendency of much goddess feminism. Woodman uses, as narrative devices, introspection, dreams and clinical creative work to search out the pregnant-virgin psyche in the writing of her texts. A particularly evocative example of the goddess in Jungian feminist analytic practice is her description of a therapeutic drama group as the womb of the great mother.

Linda Schierse Leonard In a later inspiring work, *Meeting the Madwoman* (1993), Linda Schierse Leonard takes the demeaning stereotype of the deviant, crazy female and uses it as an image of psychic empowerment.[34] It becomes a way of understanding female rage within patriarchy. Like other Jungian feminists in this tradition, she unproblematically links women and the psychological feminine, but admits that the 'madwoman' as archetypal energy is equally available to men. *The Wounded Woman* (1982) draws upon Iphigenia as an archetypal image subordinated by the father and the father culture of patriarchy.[35]

Nancy Qualls-Corbett Nancy Qualls-Corbett in *The Sacred Prostitute* (1988) finds archetypal images of the Virgin Mary, Mary Magdalene, the Black Virgin and lunar great goddesses in the practice of the sacred prostitute.[36] This pre-Christian ritual involved women choosing to serve the goddess by standing for her within the temple. Any male could come and sexually unite with the divine goddess through intercourse with the sacred prostitute.

Qualls-Corbett reads this practice as the social organization of the Jungian principle that sexuality can be a means to communion with the numinous unconscious. One task of analysis is to heal the traumatic split still deeply ingrained in post-Christian culture between sexuality and spirituality. The sacred prostitute is one myth, one archetypally infused story, that allows men and women to imagine more plural forms of sexual practice and social codification contained in the tales of the goddesses.

Jean Shinoda Bolen A popularizing classic of Jungian goddess feminism appeared with Jean Shinoda Bolen's *Goddesses in Everywoman* (1984).[37] Here the goddesses are collections of archetypal images and potentialities. They are divided into categories: 'virgin' independent goddesses are Artemis, Athena, Hestia. Those predicated more on forms of feminine vulnerability and relatedness are Persephone, Demeter and Hera, while Aphrodite stands alone as alchemical and transformative.

While these 'goddesses', as a means of describing archetypal functioning, are distantly related to Toni Wolff's four types, Bolen considers most women to have access to each archetypal image. Women are able to draw upon the range of archetypal functions and energies as required by circumstances. These goddesses are stories that play out the interior lives of women in contemporary culture.

Amplification: the myth of the Great Goddess

As indicated earlier, Jungian goddess feminism is both a set of narrative resources for innovative therapeutic practice and a profound criticism of Western culture. Jungian writers who develop the myth of the great goddess are at the point where Jungian grand theory on gender and the feminine becomes amplified into a feminist theory (or myth) of culture, history and transformation.

E. C. Whitmont's development of Neumann's three stages of human consciousness into an urgent call for a fourth stage is nothing less than a demand for human consciousness to integrate the feminine as divinity immanent within nature. The sacred is no longer to be confined to a father-god transcendent of the material or natural world. With the 'return of the goddess', the name of Whitmont's 1982 book, humanity rediscovers nature as holy: it embraces the human realm within its numinous fecundity.

Western culture thereby abandons models of consciousness dependent upon repressing the other, of which patriarchy's suppression of the feminine is only one obvious example.

Key authors

E. C. Whitmont For Whitmont, Neumann's patriarchal stage of consciousness has been disastrously exaggerated and prolonged. 'In the depths of the unconscious psyche, the ancient Goddess is arising. She demands recognition and homage. If we refuse to acknowledge her, she may unleash forces of destruction. If we grant the Goddess her due, she may compassionately guide us towards transformation.'[38] He suggests that four myths, stemming from masculine monotheism, have served to reinforce the sterility of patriarchal thinking dependent upon splitting and repression. These myths are, first, that of divine kingship, still visible in the 'magical' leaders, secondly that of human exile or the loss of paradise, thirdly that of the sacrifice of the scape-goat and, as a fourth, the inferiority of the feminine. Today's society needs the goddess to 'return' because patriarchal, atheistic, planet-exploiting attitudes are, to Whitmont, directly linked to masculine monotheism.

Unlike Jung, Whitmont believes that Christianity (and the other great monotheisms) cannot be reformed to release its suppressed 'other'. Whether that other be darkness, death, the body or the femi-nine, masculine monotheism will not cease to split the human psyche. Monotheisms are neurotic, one-sided structures devoted to transcen-dent and triumphant powers over nature.

The great goddess is rising because she is a sign of the other that monotheistic patriarchal consciousness has deeply repressed. 'She' is returning through individual psyches and in cultural movements such as new forms of spirituality, environmental campaigns and eco-feminism.

Anne Baring and Jules Cashford Baring and Cashford's 1991 volume, *The Myth of the Goddess: Evolution of an Image*, provides the most comprehensive exposition of Jungian goddess feminism as a lens through which to view the span of human culture and tech-nology.[39] Moving from an analysis of neolithic 'goddess cultures' to post-industrial alienation, this is grand theory more earnestly sub-stantiated than even Jung's ambitions. Its myth of world history is explicitly a feminist argument for a revolution in consciousness. 'The moral order of the goddess culture . . . was based on the principle of relationship . . . The moral order of the god culture . . . was based on the paradigm of opposition and conquest: a view of life, and particularly nature, as something "other" to be conquered.'[40]

Importantly, this myth of the great goddess cannot be read as an essentialist call for a 'woman-religion' to replace masculine monothe-ism. Originally non-gendered, the great mother provided a narrative to figure a relationship between creator and created, eternity and time. The divine mother as 'Zoe' or source of life gives birth to her son-lover as 'bios', the biosphere of created life within and subject to time. The 'bios' is created life as nature and humanity within nature. It lives in time and dies back into the source of the divine mother. 'She' is not feminine or masculine, but is the divine source of all gendering possibilities.

Masculine monotheism distorts the great-mother story. In splitting apart the divine from nature, it creates a split in human conscious-ness. The unfortunate results are the binary polarities of gender and consciousness based upon the repression of the other.

The myth of the great goddess offers yet another fantasy of psychic wholeness within Jungian studies. In this sense it is an amplification of Jung's fascination with his self-archetype, but amalgamated to pagan prehistory rather than Christian culture. However, the aim of this branch of Jungian feminism is the healing not of individuals, but of the cosmos. The sacred is not a *stage* in consciousness: it is a *structure* in consciousness. The model for subjectivity here is of the web of life, connecting human, to nature, to the divine, conscious to unconscious, feminine to masculine in the psyche. The sacred is part of nature and human beings are part of that dance. 'The Mother Goddess, wherever she is found, is an image that inspires and focuses a perception of the universe as an organic, alive and sacred whole, in which humanity, the earth and all life on Earth participate as "her children" . . .'[41]

The goddess and the feminine principle: some conclusions

The achievement of Jungian feminism (grand theory)

Despite well-documented misogyny, Jung had some valuable thoughts about gender and the feminine, which were picked up by his pro-feminist successors. These ideas include the exploration of 'the feminine' in symbols and myths, proclaiming the presence of the feminine and masculine in each gender, protesting at the harm done to psyche and culture through repression of the feminine, and an insistence on full individuation for women in analytic practice. All this does not remove the stigma of Jung's reductive and misogynistic language, the slippage of gender into biological sex and the equation of women, the feminine, Eros and diffuse consciousness. A particular problem is Jung's positing of female psychology as opposite and complementary to men's.

Traditional Jungian feminism, taking Jung's writings as grand theory, has addressed many of the issues that feminists criticize in Jungian psychology. There has been a movement from considering women as 'the other side' of the male psyche and towards exploring their complexity as not dependent upon a binary structuring of gender. Jung's insistence on psychic contrasexuality has been developed: terms such as animus and anima have been revised in ways that are aware of cultural limitations in Jung's writing.

Usefully, there has been a growing emphasis on cultural factors in the expression of gender and of the role of patriarchal structures in women's psychological difficulties. As in the wider culture, the terms 'women' and 'the feminine' are now separable, but remain in a nebulous relationship. Generally, what still distinguishes Jungian feminists of grand theory is the sense that gender is somehow a stable category. They seek a source for gender's stability either in Jung's texts, or in his preferred source material of cultural mythologies, or in both, *before* considering the influence of material culture.

Goddess feminism: an evaluation

Jungian goddess feminism is a feminist attempt to revolutionize the understanding of the psyche, and of human culture and history. To much of Western culture, and, indeed, much of Western feminism, goddess feminism is perceived as antipathetic to the concentration on embodied material politics. Why should modern feminists remake and reabsorb ancient stories of goddesses in a post-religious, post-industrial age? If goddess feminism is not to be a literal religion (which it is not in Jungian feminism), then what is it for?

Jungian goddess feminism can be defended both theoretically and in terms of material practice in a number of pragmatic ways. In the first place, the theoretical defence is that of Jung's speculation that traditional religious mythologies of all kinds and all cultures contain archetypal material. Therefore, any new attention to myths of goddesses may rectify centuries of one-sided concentration of masculinity in the divine. Such unequal focus on one gender has distorted the psychological potentials of both women and men (arguably to the greater detriment of women).

For the practice of analysis from a feminist perspective, goddess feminism offers opportunities for feminine fictions of empowerment and agency, for Jungian goddess feminism is a matter of the psyche and the imagination, not a literal replacement of a religion. To many therapists and feminists it is less viable as a branch of feminist theory than as an experiential and pragmatic means of aiding wounded women.

I would suggest calling Jungian goddess feminism the fantasy literature of psychology in two senses. It does enable splendid fantasies to be constructed in analysis. Secondarily, in a literary sense, texts expounding goddess feminism could be linked to the tradition of feminist science fiction or fantasy novels. For example, feminist fantasy novels are very close in tone *and intention* to the work of E. C. Whitmont.

Considering goddess feminism as feminist fantasy fiction places it on the disputed margins of literature and psychology. Here, Jungian goddess feminism is seen to be transgressive and Gothic to both main-stream psychology and to secular modernity itself. It offers a prag-matic rather than theoretical feminism in providing fictions of subjectivity that lead into notions of gender and personality as 'per-formative'. Gender is seen as a process, as a form of social and psy-chological 'drama', rather than as a centred stable entity. See chapter 6 for more on the feminist linking of literature and psychology in postmodernity.

I would also point out the potential value of goddess feminism as a means of rethinking crucial debates about gender and culture outside, or at least less in the tradition of, a post-Christian monotheistic culture. At a deeper level, goddess feminism allows us to unpick the binaries of theory that has dominated cultural debates on gender. Even the great goddess is not a feminine version of monotheism, which forms a binary by casting out so much that is 'other'. The great goddess is immanent in nature, necessarily experienced as plural and differentiated, not transcendent of the material world, so not one, plus the 'other'. In this sense, 'goddess[es] consciousness' is multiple and differentiated; a notion able to have a fruitful dialogue with the fragmented consciousness of postmodernism (see chapter 6).

Jungian goddess feminism is the most ambitious amplification of Jungian ideas as grand theory mapped onto marginal historical (or feminist revisions of marginal historical) mythology. It is time to look at post-Jungian work on gender through the lens of Jung's character-ization of his theory as 'personal myth'.

Concluding summary

Traditional Jungian feminism derives from Jung's work as grand theory. It extends, revises and amplifies his notions of gender and the feminine to create a mutually supportive and mutually criticizing set of theories and practices. A core dynamic in Jungian feminism is the linking of theory with analytic practice, often, but not exclusively, with women.

Mythology is a characteristic means of connecting individual psychic experience of gender to Jung's works and to the wider culture. Descriptions of the 'feminine' and 'masculine' principles are used as a polarized binary, operating within culture and available to the psyches of both women and men. Gender is thereby detached from bodily sex and is conceived of as plural within any one being.

Jungian goddess feminism regards mythological narratives of god-desses as the only satisfactory means of expression and empowerment for the long subordinated female psyche. Goddess feminism can be expanded and formalized into a comprehensive myth of the human culture, psyche and technology in the myth of the great goddess. What has not yet been appreciated is some of the postmodern, post-structuralist and wider feminist theoretical context. Before we enter such contested areas, we need to look at post-Jungian work on gender, which is (rightly) very wary of the certainties of traditional Jungian feminism.

FURTHER READING

General

Douglas, Claire, *The Woman in the Mirror: Analytical Psychology and the Feminine* (Boston: Sigo Press, 1990).
An invaluable historical account of gender and the feminine in Jung's writings and those of post-Jungians.

Extension and revision

Claremont de Castillejo, Irene, *Knowing Woman: A Feminine Psychology* (Boston: Shambhala, 1973).
Breaks with some of Jung's misogynistic assumptions and suggestively revises archetypal gender.

Jung, Emma, *Animus and Anima* (Woodstock, Conn.: Spring Publications, 1957).
In this early work of extension, Emma Jung is both positive and incisive about Jung's negative animus.

Ulanov, Ann, *The Feminine in Jungian Psychology and in Christian Theology* (Evanston, Ill.: Northwestern University Press, 1971).
A very influential work in extending both Jung's notions of contrasexual gender and his rethinking of Christian theology.

Young-Eisendrath, Polly, with Wiedemann, Florence, *Female Authority: Empowering Women through Psychotherapy* (New York: Guilford Press, 1987).
Emphatically criticizes Jung's limitations on gender and revises his concepts to empower women through individuation.

The feminine principle

Harding, M. Esther, *Woman's Mysteries: Ancient and Modern* (1935; New York: Harper & Row Colophon, 1976).

Powerfully imagined progenitor of much Jungian feminism. Harding amplifies Jung's theories surrounding mythology.

Leonard, Linda Schierse, *Meeting the Madwoman: An Inner Challenge for Feminine Spirit* (New York: Bantam Books, 1993).
A thoughtful reimagining of negative feminine stereotypes as a means of psychological transformation.

Woodman, Marion, *The Pregnant Virgin: A Process of Psychological Transformation* (Toronto: Inner City Books, 1985).
Evocative exploration of the feminine. Woodman links myth to analysis to bodywork and theatricality.

Jungian goddess feminism

Baring, Anne, and Cashford, Jules, *The Myth of the Goddess: Evolution of an Image* (Harmondsworth: Viking, 1991).
Exhaustively comprehensive reinterpretation of history and culture from the neolithic to the present day in terms of Jungian goddess feminism.

Brinton Perera, Sylvia, *Descent to the Goddess: A Way of Initiation for Women* (Toronto: Inner City Books, 1981).
Popular and influential analysis of the 'dark side' of the feminine through the Sumerian myth of Inanna.

Paris, Ginette, *The Sacrament of Abortion*, translated from the French by Joanna Mott (Dallas, Texas: Spring Publications, 1992).
A fascinating study of contemporary attitudes to abortion from the perspective of ancient goddesses, rather than modern post-Christian culture.

Whitmont, E. C., *Return of the Goddess* (New York: Continuum Publishing, 1982).
Indispensable setting-out of the framework of this approach.

4

Jungian Feminisms?

> Thus it is that I have now undertaken . . . to tell my personal myth. I can only . . . 'tell stories'. Whether or not the stories are 'true' is not the problem. The only question is whether what I tell is *my* fable, *my* truth.
>
> (Jung, *Memories, Dreams, Reflections*, 1963)

> Jung was anima-inspired, and that condition must necessarily empower those who come after him to 'dream the work onward' . . . Whether or not we accept the revisionings of anima-inspired followers is a separate question.
>
> (David Tacey, *Remaking Men*, 1997)

Chapter 4 looks at the post-Jungian work on gender that does not fall into the grand-theory tradition of 'Jungian feminism'. I suggest that this more plural and diverse thinking about gender constitutes the evolution of 'Jungian feminisms'.

The production of 'Jungian feminisms' is distinguished from the 'Jungian feminism' of chapter 3 by linking it to the 'personal-myth' aspect of Jung's writing (outlined in chapter 2). It encompasses ground-breaking rethinking of gender, theory and society from those based primarily within Jungian psychology. James Hillman and the archetypal psychology he promoted are sources for such Jungian feminisms.

It is also necessary to look at the mythopoetic men's movement inspired by the poet Robert Bly for its claims to be 'Jungian' on gender. I aim to show that such claims cannot be substantiated. In addition, Jungian feminisms have gained much from thinkers prepared to use the perspectives of other disciplines. These include David Tacey, Andrew Samuels (whose work has been so influential), the grouping of feminist scholars known as Feminist archetypal theorists and the post-Jungian school of developmental psychology. I end the chapter with an example of how historical feminist work on Jung can provide analyses of the function of gender in his writing.

Introduction: Jungian feminisms

Within the field of Jungian studies after Jung, there is what is popularly known as 'Jungian feminism'. This label denotes the Jungian works on gender and the feminine covered in the previous chapter. Traditional 'Jungian feminism', as I have argued, is linked with Jung's desire to produce a 'grand theory' of psyche and culture.

However, there is simultaneously a growing critical awareness of what I have described as the 'personal-myth' element in Jung's writing. This refers to his tendency to explore the consequences of the slippery, *unknowable* nature of the psyche. Jung in personal myth is aware of the impossibility of producing a single unchanging authoritative version of the mind.

What links the work of the post-Jungians in this chapter is the refusal to treat Jung as a grand theorist whose core principles can be extended, but not disputed. Therefore, they operate in the tradition of his 'personal myth'. As analysts and thinkers have responded to these qualities in Jung, they have produced work on gender and the feminine that diverges explicitly or implicitly from those seeking definitive foundations for a psychology of women.

Consequently, much of the material of this chapter derives from Jungian thinkers who are not self-identified wholly or even partly as 'Jungian feminists'. Their work constitutes the evolution of 'Jungian feminisms' and should be placed in the wider context of feminist and gender studies.

At this point it would be useful to outline the broad developments in contemporary feminist theory. Feminist studies gathered momentum as women began to realize that male-authored systems of knowledge of all kinds, in medicine, history, religion, literature, philosophy, psychology, had either omitted or distorted the representation of women. The resulting 'feminist critique' of masculine norms (previously disguised as universal truths about human beings) became the founding direction of feminist research. In this book feminist critique of Jung's thinking about women is chiefly located in chapter 2. It is also a significant feature of much of the Jungian work on gender after Jung, considered in chapters 3 and 4.

Recognizing that it was not enough merely to criticize authoritative male texts, feminist theory entered a phase of 'women writing'. Women must represent themselves by writing *their* psychology, their history, their art, their philosophy and religion. Much of the work discussed in chapter 3 can be linked to this genre of women's self-representation.

Nevertheless, challenges to the idea of any one woman writing unproblematically for *all* women arose from both within and outside feminist activity. In the first place, feminism as a wider political and cultural movement became more self-critical. It became conscious that it could not sustain a single, simple category of 'women'. Differences of sexuality, class, race, ethnicity and cultural location meant that feminism had to address issues of power and identity within its ranks. Externally, the impact of such theories as psychoanalysis, deconstruction and postmodernism produced a serious assault on the idea of a single unified self. Such a notion of fixed identity is necessary to maintain the fiction of an unproblematic grouping together of 'women'.

In response to this new political and theoretical situation, 'feminism' became 'feminisms'. There can be no grand unified account of 'women'; 'feminist theory' becomes a strategic alliance of differing approaches to issues of gender, identity, culture and power.

My contention is that Jungian studies have now reached the point of offering Jungian feminisms rather than just Jungian feminism. This book is dedicated to exploring the new opportunities engendered by this expansion of feminist possibilities. What is particularly worth noting here is how far Jung himself provokes such a development in his questioning of straightforward conceptions of authoritative theory in the impulses that I have termed 'personal myth'.

This chapter will look at Jungian feminisms already existing within the creative arena of work on gender after Jung. All the theorists could be called 'imitators' rather than 'followers' of Jung. They imitate Jung's 'personal-myth' awareness of the difficulty of writing about what can never be securely pinned down. They do not amplify Jung's precepts to something with the ambition of a grand theory of gender, psyche and culture.

Such a characterization of these Jungian theorists means that I will be looking at two of Andrew Samuels's post-Jungian schools: the archetypal and the developmental. These two schools are post-Jungian in the sense that Samuels has defined it: operating in dialogue with, but at a critical distance from, what are generally accepted as the tenets of Jungian psychology (that is, Jung as grand theory). The third school, the classical, tries to follow Jung more faithfully and so any feminism generated by it falls into the tradition covered in chapter 3.

Of course, there is a very real danger in making too rigid a division between 'grand theorist' Jungians on gender and the 'personal-myth' aligned authors treated here. Within the previous chapter some authors are considered who are highly critical of Jung's limitations on gender and women. Just as Samuels points out that there is no clear-cut division of Jungian analysts into any of the three schools,[1] so some of the theorists discussed in chapter 3 would indeed claim some connection to either the developmental or the archetypal traditions.

Conversely, David Tacey, discussed in this chapter, is an adherent of the notion of 'the feminine principle', a characteristic of those Jungians described in chapter 3. In practice, this chapter's treatment of those influencing the development of Jungian feminisms covers those authors who *radically* revise core Jungian ideas.

Recent research in feminisms of all kinds has frequently focused upon gender as historically located. This chapter will end with an example of how feminist historical investigation can shed light on the vexed notion of Jung's anima. As a whole, chapter 4 looks at the unplanned evolution of diverse and challenging Jungian feminisms to set alongside, and to criticize, the exclusive claims of traditional Jungian feminism. Subsequent chapters of this book will explore future possibilities in this liberated, interconnected web called 'Jungian feminisms'.

Challenging from within Jungian studies

James Hillman's radical anima

The main achievement of James Hillman's radical rethinking of Jung's anima is to free women forever from having her devious unconscious qualities stamped upon them as women's intellectual inferiority. In two key articles in the 1970s, Hillman recreated Jungian psychology. He structures his revisions through a critical rereading of Jung's own texts.[2]

Consciously exploiting the personal-myth dimension, Hillman argues that the anima should not be conditioned by Jung's tendency to think in opposites. The anima is not the contrasexual (opposite-sex) side of the male psyche, nor is 'she' present only in men. In fact, the anima or 'soul' (Jung's terminology as well) is the archetypal structure of consciousness. She is a consciousness aligned with, or attached to, the 'other', the unconscious.

Anima is, therefore, a function of relationship, as Jung suggested, but not of *human* relationships, as he thought. Anima *relates* to the deeper authenticity of the unconscious and away from the facile limitations of the selfish ego. 'Eros' is not to be stuck onto the anima: it is a wholly separate function of sexuality.

Therefore women do not bear the anima or soul for men. They have souls of their own and, like males, should develop psychologically through the cultivation of the culturally neglected feminine anima. Similarly, both women and men have equal access to animus or 'spirit'.

The ego's structure is predicated upon the hero myth, a narrative of learning to despise and repress the feminine anima. However, it is the anima, not the ego, that is the true base of consciousness. She leads away from the imperious ego and towards the unfathomable otherness of the psyche. Acting through psychic images, the anima aims for the sacrifice of the ego's will to control. Ego domination includes the control of meaning. Anima consciousness means awareness of my unconsciousness. It means theory and knowledge themselves must be held provisionally, subject to continual testing and revision. 'Theory' can only be a 'personal myth'.

Hillman calls his anima the archetype of psychology and soul-making. For him neither the anima nor the animus can be restricted to either the singular or the plural; such is the elusive nature of psychic beings. Rather, the anima and animus enact a psychic marriage within, and are the perspectives by which the other is known. So the anima is frequently seen as 'one', not because that is her 'essence', but because she is viewed through a lens conditioned to see 'ones'.

Hillman is explicit about his imitation of Jung in his personal myth mode of writing psychology; he concludes his second article: 'This essay is a mythical activity of anima coming on as a critical activity of animus'.[3] In claiming not to be producing grand theory primarily (an animus activity), Hillman develops Jung's personal-myth writing into a self-conscious detaching of Jung from his unacknowledged cultural prejudices on gender.

To illuminate this Jungian feminism further, I will set Hillman's revision of the anima into the context of the post-Jungian school that he, principally, inspired: archetypal psychology.

The feminism of archetypal psychology: a post-Jungian school

Leading archetypal psychologists include Patricia Berry, Paul Kugler, David L. Miller and Edward S. Casey.[4] Archetypal psychology allies itself with poststructuralism and postmodernism (introduced in chapters 5 and 6) by making two distinct breaks with orthodox Jungian theory. In the first place it redesigns Jung's core idea of the archetype. Jung defined the archetype as an inherited possibility for form and meaning, representable only through a culturally influenced psychic image.

Instead, archetypal psychologists reject the idea of the prior existence of the archetype. The image alone is real. The archetypal image (which can be any psychic image) *is* the archetype and is the primary reality. It is more to be trusted than the pretentious perceptions of the ego.

Secondarily, archetypal psychologists consciously refuse to regard Jung as an authoritative 'master' theorist. In his book *Healing Fiction*, Hillman explores the personal-myth side of Jung as one who healed himself through the 'fiction' of his psychic imagery.[5] Following on from this recognition is Hillman's claim that the writer open to the play of the fictional psyche, such as Jung, produces *therapeutic* theoretical works, in so far as the fictional images direct and shape his or her ideas (just as Hillman asserts that the anima shaped his anima critical essays).

This intertwining of theory and fiction enables archetypal psychology to provide a sophisticated and subtle body of writings, expressly designed to undermine dogmatic statements on gender, gender roles and the feminine. Particularly useful for a Jungian feminism is archetypal psychology's downplaying of the ego: it is the product of an immature hero myth, liable to delusions of patriarchy as a baseless fantasy.

Patriarchal ideology depends upon the suppression of the feminine as inferiority. The 'feminine' can be an imprecise category merely denoting the 'other' to what dominant 'fathers' consider to be meaningful or authentic. Therefore the ego's repression of the unconscious can become a defining ingredient for all kinds of patriarchal ideas. Archetypal psychology believes the growth of the ego in a young person (of either sex) to be structured upon the hero myth of conquest and suppression of all that is 'other'. The developing ego is particularly liable to suppress the feminine anima–soul. In condemning the ego's claims to be the authentic mode of subjectivity, and by recognizing the link between the ego-hero and patriarchal social attitudes, archetypal psychology truly offers a Jungian feminism.

Another feminist contribution is made by archetypal psychology's surprising endorsement of polytheism, the belief in many gods and goddesses. However, this is *not* to merge archetypal psychology's Jungian feminism with the goddess feminism of the previous chapter.

Abandoning the notion of an antecedent archetype 'producing' its images means that archetypal psychology is not offering to supply goddesses. Rather, regarding images as primary archetypes (in order to frustrate the ego's drive to convert them into interpretations) entails *valuing* the image instead of trying to reduce it to something verbal.

So, in order to maintain the privileging of psychic images above the ego, it is necessary continually to submit to their numinosity and psychic resonance. Hillman calls such an attitude of mind polytheism, because it means giving a higher sense of reality or importance to the images. His polytheism is not the worshipping of a collection of gods somewhere 'out there'. Polytheism, as we have seen in chapter 3, provides a real opportunity for feminism in undoing the patriarchal exclusions written into monotheism. It validates other, different and feminine styles of being. Yet archetypal psychology's Jungian feminism does have limitations.

For example, the desire to dissolve the masterful claims of the ego cannot always be received by unalloyed enthusiasm by feminism. While the theoretical accounting for patriarchy and its explicit repudiation is a feminist project, the ego is also the home of rationality. Reason is part of clear thinking about equality and fairness in society. Feminism can never afford to renounce reason and justice. The attempt to degrade the ego as the chief organ of consciousness is, in effect, to dissolve the distinction between the rational and the irrational.

This can be an ethically feminist move if it removes the feminine's taint of inferiority as the irrational other. If it leads to alliances and connections beyond a binary structure of self/other or rational/irrational, then it suggests feminisms embracing differences of all kinds without privileging one above the other. Yet the danger of dissolving the conceptual rational/irrational distinction is the potential loss of rational political engagement with existing hierarchies of power.

The possible negative consequences of archetypal psychology's assault upon the ego are related to another factor inhibiting for feminism. The way that the psychic image is valued means that the notion of a cultural shaping of subjectivity and gender is *not theoretically written out*, but *is practically neutered*. This is what Hillman says about the archetype-as-image: 'Any image termed "archetypal" is immediately valued as universal, trans-historical, basically profound, generative, highly intentional, and necessary'.[6]

On the one hand, archetypal psychologists stress that more or less any psychic image may be considered archetypal. In effect, this values cultural diversity, since there are no grounds for suggesting a hierarchy of images that people 'ought' to experience. On the other hand, the valuing of the image above the ego means that any sense of cultural location is *de*valued. The ego's witnessing of history and culture is ignored. The term used by Hillman, 'trans-historical', is inimical to those feminisms engaged with material conditions.

Paradoxically, by going back to Jung's definition of the archetype, I would suggest that there is a structuring of subjectivity that does engage with a feminism interested in a cultural and material shaping of gender identity. The formless archetype supplies creative energy: the resulting image is also shaped by the subject's bodily and social integration into a culture.

For example, methods of mothering have varied enormously across cultures and histories. An archetypal image of 'mother' will partake of this diversity by being formed through a particular subjectivity, culture, society and historical moment. It can be examined as one manifestation of the ineffable multiplicity of the archetype *and* as a witnessing of specific material conditions.

By repudiating the transcendent aspects of Jung's archetype yet still stressing the superior authenticity of the unconscious or soul, archetypal psychology has produced a feminism of radical yet relatively narrow dimensions. It has not, as I have just demonstrated, exhausted the potential of Jungian ideas to generate 'other' feminisms. The poet and inspirer of the mythopoetic men's movement, Robert Bly, is interested in James Hillman's work.[7] No one would accuse the mythopoetic men's movement of feminism. However, its popular dissemination of what it claims is a 'Jungian' treatment of gender requires some consideration.

Robert Bly and the mythopoetic men's movement

Robert Bly and his followers believe that feminism has emasculated men. They hope to use 'Jungian' male archetypes in order to initiate these victimized beings into an authentic 'deep patriarchy'. The leading publication of this developing movement is Bly's *Iron John*, which has been succeeded by a number of best-selling volumes promising access to 'deep male' or 'inner warrior' 'archetypes'.[8]

A particularly provocative episode in *Iron John* can give a flavour of the anti-feminist tone of the whole. Bly urges the male initiate who has reached his inner patriarchy 'to lift or show his sword' in relations with women.[9] Disingenuously, he records: 'In these early sessions it was difficult for many of the younger men to distinguish between showing the sword and hurting someone'.[10] My most immediate reaction to Bly's sword is that this is socially irresponsible writing. If the 'sword' is not violence, then is it the threat of violence? Is it a simple bid for domination or is it some metaphor for the superior phallic purity of masculine reason? At best, Bly's book and its progeny implicitly and explicitly demean women. At worst, it inspires an anti-feminist backlash. Bly is too easily interpreted to license regressive and simple-minded forms of patriarchy.

The mythopoetic men's movement also betrays Jung. It seizes upon his theoretical terms to try to justify an attempt to re-create early twentieth-century social relations between men and women. Bly and his followers are not true to Jung in his grand-theory mode (which is why they appear in this chapter) in their dangerous oversimplification of archetypes.

To the mythopoetic men's movement, an archetype is for males a heroic masculine gender identity stamped deep into the unconscious where the horrifying contamination of feminist modernity cannot get at it. Such a notion is not Jungian theory: Jung's archetypes are not inherited images. To Jung an archetype is not of fixed gender, it is not a stable image preserved unchanged through the generations, and it can be known only through archetypal images that have a *creative* engagement with culture. Bly turns archetypes into reactionary gender stereotypes.

Unfortunately, the popularity of the mythopoetic men's movement amongst confused white males frequently results in Jungian theory as a whole being regarded with unwarranted suspicion by non-Jungian feminists. Fortunately, Jungian studies themselves have produced powerful refutations of Bly, in Andrew Samuels's *The Political Psyche*,[11] and extensively in David Tacey's *Remaking Men*, a Jungian study of masculinity in a progressive and supportive dialogue with feminism.[12]

Using the perspectives of other disciplines

David Tacey: masculinity and feminism

One of the near relations of feminist theory is the politically interested body of work known as Gender Studies. In order to be socially effective, feminism needs men as well as women to question the assumptions of their gender and its relation to culture and power. Despite David Tacey's adherence to notions of 'the feminine principle', his work belongs in this chapter for his stated ambition of bridging the gulf between archetypal theories and progressive men's studies. Gender and men's studies have been particularly reliant upon materialist and social constructivist accounts of gender.

Tacey's position is that progressive Jungian thinking gains from the input of materially oriented gender studies. Such theory has a useful function in preventing dangerous nostalgic lapses, such as the mythopoetic men's movement, of which he provides a trenchant criticism. On the other hand, men's studies needs Jung because materialism is not enough. It is not enough, either as an explanation of the psyche's passionate involvement with gender, or to supply the psychological energy for real social change.

For Tacey, gender is socially reproduced through ideology. However, ideology is not solely the instrument of materialist forces, as it possesses an archetypal foundation. Tacey affirms his support for feminism's social aims. Like most feminists, he regards the political project as far from complete.

In Jungian terms, Tacey understands feminism as the wholly-to-be-welcomed rising of the feminine principle after centuries of suppression and denigration. The task for men is to acknowledge their psychological pain at the loss of the fantasies of patriarchy. Men need to develop a higher *consciousness* within themselves by embracing their inner feminine. Seeking the inner feminine in the cause of developing consciousness is not to advocate a descent into the anima-as-mother. Tacey is well aware of the political dangers for progressive men and women of identifying femininity with the maternal. Rather, by re-evaluating psychological and sociological bonding with the *father*, sons and daughters can both experience psychologically and perceive socially, a more evolved form of the feminine. Tacey envisages an anima that produces more varied and diverse styles of gender for the psyche and for society.

A striking potential for a Jungian feminism is the way that Tacey brings an archetypal element into the understanding of social change. The 'absent father' (subject of much agonizing in men's studies) is missing either literally or emotionally for sons. This figure is 'derived from the loss and disappearance of authentic "father-energy" at an archetypal level'.[13]

Such an archetypal deficit is not the lamentable consequence of feminism. It occurs through the decline of *belief* in patriarchy, which is not the same as its *absence*. It is the task of individual men and progressive psychology to reinvigorate the archetypal paternal by learning to discard patriarchy as the only viable mode of masculinity or fathering. Embracing the higher feminine anima is the path to a more sustainable, flexible and playful style of gender for men.

Also intriguing is Tacey's Jungian narrative of the issues and problems facing materialist academic men's studies. Archetypal dynamics may be patterned through myths. Tacey portrays patriarchy as a Chronos, who, fearful of the prediction that he will be supplanted by an offspring, swallowed his male and female children. The children of the myth represent more multiple and liberated styles of gender.

In psychological terms, the devouring Chronos is preventing other styles of masculinity (his sons Zeus, Poseidon, Hades) and other feminine forms (his daughters Hestia, Demeter, Hera) from coming to birth. The fact that Chronos consumes the new indicates that a single archetypal complex has seized control, and everything in psyche and society is subsumed by his one dictatorial style. This is precisely what the new men's studies is about: releasing suppressed or devoured styles of masculinity or femininity from the all-devouring hegemonic complex that is called patriarchy.[14]

However, Tacey is critical of men's studies for what he calls 'mythological slippage'.[15] He discerns both a hostility towards the father and the overemphasized concentration on relations with the mother as a lapse from the desirable completing of the Chronos myth. What happens in the myth to Chronos is that Zeus frees his siblings by tricking his father, and all the (archetypal) heterogeneity of the gods and goddesses is let loose. What appears to be happening in men's studies, says Tacey, is a decamping from the myth of Chronos into the dangerous seductions of Oedipus. This doomed so-called hero kills off his father the better to enjoy the forbidden embraces of the mother.

Tacey points out that Freud, so ubiquitous in gender theory, fears the Oedipal destiny. Hostility to the father and the reduction of the feminine solely to the maternal are no answer. For Tacey, gender theorists have been hampered by only one myth in psychoanalysis, that of Oedipus, where the feminine is confined to mother. If progressive and feminist theorists would only look at Jung, they would discover an archetypal feminine not reductively confined to mothering.[16]

Tacey is a true imitator of Jung also in his use of the 'personal-myth' methodology. Noting that feminism asserts the value of the personal in theoretical thinking, he, like Jung, describes his own psychic engagement with gender.

I would describe Tacey's work as a stimulating contribution to Jungian feminisms both despite, and because of, his focus on masculinity. A Jungian theorizing of masculinity designed to promote the social struggles of feminism is itself a feminist activity. The stress on the personal element in theorizing and in gender identity is here not essentialist in claiming a secure purchase upon an eternal masculine. It reaches out to, and makes room for, others of all kinds.

Feminist theorists looking at Jung from other disciplines

Demaris S. Wehr   Demaris S. Wehr's 1987 book, *Jung and Feminism: Liberating Archetypes*, appears at first to take a rather jaundiced and reductive view of the complexity of her two topics.[17] She sets up an opposition between 'feminism' (signifying here gender as culturally contextual) and Jung/Jungians, for whom, she says, 'the feminine is indeed biological, innate, even ontological [of being]'.[18]

A reduction of Jungian theory to biological essentialism, with gender as virtually detached from cultural influence (implied in the 'ontological'), might well be assented to by Jung in his more prejudiced moods and by some of the 'Jungian feminism' discussed in chapter 3. Wehr quotes Ann Ulanov on the 'irreducibility' of the feminine principle, even if subject to *some* cultural distortion.

Yet such a straightforward opposition between feminism as culturally constructivist on gender and Jungian theory as completely essentialist and conservative cannot be maintained by a careful scrutiny of Jung's work (see chapter 2), nor is it fair even to some of the metaphysical Jungian feminism of chapter 3. Wehr goes on to make this point herself in a more nuanced consideration of Jung's archetypes.

The major contribution of Wehr's work lies in her linking insights from theology to a sociology of knowledge. This enables her to read Jung's description of archetypal gendering as portraying socially conditioned reality as experienced in patriarchal culture. She interprets much of Jung's own accounts of gender as providing a mirror of cultural stereotyping. The danger inherent in Jung's theory is that accounts of archetypal expressions in one patriarchal culture may be taken for timeless truths about women. The creation of 'grand-theory' (my term not Wehr's) Jungian feminism of the feminine principle is an example of such a congealing of socially contingent ideas into restrictive unyielding codes.

However, Wehr is not principally a materialist feminist critic, as her position in feminist theology would indicate. She seeks a productive union between Jung and feminism by drawing upon the potential of Jungian psychology to explore religious experiences positively. Also she realizes the potential of the Jungian psyche to heal those damaged by patriarchy.

Without using the terms, Wehr outlines *a* 'Jungian feminism', retaining only the personal-myth aspects of Jung. She values the Jung who posits a meaning-making, intrinsically religious, creative and culturally engaged psyche. This Jung she distinguishes from the 'grand theorist' who made reductive pronouncements about women.

Naomi R. Goldenberg   Naomi R. Goldenberg's fascinating approach to Jung from a feminist perspective very acutely accuses 'Jungians' of simplifying the textual complexity of Jung's writings. Effectively, she accuses much of Jungian studies of condensing him solely into 'grand theory',[19] a point with which I would concur.

Unlike traditional Jungian feminists, Goldenberg finds no redeeming potential in the theory of the transcendent archetype, perhaps because she still considers it as gender determining. In arguing that 'feminist scholars must examine the very idea of the archetype in Jungian thought if sexism is ever to be confronted at its base',[20] she appears to suggest that culture can play no role in psychic gender for Jungians. This position is not a necessary consequence of the theory of archetypes, as I have shown. To Goldenberg, the alternative to challenging Jung's notion of the archetype is either to accept patriarchal sexism as unchangeable, or to search for 'feminine' archetypes (as in goddess feminism). This latter option she dislikes for its detachment of gender from cultural conditions.

She seems to have fallen into the trap, which she herself identifies, of reading Jung exclusively in his dogmatic mode, thereby missing the possibilities of his *androgynous* archetypes, which are representable only through culturally influenced archetypal images.

Where Goldenberg's attempt to find a Jungian feminism ends is with a position taken by James Hillman's archetypal psychology. She does away with the transcendent archetype as such, in favour of the pure archetype-as-image. Despite references to Hillman, Goldenberg's emphasis is very different in insisting upon keeping the archetypal image as a vehicle of *cultural* expression. Culture and history play a formative role in the images generated by the psyche. This Jungian feminism is a combination of three elements: the challenge to Jung as master-theorist, the stress on the psyche as creative and religious *and*, thirdly, a strong role for culture in shaping subjectivity and gender.

Feminist archetypal theory

Both Wehr and Goldenberg are associated with the interdisciplinary project of feminist archetypal theory, best represented in the book *Feminist Archetypal Theory: Interdisciplinary Re-Visions of Jungian Thought*, edited and introduced by Estella Lauter and Carol Schreier

Rupprecht.[21] In spite of the acknowledged link to archetypal psychology, there are crucial differences in the approach of these feminist scholars from fields as diverse as religion, psychology, literature and the visual arts. It is, therefore, necessary for this book to keep the term 'archetypal psychology' for the Hillman-inspired movement, and 'feminist archetypal theory' for those scholars so defined by Lauter and Rupprecht's work. Both archetypal psychology and feminist archetypal theory reject the transcendent archetype for the immanent image. From this point differences start to emerge.

Lauter and Rupprecht's introduction describes the convergence of scholars and theoretical methods through academic conferences in the late 1970s and early 1980s. Interestingly, to Hillman's condensation of the archetype into image, Lauter and Rupprecht add work by Erich Neumann in 1959 to suggest that such images will be coloured by culture.[22]

With this deliberately dual inheritance, feminist archetypal theory can insist upon the pressure of society and ideology registering in the psychic image. This enables feminist archetypal theory to situate itself as a feminist intervention in the humanities. It offers innovative and even emancipatory accounts of the category, 'women'. 'In the case of feminist theory, if we regard the archetype not as an image whose content is frozen . . . but as a tendency to form and re-form images in relation to certain kinds of repeated experience, then the concept could serve to clarify distinctively female concerns that have persisted throughout human history.'[23] Such a theory possesses intriguing connections to a number of anxieties and issues surrounding contemporary 'feminisms'. On the surface, feminist archetypal theory appears to be essentialist in assuming an uncontestable grouping called 'women' across cultures and throughout history. This is not really the case. 'Women' in feminist archetypal theory will produce culturally contingent images, so preserving and expressing *any* form of 'differences' including those of race, sexuality, culture, history, health, age.

There is no basis in feminist archetypal theory for generating a 'norm', an account of what images 'ought' to be, so producing a hierarchy amongst them and, by extension, amongst women. For this Jungian feminism, an archetype can never be fully known 'until all its manifestations – past, present and future – are brought to light'.[24] This is the same as asserting that it can never be fully 'known' at all. Therefore, no fundamental or ideal models can be produced.

Lauter and Rupprecht similarly do not assert any absolute or simple difference between those images produced by women and those derived from the male psyche, despite the hint of essentialism in their search for 'distinctively female concerns' in the above quotation.

Feminist archetypal theory is consciously in the realm of Jungian theory where the psyche is vitally connected to the body, yet is not governed by it. Lauter and Rupprecht argue that the experiential context of the image is necessary to its discussion (a psychic image cannot simply be explained, because that would be to deny its primary imaginary quality, as Jung would agree).

'Experiential context' of the archetypal image can include the body, but the body is not to be regarded as the transcendent source of the image's significance. Whatever the body 'is' is also subject to archetypal fantasies. Some such fantasies may be patriarchally distorted. Further challenges to the category of the sexed body as a 'natural' entity as opposed to a 'cultural' gender are considered in chapter 6.

Of course, feminist archetypal theory repudiates Jung as a patriarchal authority and what Rupprecht has called his 'prison-house of language'.[25] Patriarchal language is particularly apparent in Jung's description of the woman's animus (see chapter 2 for examples). Rupprecht has coined the term 'animity', to signify a process of 'befriending the soul' or unconscious, in order to replace the constrictions of Jung's binary anima/animus.[26]

Feminist archetypal theory is a Jungian feminism devoted to uncovering the traces of women's unconscious in the arts and across cultural boundaries. It can be socially oriented in looking for cultural pressures and effects within the feminine psyche. Yet it can never be a materialist feminism, because it retains the core Jungian notion of the creative *otherness* of the unconscious. Psychic images will be affected by, but never determined by, the culture and the ego's witnessing of it.

What most Jungian feminisms will probably have in common is Jung's defining concept of the irreducible and transformative 'otherness' of the unconscious. Feminist archetypal theory combines this principle with a successful renunciation of hierarchies amongst women and their archetypes-as-images.

Developmental psychology: a post-Jungian school

Developmental Jungian psychology is one of the three post-Jungian schools set out by Andrew Samuels in 1985.[27] There he described those dedicated to maintaining Jung's techniques (the classical school), those modifying the theory of the archetype (archetypal psychology) and those seeking a creative rapprochement with the Freudian tradition (the developmental school).

What particularly characterizes developmental Jungian theorizing is the reconsidering of links and dissimilarities between Jung and

Freud, and psychoanalytic pioneers after Freud. Developmental psychology is especially interested in Freudian accounts of early childhood. 'Object-relations' psychoanalysts such as Melanie Klein, Wilfred Bion, Donald Winnicott and John Bowlby took these up. Thinking about early childhood using object-relations leads to a consideration of transference and counter-transference in analysis.

Transference signifies the way an analysand unintentionally projects his or her inner turmoil upon the analyst. In effect, the analyst becomes a screen for part of the analysand's psyche. Freud realized that transference would play a vital role in the talking cure. Counter-transference is the reciprocal move on the part of the analyst. Jung was the first practitioner to argue that the analyst's psyche would also engage in unwitting transference, and that it, too, could be a valuable tool.

Despite developmental psychology's wish to build bridges between psychoanalytic practice and the Jungian legacy, real differences remain. Freudian theory is both reductive and backward-looking in its stress on early infantile states as the 'scene' to be primarily investigated. By contrast, Jung urged for a prospective and forward-driving notion of the psyche. Dreams and psychic symptoms are geared towards *future* evolution of the personality. What the person might *become* is even more important than where he or she has *been*.

Consequently, although Jung was content to include Oedipal structuration into his overall scheme, the early years of a person could never be of such overwhelming significance. It is the creative, prospective encounters with the superior potentials of the unconscious that Jung regarded as first principles.

Object-relations theory derives from Freudian psychoanalysis with a crucial modification. Where, for Freud, the infant is primarily driven by instincts, in object-relations a child possesses from birth the capacity to relate to its caregivers. Here the 'object' takes on two significances: it is the person to whom the child seeks to relate, and also a set of motivations attributed to the 'other' by the infant (although actually located in the child).

In suggesting that a child from birth brings the ability to interact with caregivers, object-relations moves closer to Jung and his belief in an inherited potential for certain mental capacities. Developmental Jungian theory has identified suggestive parallels and fruitful differences in the emphases of Melanie Klein and Jung in early mental bonding to the mother.

As Hester McFarland Solomon points out, Klein's language of the infant's early appreciation of the mother as 'part-objects' and not as a separate mirroring 'other' can be translated into Jungian language as archetypal images of the mother.[28] These images are formed through the child's very early experiences of the mother's body. When Klein suggests that an infant's fantasy will produce shifting notions of a 'good' and 'bad' breast, Jung offers dual aspects of the mother archetype as both nurturing *and* destructive.

Although the two sets of positions diverge, in developmental Jungian theory, Jung and Klein need not entirely divorce. In mapping the infant's psyche, Klein's ideas of part-objects largely refer to the child's paranoid state prior to achieving a separate sense of self. Irrational images and memories of mothering are repressed into the unconscious and may be relived through later analysis.

Jung has a richer, more romantic notion of the destructive/nurturing mother. She lives in a person's unconscious in ways devoted to the future growth of the personality, even in her destructive form. Developmental psychology remains Jungian in its maintenance of the forward-driving creativity of the archetypal parents. Yet linking with object-relations theory means that it has a method that can focus upon early parent–child interaction (mother or father) in analysis.

In placing Jung's archetypes in the context of very early psychological development, developmental thinkers are not contradicting Jung. They are merely reversing his preference for focusing upon the second half of life.

One result of developmental psychology is the possibility for Jungian feminisms more coherent with Freudian psychoanalytic feminist theories. See chapter 5 for more on this. It is already possible to see how a Jung/Klein treatment of the mother could be used critically to examine a subject's psychological investment in mothering and its role in the emerging person. Such a Jungian–Kleinian feminism would be open to exploring the social–psychic processing of the literal embodied mother. It could also seek to build upon a meaningful sense of 'mother' in the psyche, not limited in richness to the ego's actual experience.

If 'mother' can be creatively revised, then gender too can be freed up from either the deficiencies of personal history, or the shaping conventions of a particular society. As a way of further exploring Jungian feminisms that focus on the developing child, I will briefly look at some of Andrew Samuels's work on 'the father'.[29]

Andrew Samuels on gender and theory (for feminism)

Andrew Samuels's affinities with the developmental school have contributed to a radical analysis of the father-relation in feminist-friendly ways. Increasingly concerned to link Jungian ideas with progressive, left-leaning politics, his ongoing project linking politics with psychology has been influential and revisionary.[30] Critical of object-relations' almost exclusive stress on the mother–child interface, Samuels's treatment of fathering suggests possibilities for pro-feminist thinking about the role of gender in society. Only some of his work productive for Jungian feminisms can be touched upon here.

As with many Jungian gender theorists, Samuels is sceptical of Jung's cultural biases concerning women, including his lapse into bodily essentialism on gender. While not discarding the concepts of anima and animus, he argues that contrasexual images in the psyche are metaphors for 'otherness', not representations of a particular set of gendered characteristics. An image of a being with another anatomy stands for whatever is currently unknown or may, perhaps, be unknowable. Relations between consciousness and anima or animus are not to be mistaken as endorsing stereotypes of gender. 'The difference between you and your animus or anima is very different from the difference between you and a man or a woman.'[31] Samuels is also highly suspicious of what he calls 'Jungian feminism', by which he means the grand-theory practitioners of chapter 3. He is particularly critical of the concentration upon 'the feminine principle', seeing it as both theoretically and politically flawed. It is theoretically flawed because it amplifies Jung's fantasy of opposites upon gender to even more theological proportions. 'It is assumed that there is something eternal about *femininity* and, hence, about *women*; that women therefore display certain transcultural and ahistorical characteristics; and that these can be described in psychological terms.'[32] The result politically is that the cultural contribution to gender is ignored, so that 'Jungian feminism' aims at a simple reversal of power positions. Such opposition is tempered by Samuels's careful assessment of *why* Jungian studies felt the need to amplify 'the feminine principle'. This motif and its more inflated form of goddess feminism supplied a means of celebrating women from within Jung's ideas, as well as providing a standpoint from which to criticize capitalist patriarchal culture. Samuels acknowledges that goddess feminism may have a *practical* role in generating imagery to deal with women's pain and struggle, *if* it is employed as a *metaphor*. If such therapy turns literal, into claims of eternal qualities in women, it risks becoming essentialist and prescriptive.[33]

Samuels does not describe himself as a Jungian feminist. In part this is because he sees Jungian feminism as the single entity clustering around the notion of the feminine principle (he is not yet thinking in terms of 'Jungian feminisms'). Also, Samuels's attachment to progressive causes ranges wider than gender relations and the feminist label would be too constricting. However, some of Samuels's work does provide a framework for a Jungian feminism in revisioning gender in a creative dialogue with psychoanalysis.

First, what Jung called the anima and animus is equally available to both women and men – there is no question of women being 'alien' to logical and intellectual thinking. He also stresses the need to question the innateness of heterosexuality, a position implicit in Jung's androgynous collective unconscious. Samuels prefers to rethink Freud's notion of the infant as sexually undetermined or 'perverse' as 'a vision of there being available to all a variety of positions in relation to gender role – without recourse to the illusion of androgyny'.[34]

In *The Plural Psyche* Samuels describes his theoretical position as that of 'pluralism', meaning a drawing-upon different psychologies without attempting to synthesize them, or to structure a comparative hierarchy. Such a theoretical model is explicitly part of a political project: it offers a way of engaging with differences of all kinds between people of different genders, ethnicities and classes, and also the differences *within* the individual psyche. This stance is implicitly a call for Jungian feminisms, not an exclusive Jungian feminism.

Crucially, in *The Plural Psyche* Samuels suggests that difficulties concerning fathering can lead to 'gender certainty' in ways problematic for both daughters and sons. 'The father' is a created, not a biological, relationship.[35] Fathering is predominantly psychological and cultural. Its constructed role impacts upon the (originally biological) mother–infant condition and converts it into a cultural mother–child relationship.

Recognition of the socially constructed father allows a greater sense of the mothering relation as socially contingent. The father need not be the biological male parent. Viewing him as a created relation enables Samuels to posit a father-of-whatever-sex; 'others', women included, can construct this role.

The key issue with fathering in terms of gender is that a sense of a 'lack' in the father as being deficient in some way can result in a psychological congealing of gender identities. This is because an insufficient bonding with 'a father' leads to ideas of the feminine becoming exclusively centred on the mother *as just this one role*. Femininity equals motherhood in a squeezing of gender possibilities into narrow conventions injurious to both daughters and sons.

What daughters also need, argues Samuels, is what he calls 'erotic playback' from their fathers.[36] A father's emotional energy should contain sexuality in order to give his daughter a sense of emotional and psychological selfhood beyond mothering. This is *not* to sanction acted-out sexuality between fathers and daughters: literal incest is unequivocally damaging.[37]

Rather, in being apparently 'Freudian' in considering emotion and psychic energy as sexual, Samuels is equally Jungian in suggesting that erotic energy can come to signify *something else*: more plural gender possibilities. The value of erotic playback between fathers and children is that more imaginative versions of gender, even 'gender confusion', could result. Samuels calls for an analytic practice that enables a person to live with the tension between gender confusion (which enables gender to be rethought against social norms, yet might entail pain), and gender certainty (needed for a sense of stability yet tending to anchor itself on traditional gender expectations).[38]

This 'Jungian feminism' develops a liberatory concept of fathering in ways vitally linked to Freudian psychoanalysis. It remains a *Jungian* feminism in using the forward-driving notion of the psyche as well as the plural creative unconscious to reorient restrictive conventions of gender.

The creativity of the unconscious also aids Samuels in *The Political Psyche* when he seeks a politically liberating paternal in society. Such a being can mitigate the restrictive effects of Jacques Lacan's phallic father, so long held responsible for the social formation and perpetuation of patriarchy. Samuels provides a father of gender confusion to set against Lacan's symbolic father of gender certainty.[39] The next chapter will look at further opportunities for Jungian feminisms in this revisionary reading of Lacan.

History, feminism and Jung

I want to end this chapter on existing work in Jungian feminisms with an example of the possibilities of historical feminist critiques of Jung, drawing upon Samuels's discussion of gender confusion.

In chapters 1 and 2, I showed how Jung's personal involvement with female mediums revealed a gender politics at the genesis of his psychology. Women in Jung's life and writing become displaced into the characteristics of the anima, the feminine part of a male's psyche. Jung's attraction to the female medium was not simply a fascination with a certain female personality, despite its repetition in later life with the medium-like Sabina Spielrein and Toni Wolff. In fact, Jung's attraction to mediums seems to be bound up with the desire to *become* a medium in his later work. The medium continues as a woman in his emotional life in the person of Toni Wolff.

Most significantly, Jung becomes highly mediumistic in his contacting of unconscious figures within, notably his anima. A gender politics marking Jungian psychology as masculine theory redefines the troubling excesses of spiritualism, predominantly associated with women. In gender terms we have masculine-authored psychology seeking to neutralize its own 'other' (feminine), mental phenomena that until now defy 'scientific' explanation.

What is 'other' to the rational, theoretical mind of the ego is the unconscious. Jung's prime image for the unconscious is the feminine anima. He takes over the role of the medium in order to posit a theoretical relationship to the other as feminine. The feminine as real woman becomes displaced in Jungian theory to the feminine as anima, the 'other' to theory and clear thinking itself.

Yet this historically based feminist critique needs to recognize the ambivalence within Jung in his personal and psychic history. In his shifts between his desiring the female medium and taking on the role of the culturally defined 'female' medium, he is, in Andrew Samuels's terms, tracing a continuum between 'gender certainty' and 'gender confusion'.

To the extent that the medium is culturally marked as a feminine position (in typical practice and because 'other' to the prevailing medical orthodoxies), Jung's psyche also genders the medium in the persistence in his emotional life of medium-like women. Jung moves between gender certainty in fascination with the feminine as another, separate person, and gender confusion in taking on the 'feminine' medium position himself, in order to get closer to his 'other' within.

It is surely significant that, when medium himself, Jung most of all focuses upon his feminine anima, *as if he needed the unconscious to be feminine* to try to protect his (masculine) ego from being overwhelmed by it, *in order to keep the ego masculine*. Perhaps his tendency to think in gendered opposites, most obviously in the emphasis upon the anima as a devious unconscious opposite to his absolutely masculine consciousness, demonstrates inner vulnerability. It shows a need to shore up his identity against the chaos threatened by gender confusion.

James Hillman's anima theory suggests that we abandon the masculine heroic ego and aim for a consciousness that is anima based, attached to the unconscious and the feminine. Maybe Jung had already reached this position in his gender confusion between his desire *for*, and his desire to *be*, the 'feminine' medium linked to the spirits as unconscious powers.

Moreover, the oscillation in Jung between gender confusion (as a medium) and gender certainty (rigidly defining his consciousness as masculine reason, condensing ideas of women into his unconscious anima) is a version of his dual tendency to grand theory and personal myth. The concepts making up grand theory are heavily reliant upon the tension of opposites, especially opposites structured as gender. Grand theory is therefore the product of the drive to gender certainty, whereas personal myth's acknowledgement of the inability to reduce otherness of the unconscious to a set of symmetrical concepts could be read as Jung's personal loyalty to gender confusion.

Jungian studies may be slow to recognize the situation, but they have now embarked upon an era of Jungian feminisms. These will serve to mitigate and diversify the grand-theory-influenced Jungian feminism mapped in chapter 3. Chapter 5 will follow up archetypal psychology's interest in poststructuralism and developmental psychology's positive engagement with psychoanalysis. It will consider new Jungian feminisms in deconstruction and post-Freudian theories of gender, two areas prominent in the wider feminist debate. Afterwards, chapter 6 will look at the potentials for Jungian reading of alchemy and the body. From these it will outline a Jungian role for key feminist concerns: of narrative, the Gothic, the sublime and postmodernism.

Concluding summary

Pro-feminist Jungian thinking on gender has moved on from the creation of a psychology for all women, known as 'Jungian feminism', to the more diverse and differentiated 'Jungian feminisms'. I link Jungian feminisms to the 'personal-myth' aspect of Jung's writing because it allows, even promotes, developments of Jung's ideas that refuse to treat Jung as an authoritative 'grand theorist'.

Two post-Jungian schools, the archetypal and the developmental, can be associated with 'personal myth' in adopting the reflexive, self-critical dimension of Jung to structure feminisms. Neither school is principally defined as 'feminist'. In addition, both from within Jungian studies and from the perspective of other disciplines, critical treatments of masculinity now connect Jung to progressive debates on gender. This acts as a welcome counterweight to the reactionary oversimplification of Jung.

And, finally, historically located feminist research can place Jung in the context of his contemporary cultural anxieties over gender, women, psychology and the status of institutionally endorsed 'theory'. The feminism that seeks an alliance of theoretical feminisms (owing to 'difference' and unique cultural contexts) meets in Jung's personal myth an answering voice. As well as being the progenitor of the monolith 'Jungian feminism' with its tendency to view gender as 'one', Jung is also the sponsor of 'Jungian feminisms'.

FURTHER READING

James Hillman's anima and archetypal psychology

Hillman, James, 'Anima', *Spring: A Journal of Archetype and Culture* (1973), 97–132.
Hillman, James, 'Anima II', *Spring: A Journal of Archetype and Culture* (1974), 113–46.
Engaging and persuasive rethinking of Jung's anima in ways sympathetic to feminist analysis.

Hillman, James, *Archetypal Psychology: A Brief Account* (Dallas, Tex.: Spring Publications Inc., 1983).
Accessible introduction to archetypal psychology; contains a comprehensive bibliography of works by James Hillman up to 1983.

Jungian feminisms in the humanities

Barnaby, Karin, and D'Acierno, Pellegrino (eds), C. G. *Jung and the Humanities: Towards a Hermeneutics of Culture* (London: Routledge, 1990).
Fascinating collection with influential pieces by other archetypal psychologists such as Paul Kugler and feminist archetypal theorist Carol Schreier Rupprecht, and a round-table discussion including Robert Bly.

Goldenberg, Naomi R., 'A Feminist Critique of Jung', in Robert L. Moore and Daniel J. Meckel (eds), *Jung and Christianity in Dialogue: Faith, Feminism and Hermeneutics* (Mahwah, NY: Paulist Press, 1990), pp. 104–11.
Trenchant criticism of Jung's limitation on gender, combined with a call for a more archetypally oriented feminism.

Tacey, David, *Remaking Men: Jung, Spirituality and Social Change* (London: Routledge, 1997).
Tells you everything you need to know about the mythopoetic men's movement and what is wrong with it. Readable and convincing attempt to conjoin academic men's studies with progressive Jungian theory.

Wehr, Demaris S., *Jung and Feminism: Liberating Archetypes* (Boston: Beacon Press, 1987).
Oversimplifies an 'opposition' between Jung and feminism. Goes on to make a valuable argument for his integration into feminist thinking in the humanities.

Feminist archetypal theory

Lauter, Estella, and Rupprecht, Carol Schreier, *Feminist Archetypal Theory: Interdisciplinary Re-Visions of Jungian Thought* (Knoxville, Ten.: University of Tennessee Press, 1985).
Comprehensive introduction to this important Jungian feminism. Includes essays on literature, visual art and feminist therapy.

Developmental Jungian psychology and Andrew Samuels

Samuels, Andrew, *The Plural Psyche: Personality, Morality and the Father* (London: Routledge, 1989).
The call for 'pluralism' to embrace Jungian studies makes the case for 'Jungian feminisms' without using the term. Highly innovative and progressive work on gender in the context of Jung, Freud and their legacies.

Samuels, Andrew, *Politics on the Couch: Citizenship and the Internal Life* (London: Profile Books, 2001).
Fascinating and optimistic reading of psychology and politics together. Very accessible and blends political with psychological approaches to gender.

Young-Eisendrath, Polly, and Dawson, Terence (eds), *The Cambridge Companion to Jung* (Cambridge: Cambridge University Press, 1997).
Contains helpful introductions to both archetypal and developmental schools with extensive bibliographies.

5

Jungian Feminisms in Deconstruction and Post-Freudian Feminism

The names I give do not imply a philosophy, although I cannot prevent people from barking at these terminological phantoms as if they were metaphysical . . .

(Jung, *The Practice of Psychotherapy*, 1954)

Thus the insinuations of the anima, the mouthpiece of the unconscious, can utterly destroy a man.

(Jung, *Memories, Dreams, Reflections*, 1963)

This chapter looks at Jung in the light of two powerful movements in feminist theory: deconstruction and post-Freudian feminism. It considers Jungian writing in relation to the work of Jacques Derrida, and the psychoanalytically oriented feminism of Luce Irigaray, Hélène Cixous and Julia Kristeva. I aim to suggest a relationship between Jung and deconstruction that would provide expanding opportunities for Jungian feminisms. Additionally I will show how the influential feminisms of Irigaray, Cixous and Kristeva set up echoes and correspondences in Jung's work, without eroding the real differences between them.

Introduction

The previous chapter placed innovations in post-Jungian gender in the context of the diversifying of feminist theory, as well as Jung's 'personal-myth' forms of writing. Feminist theory has evolved away from accepting a simple category of 'all women everywhere'. It has moved towards an understanding of multiple differences of gender identity. This development in feminism owes a great deal to productive encounters with deconstruction and psychoanalysis.[1] These encounters can be characterized in two ways: as feminist theory 'learning from' and as 'making strategic use of' these complex intellectual resources.

From deconstruction, feminism learned of philosophical challenges to the types of knowledge that had long denigrated the feminine as part of their structuring as 'truth', 'science' or 'philosophy'. 'Language', for deconstruction, is not a transparent tool for communication or knowledge. Rather, it is an unstable entity that constructs fragile cultural forms and disputes the very possibility of a unitary gendered self. Consequently, deconstruction can be used *strategically* by feminists to undermine traditional ideologies or myths that have historically oppressed women.

From Freudian psychoanalysis, feminists learned to regard subjectivity and gender as a web of psychic and social structuring that is never fixed and complete. A person's interior landscape is always an ongoing process. Despite Freud's belief in the ultimate inferiority of the feminine mind, psychoanalysis, particularly as extended in the work of Jacques Lacan, provides opportunities for feminists to explore the psychic pain of patriarchy, and to imagine ways of rethinking gender.[2]

The so-called French feminists, Luce Irigaray, Hélène Cixous and Julia Kristeva, have performed particularly significant work strategically linking deconstruction and psychoanalysis.[3] What feminist theory has largely not yet done is to bring the psychology of C. G. Jung into this fertile arena. Therefore this chapter aims, first, to read Jung in relation to deconstruction. I will then turn to some of the key ideas of the French feminists that seem to resonate with Jung's own complex reactions to gender.

One aspect of my method here needs to be carefully stated: I am not trying to 'convert' Jung into deconstruction, or to argue that his psychology is really an early version of the feminism of Irigaray, Cixous or Kristeva. Instead, I propose to explore echoes, correspondences and differences between Jung's work and these areas, in the cause of Jungian feminisms.

It would be a betrayal of the complexity of Jung's *Collected Works* to attempt to absorb him totally into something countered and contradicted in some aspect of his writing (for he could never be a 'pure' deconstructionist and is certainly not a feminist in intention). Any attempt to remake a thinker into a feminist by ignoring significant parts of his or her work is similarly a betrayal of the feminist principle of respecting 'difference'.

First of all, this chapter needs to introduce deconstruction and its context in the cultural movements of structuralism and poststructuralism.

What is structuralism, poststructuralism and deconstruction?

Structuralism was a development in the social sciences and humanities that regarded cultural meaning as the product of fundamental, yet often unrealized, structures.[4] A cultural unit, whether it be a family pattern, a novel, or even a single word, acquires meaning *only* in relation to the other cultural units in its particular social sequence. Instead of the individual cultural entity possessing its own, separate, meaning and identity, meaning is *constructed* unwittingly out of the *relationship* the individual item of culture has with its entire structural system.

For example, the novel *Middlemarch* has no intrinsic significance of its own. The culture attributes meaning to it because it differs from *Adam Bede* (another novel by George Eliot) and because it occurs in the categories of nineteenth-century British novels, the novel as a whole, literature, prose narrative and the system of language. Within the novel, structures will construct meanings of words and sentences only in relation to other words and sentences. *Middlemarch* does not possess its own unique relationship to 'reality', 'truth' or 'the world'.

For structuralism, language is not a transparent window onto the world. Rather, language is conceived of as a system that constructs meanings through connections and differences between words. Cultural units, including words, operate as 'signs', organizing meaning on a principle of how the sign differs from its adjacent one. For example, the word 'fog' signifies what it does because it is not 'dog' or 'bog'. The word-as-sign works by its *difference* from the other words, not by any intrinsic bond to 'reality', here the cloudy substance. The 'real thing' that the word refers to is called the 'referent' and is not part of the language system.

Signs of all kinds are divided into two aspects: the 'signifier' is the material form (the letters on the page in the case of a written word), while the 'signified' is the meaning, the cultural significance. In the case of the sign 'fog', the signified is my understanding of what fog is. It is not the substance itself, the referent, which stands outside as wholly separate from the mechanism of language.

Poststructuralism is the radical challenge to the stabilities of structuralism. Whereas structuralism presupposed that cultural systems, however separate from 'reality' or nature, could at least keep meaning from shifting or wobbling, poststructuralism renounces any such confidence. Structuralist analysis assumed the relative stability of the underlying structures and cultural codes. Poststructuralism pushed some of these presuppositions to a crisis point.

Structuralism split off language and culture from the belief in a 'natural' relationship to 'the word' or 'reality'. In turn, poststructuralism took the next step in splitting off the signifier from the signified. There is no 'natural' bond here either. The signifier and signified, material mark and attributed significance, do not stick together. They slide over each other, so that meaning is forever slipping away when words are used. As a result, meaning, language and culture have to be rethought as radically unstable. If words cannot mean reliably, then forms of knowledge and power expressed in words also cannot be fixed, cannot be regarded as stable and 'true', in the sense of unchanging. Furthermore, instability of language means that even subjectivity, including a sense of who I am, is not secure. If meaning is forever slipping away, then so is *self*-expression: when 'I' speak, I cannot give myself reliable meaning or even a secure narrative of who I am. Subjectivity is revealed as a product of language. Like language, it is fragile and subject to slippage.

Deconstruction is the form of poststructuralism associated with the work of Jacques Derrida on language.[5] Structuralist analyses demonstrated that many Western cultural forms are dependent upon a system of binary oppositions in order to construct their meaning. A binary opposition works by one term excluding and in that way defining the other term. For example, 'male' gains its meaning by being structured as 'not female'.

Other common cultural binaries are masculine/feminine, body/mind and nature/culture. In such a structure one term inevitably becomes privileged above the other in a hierarchy. One term becomes the 'other', whose exclusion defines the prior category. Such binary hierarchies can often be shown to underpin 'common-sense' notions, such as traditional beliefs in the inferiority of women.

Christopher Norris has defined Derridean deconstruction as an activity inimical to binary oppositions: it 'seeks to undo both a given order of priorities and the very system of conceptual oppositions that makes that order possible'.[6] What Derrida points out is the *metaphysical* bases of beliefs about language as a stable system of meaning. Traditionally philosophy has relied upon a binary opposition between speech and writing in which speech is regarded as superior because the *presence* of the speaker acts as a guarantor of 'his' meaning. Writing, on the other hand, without the author present to back up his words, is all too often open to misinterpretation.

Such a binary opposition gives rise to 'logocentrism', which is the idea that there can be a full and *present* meaning of the word. A word can unambiguously mean what it says, and say what it means. Logocentrism, argues Derrida, is *metaphysical* because it is an object of belief rather than a logical consequence.[7] This is because, in fact, speech is *not* prior to writing. It is the system of language enshrined in writing that gives speech its capacity to 'mean' anything in the first place. Logocentrism relies on an assumption of secure meaning that the slippery nature of the language system cannot supply. Hence logocentrism is metaphysical, something posited as *outside* the verifiable world.

Against metaphysical logocentrism, Derrida demonstrates slippage of meaning in the sliding of the signifiers over signifieds. Despite the logocentric cultural pretence that words have stable meanings, this is really not the case. Any cultural system that desires to maintain some semblance of unity between signifier and signified requires a powerful 'god-term', a word of ultimate significance (like God, Truth, Man, Materialism) that purports to pin the rest of the system of meanings together.

The god-term acts as a 'transcendental signifier/signified', since it tries to 'transcend' the inherent capacity of language to slip and spill its cargo of meaning. Once the transcendental sign can be shown to be a myth (a form of metaphysical logocentrism), signs are revealed as operating upon principles of difference from each other (the structuralist position) and *deferral* (the poststructuralist addition). They will defer a fixed meaning infinitely in a continual sliding of signifier over signified.

Instead of having a 'set' system of structures, as if it was a crystal, language has the ever-moving quality of a liquid, spilling and disseminating meaning. This 'liquid quality' of difference and deferral, Derrida put together in his invented word, *différance*. It expresses his perception of his perception of a radical instability of language, and therefore of culture, knowledge and human subjectivity. The systems and underlying cultural codes that the structuralists were proud of discovering are, in fact, very fragile *fictions* in their claims to organize truth and significance. Deconstruction does what the word indicates: it shows texts simultaneously constructing and destructing in their claim to offer knowledge and meaning.

Derrida's deconstruction of the ways in which texts set up a notion of 'truth' shows that binary oppositions are not 'natural' categories but fictions. Binary oppositions always require a 'supplement' or something from 'outside' (so something metaphysical), which is then

offered as the originating principle. Yet, this supplement, as metaphysical origin, is not a fixed point of authorization; deconstruction
reveals that it is produced by the text itself. The so-called origin is, in
actuality, a supplement generated by the text or cultural system (a
text, for Derrida, encompasses all form of human signifying), in a
vain attempt to stabilize its capacity for meaning. In deconstruction,
all texts can do is to demonstrate their own metaphorical nature.
They are never able to give a fixed transparent version of 'truth'.
Theories of all kinds become another variety of 'literature' or
'fiction'. Read deconstructively, theories are criticisms of their own
attempts to speak authoritatively.

At this point, feminism's interest in deconstruction becomes explicable. As a technique for dissolving the power of philosophies that rely
upon binary oppositions that suppress the feminine, deconstruction is
invaluable. Yet feminism becomes ambivalent about deconstruction
when it comes to its desire to strengthen female subjectivity and to
lobby for political change. Here the impact of deconstruction on categories such as 'women' means that its efficacy is highly dubious. If subjectivity is so polluted with *différance* that terms such as 'women' have
no stable meaning, then deconstruction may well be useful as a recognition of multiple differences; yet it has its limitations as a political
creed. After all, if the category 'women' is regarded as a fiction, then
who will take seriously arguments about women in the labour force?

Therefore, feminist theories tend to embrace deconstruction warily
and in part only. Deconstruction is employed as a technique to challenge patriarchal institutions and ideas. It is not embraced whole-
heartedly as feminism's philosophical position.

Perhaps it is feminism's partial adopting of deconstruction that has
lead to its dual existence in contemporary critical culture. Critics of
all varieties have seized upon deconstruction as a method to untie
texts and dethrone institutional meanings. However, Derrida has
stressed that such a characterizing of deconstruction as just a critical
tool has missed the full implications of his work.

Deconstruction is . . . not a method, nor is it a set of rules or tools . . .
On the one hand, there is no 'applied deconstruction'. But on the other
hand, there is nothing else, since deconstruction doesn't consist in a set
of theorems, axioms, tools, rules, techniques, and methods. If deconstruction, then, is nothing by itself, the only thing it can do is apply, to
be applied, to something else . . . There is no deconstruction, deconstruction has no specific object . . . Deconstruction cannot be applied
and cannot *not* be applied.[8]

In this understanding of deconstruction, it is not a technique, but, as Julian Wolfreys puts it, an 'event' within texts and structures.[9] It is *there*, whether we are aware of it or not. Deconstructive readings are the revelation of unrepeatable crises of meaning within/upon texts. In addition, Derrida stresses a limit to the 'play' of deconstruction when he argues that metaphysical thinking is inescapable. There will always be, in every deconstructive reading, an irreducible metaphysical residue that is impermeable to deconstruction.

If feminism has had a hand in domesticating Derrida's philosophy as a critical method whose radical nature can be restricted, then it is worth considering deconstruction both as a technique and as an 'event' in relation to Jung.

Jung and structuralism, poststructuralism and deconstruction

To return to Jung, the theory of archetypes as basic, inherited structuring principles within the psyche puts Jung squarely in the tradition of structuralism. Of course, archetypes are not structures in the sense of fixed entities, as they are definitely not inherited images. What archetypes generate in the individual psyche varies widely with cultural, social and personal circumstances. Yet archetypes *are* structuralist in suggesting an underlying (if unfathomable) code.

Jung is being particularly structuralist when he argues that archetypes are like the structuring behind plant families: they do not materially 'exist' but are an energy shaping actual related forms.[10] Jung, the structuralist, is also Jung, the grand theorist, architect of a *systematic* account of psyche and culture. However, as I have suggested, there is an-Other Jung, that of personal myth.

Jung in poststructuralism and deconstruction

Deconstruction has polarized into what I will call, for the purposes of this book, 'feminist method' and 'philosophical event'. Feminists and other politically motivated critics may choose to limit the consequences of deconstruction for strategic ends. How far a theory may be *conscious* of its own deconstruction is another matter.

Jung's writings, particularly in what I have called the 'personal-myth' mode, are both aware and not aware of their own deconstructive potential. This ambivalent state of awareness is part of Jung's unique properties for psychology and feminism, for it is fundamental to his conception of the psyche. Therefore, I am going to look at the possibilities for Jung to become a thinker in deconstruction (not a deconstructionist *per se*), always in tension with his logocentric drive to be also a grand theorist.

When Jung writes authoritatively about the anima, animus and the female psyche attuned to Eros, he is being logocentric in assuming that these names have a full, present and stable meaning. In Derrida's sense, he is being metaphysical; in mine, a grand theorist.

On the other hand, the Jung of personal myth is not a simple deconstructionist. What I have called 'personal myth' covers a number of non-totalizing attitudes. As in the first quotation at the head of this chapter, it *includes* the overtly deconstructive refusal to be considered as providing a theory or a philosophy as metaphysical. Personal myth also stands for his belief in a theory being limited in scope by the personal psychology of the theorist. Yet crucially it is, as well, the very *non*-deconstructionist assertion that his theory is a 'true' personal myth because it is the truth of his own psyche, his own story of being, personal and true to himself.

The sense of a theory as a personal *myth* does gesture towards deconstruction if it suggests a constructed fiction. However, Jung often writes about his personal myth as a *local truth*, personal and true to himself as his own private metaphysics. The idea here of coexisting separate local truths in the subjectivity of every person aligns Jung with postmodernism more obviously than with deconstruction.

Frequently, in writing in the style of personal myth, Jung is least poststructuralist in tone, more apt to claim 'fixed' knowledge of his unconscious and anima. The first quotation heading this chapter demonstrates Jung in deconstructive guise when not thinking about himself: 'The names I give do not imply a philosophy, although I cannot prevent people from barking at these terminological phantoms as if they were metaphysical . . .'.[11] Then there is an expression of his experience of the anima in his personal myth that may have acute and essentialist consequences for women and gender. An essentialist attitude to gender, especially claiming 'knowledge' that 'all women are like this', is, of course, crudely logocentric and metaphysical in deconstructionist terms. 'Thus the insinuations of the anima, the mouthpiece of the unconscious, can utterly destroy a man.'[12]

I have previously argued that, when Jung described the start of his distinct theory in the discovery of the anima, the struggle for meaning took the form of a struggle with the feminine. In a move that is simultaneously both profoundly deconstructionist and essentializing-metaphysical, the anima is characterized as an unreliable woman, insisting on 'art' when Jung wants to found/fund a 'science'. 'She' is the key; she is portrayed as the origin of Jung's psychology – in the dual sense of his interior creative psyche *and* source of his system of ideas.

Inescapably for Jung, the unconscious is more significant in the psyche and cannot be appropriated by it. By implication, then, a theory, in so far as it is a rational system and so a child of the ego, cannot contain or wholly define the unconscious. The unconscious possesses an irreducible otherness to the definition and systemization of theory.

In founding his theory upon the unconscious other as feminine, Jung is essentialist *and* makes a deconstructionist manoeuvre. The slippage occurs in his writings between feminine other as *his* unconscious and female other (women) as more 'unconscious' than men. What is simultaneously deconstructionist is that feminine otherness is also sited (and cited) as beyond the scope of his ego perceptions. The feminine is inside as anima as his irrational inferiority and outside as that which is unconscious in the theory: the unconsciousness of Jungian psychology as grand theory.

The feminine other is Jung's supplement generated in his psyche that purports to originate both his psyche and his theory. The feminine does so because the anima stands for the unconscious as the *source* of the psyche, including the source of the ego.

In this sense, the feminine is the irreducible metaphysics that cannot be deconstructed out of Jung's psychology – his personal-myth interior self and his grand theory – because it is both the *origin* and the absolute other, the *beyond* of it. The irreducible femininity both is the other everywhere deconstructing Jung's metaphysical concepts or god-term (because the unconscious cannot be wholly defined by the ego and will challenge the ego's attempt to securely map the psyche), and is congealed in Jung's thinking as the otherness-as-inferiority of the feminine as women.

Both the grand-theory and personal-myth aspects of Jung's writing generate this dichotomy between a radical femininity refusing definition and limitation for the ego and sexist essentialism. The feminine is the absolute other, the 'outside', not even limited to gender. And the feminine is also the stereotyping and essentializing function of the anima writing. Grand theory and personal myth, mutually implicated and intertwined, contain Jungian psychology's internal deconstructive drive in the creative, irreducible otherness of the unconscious.

Yet, as well as deconstructive elements, grand theory produces metaphysical concepts in its urge to organize meanings of psyche and culture into a system that can then seek authority. Personal myth, on the other hand, in its claim to be a 'local truth' of Jung's own psychic experience, paradoxically feels licensed to contaminate its self-description with cultural prejudice.

Jung can argue that his anima has inferior qualities because it stands in a binary, opposing relationship to his superior intellect, and reflects his own personal experience of women. His justification for the subsequent essentialist prejudice is that this is just his 'local truth', his theory as personal myth. It is his writing about the anima that provides the most acute point of slippage between personal myth and grand theory, since the anima is both the unknowable, irreducible 'other' (feminine) of theory and the essentializing, overdetermined cultural prejudice within it.

A last word on the unconscious as the irreducible metaphysics of Jungian psychology. The concept of the unconscious remains metaphysical as it is the proposition that Jungian writings cannot escape: the unconscious is unknowable, ungraspable, and therefore it cannot be theorized, translated into the ego's, rational terms. Jung was explicit about this: 'the concept of the unconscious posits nothing; it designates only my unknowing.'[13] In having its metaphysical irreducibility as 'unknowableness', Jungian theory becomes deconstructive to the point of challenging deconstruction as a 'method' and revealing it as an 'event'. If the irreducible metaphysical of Jungian theory is the deconstructive 'feminine' unconscious, then that is like saying that deconstruction itself is metaphysical. It is true. Deconstruction is metaphysical when it is a 'method', a set of valued tools to be applied, rather than an 'event'. Jungian ideas reveal the metaphysical residue within deconstruction.

Before looking further at Jungian deconstruction, it is worth returning to Jung in grand-theory mode. Here he is highly logocentric in the presentation of his ideas. The theory of archetypes suggests multiple 'gods of meaning' in the psyche. Jung even supplies his own transcendental sign in the 'self'. This governing archetype helpfully often manifests itself as a god-image, as if to confirm its logocentric properties. This is Jung the grand theorist as structuralist, rather than as deconstructionist. In the Jungian psyche of grand theory, the archetypal image is a signifier derived from its archetype-signified. All defer to the superior archetype of the self with its potential to structure unity and wholeness for subjectivity.

The Enlightenment intellectual revolution in favour of rationality cemented the tendency to binary oppositions in thinking about the human mind. Jung, the grand theorist, demonstrates his Enlightenment heritage in having his psychology organized in oppositional pairs. All the important concepts are arranged in mutually constituting binaries such as conscious/unconscious, ego/self, anima/animus, Eros/Logos, extraversion/introversion.

However, it would also be correct to say, as theorists such as Christopher Hauke have done, that Jungian psychology is devoted to criticizing and deconstructing Enlightenment forms of consciousness.[14] Given the overwhelming presence of the deconstructing unconscious (the unconscious 'makes' as well as unmakes meaning in a perpetual challenge to stable ego-concepts), Jung's oppositional pairs are *designed* to deconstruct into each other. The process by which the psyche constructs and destructs, 'deconstructs', relations between opposing terms Jung called 'individuation'.

Again, another look at archetypal images, which suggest a logocentric connection to archetypes, recalls Jung's stress on regarding the images as primary. Keeping the images primary means not slapping on 'ego' interpretations by translating them into words. Psychic images direct attention to the unknowable 'deconstructive' aspects of the psyche.

On the one hand, the *concepts* of archetypes and archetypal images are grand theory and logocentric. On the other hand, archetypal images are signifiers without fixed, knowable signifieds. They are subject to slippage and denied logocentric fulfilment. What Derrida alleges about language finds a distinct echo in Jung's depiction of psychic imagery. Archetypal images demonstrate *différance*, differing from each other and infinitely deferring a fixed meaning.

Indeed, given the significance of Jung's unconscious to his psychology as a whole, we could argue, in Derridean language, that his concepts exist 'under erasure'. Theoretical meanings, like any others, cannot be secured, hence the 'erasure' of their claims to fixed truth and authority. In *Writing and Difference*, Derrida linked Freud to his deconstruction in the radical otherness of the psychoanalytic unconscious, despite the logocentrism present in Freudian writings. I would like to suggest that aspects of Jung's work bear an even more intimate relation to the project of deconstruction.

One obstacle to placing Jung as a thinker in deconstruction is his use of scientific language, in particular words such as 'facts' and 'empirical evidence'. Often he will describe himself as an empiricist in an adjacent paragraph to statements that he is not offering a 'philosophy' or a 'theory', and that the unconscious is 'inconceivable'.[15] Here he is presenting himself as a straightforward recounter of 'the facts' rather than a devious spinner of theory. His so-called empiricism bears further examination.

'Empiricism' is the scientific and philosophical approach stressing the importance of observable, measurable, quantifiable and repeatable data. Moreover, it includes an assumption that there is an objective reality exterior to the observer. Methods for studying this reality can themselves be objective and the resulting hypotheses can be proved or disproved in repeatable experiments.

The problem with Jung's 'empiricism' is that what he takes as 'empirical evidence' and 'facts', are psychic images, dreams and psychological symptoms. These imply what he calls an 'objective psyche', meaning that the unconscious is capable of producing such material without reference to or deriving it from the subjective ego. This is not classical empiricism, nor does it constitute scientific 'facts', because psychic images are interior to one person. By definition, such images are not available for objective study, not repeatable and, indeed, not 'objective' in the usual sense at all. I prefer the term 'autonomous psyche' to Jung's 'objective psyche'.

If Jung is not empirical in the classical scientific sense, that need not harm his value for today's psychology and feminism. It also means that his highly logocentric language of empiricism need not detract from his potential as a thinker in deconstruction.

Jungian thinking in deconstruction and feminism

So what are the possibilities for deconstructive Jung as a Jungian feminism? Broadly, the deconstructive strand in Jung's work enables a feminist critique of its sexist essentialism and logocentric pronouncements on gender. Jung's misogynist and culturally stereotyped views of women can be criticized from within Jungian theory.

In the first place, post-Jungians have seized upon this potential in order to reframe Jung for more progressive engagements with gender. In particular, archetypal psychology deliberately rethinks Jung in a poststructuralist context. By rejecting the metaphysical aspect of archetypes, by sticking to the images and by using the Jungian unconscious to dispute the authority of his precepts, archetypal psychology declares itself a poststructuralist development, sympathetic to feminism.

Secondly, the deconstructive reading of Jung offered so far in this chapter suggests further ways of interrogating 'the feminine', as both a radical refusal of fixed forms of knowledge and an essentialist residue in Jung's writing. A Jungian feminism could go on to explore Jungian key texts for their ambivalent ways of framing gender.

A third way in which a feminism might strategically employ a deconstructive Jung is to use his theories to read external feminist issues. Take, for example, the perennial feminist question of whether gender is an innate essence or whether it is wholly culturally constructed. This binary opposition within feminism might be usefully deconstructed via Jung in the cause of teasing out the mutual implications of 'essence' versus culturally and historically 'constructed'.

Instead of a fixed opposition between essentialism and social constructivism, it becomes clear that, if gender is *wholly* socially formed, then that is to be essentialist in another way. If 'history' is *wholly* determining on gender, then that too is an essentialist position; the essence shifts from biology to history. Thinking about archetypes may be helpful here. In deconstructive language the innate essence/history binary on gender cannot stop positing a metaphysical residue, an essence, either in biology or in history. The relationship between archetypes and archetypal images provides another way by thinking through this binary archetypally. The metaphysical residue inherent in archetypes is a creative energy, not a fixed stamp of gender identity. Archetypal images are created in a dialogue between biological inheritance and culture.

As a metaphysical residue, archetypes remain radical, since they are also the irreducible unknowableness of the unconscious, making and undoing the ego's understanding of gender. By structuring gender as a creative dialogue with the unknowable, in which history and culture have a formative role, more radical and feminist versions of Jung can be glimpsed.

Jungian deconstruction as an event

To Derrida, deconstruction cannot be applied and cannot *not* be applied. This notion of something only existing 'in action' or in practice, and therefore not as a separate set of principles, sets up a strong echo in Jung. I have argued that Jungian psychic imagery and dreams do show correspondences with Derrida's thinking about language, its slippages and *différance*. In addition, Jung frequently reminds readers that archetypal imagery must be considered in the setting, the personal circumstances, of the person generating it. Psychic imagery should not be ripped out of context and used to demonstrate general principles, however much Jung, the grand theorist, was prepared to do precisely this.

Therefore it would be possible to argue for this deconstructive echo – that Jungian psychology cannot be applied and cannot not be applied. The Jung who insists on context is not just thinking about an individual's cultural history. He is trying to keep the living rootedness of dreams and images with the radical unknowableness of the unconscious (of the analyst as well as the analysand). For this Jung, Jungian psychology *does not exist* except in *application* to a particular psychic text because of the deconstructive presence (and 'presence' here shows the metaphysical residue) of the unconscious, the 'other', within the theory. Jungian practice, working with dreams, is deconstruction as an 'event'. 'The picture is concrete . . . only when it is seen in its habitual context . . . we must let it remain an organic thing in all its complexity . . .'[16]

Finally, what I have suggested about an echo between Jung, poststructuralism and deconstruction can be shown most starkly by substituting 'Jungian psychology' for 'poststructuralism' and 'psyche' for 'language', in the following.

> [People] assume that poststructuralism is a knowledge of language when it would be safer to see it as an argument against the knowability of language, which shifts attention away from knowledge of language towards the language of knowledge.[17]

Put in Jungian terms, this becomes:

> [People] assume that Jungian psychology is a knowledge of psyche when it would be safer to see it as an argument against the knowability of the psyche, which shifts attention away from knowledge of psyche towards the psyche of knowledge.

Jung and post-Freudian feminism

Jung and Jacques Lacan

As with deconstruction, I am not attempting to 'translate' Jung entirely into the presuppositions and conclusions of other theorists, for that would be to belie both the complexity and 'difference' of Jung's work. However, in the cause of Jungian feminisms, there are suggestive echoes between Jung and Lacan's revision of Freud. For example, both Jung and Lacan are structuralists when they consider prelinguistic structuring elements to be present in the unconscious. Also like Jung, Lacan regards conscious identity as radically dependent upon the unconscious. Where Jung optimistically liked to concentrate on the potential 'wholeness' afforded by union with the unconscious, Lacan, pragmatically, speaks of 'lack'. To both theorists, such an unconscious union is impossible (except for brief moments of ecstasy) and is a focus for a person's desire.

Nevertheless, Lacan's core ideas do differ from Jung's in crucial ways. Lacanians consider that the infant prior to the Oedipus complex exists in a state called the 'imaginary' in a symbiotic bond with the mother. At this point the mother is without a gender, since she is pre-Oedipal, before the psychic splitting necessary for gender definition. The imaginary begins for the infant through what Lacan called 'the mirror stage'.

Here the child starts to have a sense of an image of him- or herself, perhaps in an actual mirror, or perhaps is 'mirrored' by relating to a caregiver. To make a connection with his or her own image (as something over which the child has agency) is to start to imagine his or her own bodily boundaries. The infant mis-identifies him- or herself as unified. In turn, this entails starting to split off from the boundless profusion represented by immersion in the maternal.

The Oedipus complex erupts as the father (the 'father' can be the actual biological parent or just a third 'force' in the orbit of the mother–child bond) effects the final split from the pre-Oedipal mother. Via the Oedipus complex the child enters what Lacan calls the 'symbolic' order of culture and language as a separate and gendered being. What the Oedipus complex does is to split the subjectivity of the child as it renegotiates relationships to two parents.

Fear of castration means recognition that fusion with the mother is now forbidden. Subjectivity splits as the child represses the imaginary and its maternal profusion into the unconscious. Thereby the ego-unconscious relation is structured as one of endless desire for that fulfilment of subjectivity eternally lost in the repression of the maternal bond.

What particularly appeals to post-Lacanian feminists is Lacan's connection of subjectivity, language and gender. In effecting the Oedipal split, the 'father' takes on metaphorical form in the symbolic order as the Law of the Father, propelling the child into the symbolic order and away from the fusionary realm of the imaginary. The symbolic order is the language, conventions and symbols valued by a particular culture.

For feminists, Lacan provides an explanation of gendered subjectivity as constructed *and* deeply psychically implicated as an account of how cultures reproduce constrictions on gender identity. Oedipal splitting results in the taking-up of a gendered position in the acquisition of language. Freud's penis becomes, for Lacan, a symbol, the paternal phallus, to which females and males acquire a different gendered relation. If language is entered through splitting, then language itself becomes the marker of a 'lack' of psychic wholeness. Language is driven by desire.

For Lacan, the poststructuralist sliding of signifier over signified results from the pressure of the unappeasable desire of the person. She or he is seeking the wholeness that has been forever repressed into the unconscious. The desire to secure unsecurable meaning is one with the desire for unattainable, fixed, whole subjectivity.

Irigaray, Cixous and Kristeva are feminist post-Freudian post-Lacanians, who make use of deconstruction to investigate gender, subjectivity and language. Before looking for a Jungian entry into their work, it is worth considering an example of a post-Jungian revision of Lacan, in the cause of feminism and progressive politics.

Andrew Samuels's post-Jungian revision of Lacan and the father

In the previous chapter I described some of Andrew Samuels's work on fathering as particularly productive for a Jungian feminism of gender identity. In *The Political Psyche*,[18] Samuels addresses the political understanding of Lacan's father as the progenitor of the symbolic order and of fixity, convention and narrow notions of gender.

Lacan's father is a paternal function in psychic structuring, not a particular person. Yet 'his' role in communicating the symbolic order, and with it the dominant values of the culture, means that 'he' is regarded as repressive and patriarchal. The paternal function inscribes gender identity. This occurs despite both genders similarly 'lacking' the phallus, since it has become a fantasy object standing for omnipotence and the 'full' subjectivity, impossible after the psychic splitting in the Oedipal stage. However, for the masculine, not having the phallus is a kind of 'having', since it is the charge of the feminine being to 'be' the phallus for the masculine.

Lacan's reading of the father puts a patriarchal privileging upon masculinity in relation to language and culture. In effect, the symbolic is the realm of masculine signifying with the feminine repressed into the imaginary. The feminine is to be found in the domain of the 'other', without which the symbolic cannot be. Since it is not native to the symbolic, the home of language, representation and cultural conventions, the feminine cannot be signified.

Yet, in Jungian terms, this gendering of the symbolic as masculine through the phallus as a privileged signifier has to change.

If we add a Jungian perspective to the Lacanian symbolic, then something more creative and productive for feminism occurs. For Jung, repression is only part of the founding of the symbolic. The creative *androgynous* unconscious is active *as well* in bringing to birth a conscious ego. To Jungians, a phallus may accrue power in the symbolic, but that will be a cultural, not a psychic contribution. If a culture ascribes power to the phallus and masculinity, then that will affect the formation of subjectivity, but not through any necessary, bodily based structuration.

For a Jungian, a female body is as capable as a male body of becoming a powerful symbol. This is because, although the body contributes to meaning, it does not govern it. The deconstructive androgynous unconscious is a necessary ingredient to the cultural symbolic in Jungian terms. We can argue for a 'Jungian symbolic', in which the feminine is not excluded because it is already *there* in the androgyny of the archetypes. Indeed, Andrew Samuels makes precisely this point about the anima and animus as anatomical metaphors for otherness.[19]

Samuels subtly evokes a Jungian mitigation of Lacan in his theorizing of the interaction between gender certainty and gender confusion (see chapter 4). Jungian ideas allow Lacan's overwhelming phallus to be viewed as a cultural product, not a necessary determining psychic factor. The idea that more engaged fathering can allow a creative incursion of gender confusion is a practical demonstration of how Lacan's politically inert phallus can be rethought. 'The existence of gender confusion in itself suggests that neither the symbolic nor social behaviour are givens, and hence can be challenged.'[20] The possibility of gender confusion proves that Lacan's patriarchal phallus stamping fixed definitions on the symbolic, and especially gender, is not the *only* psychic possibility for the paternal. Under gender confusion, the father can become a symbolic means to progressive, pro-feminist politics. As a consequence, the excessive focus upon the pre-Oedipal mother (not always helpful to feminism) can be abandoned.

Samuels cites observational studies on mothers and babies in support of his Jungian contention that Lacan's picture of the paternal phallus ruthlessly slicing apart a mother–baby fusion is itself a cultural fantasy.[21]

Feminism's fascination with Lacan is explicable by his apparent anti-essentialism in showing gender and social identity as constructed. Anti-essentialism becomes severely strained, however, in his belief in the phallus as a key linguistic marker. The phallus has only a *metaphorical fantasy* relationship to the male body, with neither sex actually possessing it. Samuels persuasively points to the 'eternalism' in Lacan's depiction of the paternal function: it assumes a remote, authority-bearing model of fathering, no longer necessary.[22]

The Jung visible in Samuels's rescuing of the father for progressive politics is the Jung thinking deconstruction, whose unconscious radically problematizes the masculine, or father's ego-tistic claim to dominate signifying. Yet Jung too is beset by 'eternalism' in his own theoretical models characterized by unacknowledged likeness to outmoded styles of gender. Here, we return, yet again, to the anima as she comes to obscure his view of women as foreign to logical thought, and better suited to a life devoted to caring for others. One further method of exploring Jung's 'eternalism' is by way of Luce Irigaray's criticism of Lacan's phallus.

Luce Irigaray and the phallic anima

Initiation into Lacan's symbolic order entails both the splitting of subjectivity with the entry into language and the siting of sexual difference around the symbolic phallus. Luce Irigaray's early work was highly critical of Lacan's binary gendering. Via the symbolic phallus, the masculine 'has' the fantasy phallus and the feminine must 'be' the phallus for the masculine. Such a binary notion structures gender in a fantasy relation to biological difference. Neither gender unproblematically 'has' the phallus in a symbolic that has split the person off irretrievably from 'imaginary' fantasies of wholeness and sufficiency.[23]

Lacan's structuring of gender formation is a binary that locks the feminine into merely performing a mirroring function for the masculine. To Irigaray, this means that Lacanian thought is really only about one sex, the masculine. The feminine does not exist within Lacanian theory. In *This Sex which Is not One*, Irigaray argues that the feminine both is not *one* because feminine sexuality is multiple and so cannot be contained in a binary logic of symmetry with the masculine. Also, the feminine sex is *not* one because 'woman does not exist' in the limitations of Lacanian thought.[24] Such a well-known feminist challenge to Lacan finds a productive echo in Jung on the vexed matter of the anima.

First of all, in Jungian psychology the anima takes on much of the phallic function outlined by Lacan. The Jungian unconscious is autonomous and goal oriented. Oedipal splitting is not the overwhelming means of generating ego-subjectivity, since the archetypal energies of the unconscious also take a role. Rather than the unconscious as an amorphous condition that fatally splits, the Jungian unconscious is helpful: it *wants* to give birth to the ego.

As the chief organ of a male's unconscious, the anima (modelled in the first instance on psychic images of the actual mother) plays an active role in detaching the child in pre-Oedipal bonding. It is the anima who principally forms an oppositional and compensatory role in the binary structuring of gender. The anima works like Lacan's phallus.

What is also apparent in Jung's writing about the anima is 'her' expansive properties as she comes to obscure and essentialize his ideas of the feminine and of women. In portraying his own anima, and then generalizing to describe her role in the subjectivity of men, Jung suggests that women are, and should be, the carriers of anima images for men. Truly, the anima is not only a 'phallus' in the Lacanian sense of propelling the child into the symbolic and acting as the chief marker of sexual difference. The anima is additionally phallic, since it is what the masculine ambivalently 'has', and is what the feminine ambivalently must 'be' for the masculine.

From the point of view of Jung generalizing from his own anima to characterize the psychology of all women, we could say with Irigaray that 'the feminine' does not exist within Jungian writing. This brings us back to the dual appearance of the feminine in Jung when looked at through the lens of deconstruction: the essentializing anima and the absolute, irreducible 'other'. It is the more radical deconstructive properties of archetypes that allow ways of rethinking Jung for feminisms.

Irigaray's sensible transcendence and Jungian alchemy

Jungian alchemy will be treated in more detail in the next chapter. Broadly it consists of a projection of psychic individuation upon certain material processes in the external world. Jung came to believe that the medieval alchemists who spent their lives attempting to convert lead into gold were unwittingly trying to speed up their own individuation by projecting their archetypal unconscious onto the matter in their test tubes. Jung's alchemical writings set up a number of echoes with post-Freudian feminism, as the following arguments will demonstrate.

Irigaray argues that Lacan's theory is just one example of the erasure of the feminine from patriarchal societies. Such an erasure is largely a question of culture and is rooted in religions that celebrate masculinity in a singular, phallic-like form. In a symbolic dominated by such a monolithic conception of gender, what is needed is a means of representing the excluded feminine. She calls for a symbolic grammar for women.

The proposed grammar would represent feminine multiplicity and being, outside of, and independent of, the monotheistic masculine heritage. There needs to be a recognition of two transcendencies: a feminine multiple transcendency in addition to the masculine 'one'. Transcendencies, for Irigaray, are grammars of enlarged subjectivity possible in spirituality and religion, one of which has been culturally 'forgotten'.

> Man has been divided between two transcendencies: his mother's and God's – whatever kind of God that may be. These two transcendencies are doubtless not unrelated but this is something he has forgotten . . .
>   He was born of an other who is always Other – inappropriable. For centuries, at least in the so-called western tradition, that transcendency has seldom been recognized as such.[25]

Irigaray's 'sensible transcendence' is a reinvention of a feminine transcendency as rooted in the body. This transcendency is material and maternal in order to inject flesh and blood into the symbolic order. It encourages men and women to contemplate the mystery each represents for the other.[26]

Such a call for the feminine to be inserted into the symbolic, into the grammar of culture, does not need to go to Jungian goddess feminism in order to find correspondences. It is true to say that goddess feminism, and in particular the myth of the great goddess with the divine as multiply gendered, immanent and fleshly, does closely resemble Irigaray's intentions here. However, the core principles that traverse the Jungian tradition and Irigarayan innovation are also to be found in Jung's work.

First, a transcendent maternal intimately linked to the body is native to Jung's portrayal of mothering as archetypal. For the infant, the mother becomes the first carrier of archetypal images, principally the 'mother' as archetype, and the anima. In conceiving of the mother as an archetypal image structured through bodily connection, Jung liberates the psychic mother from merely pointing backwards to regression. The archetypal mother partakes of all the multiple plurality and numinous resonances of archetypal images. This means that the mother can stand for the divine, spirituality, the body and, crucially, the *future* direction of the person's psyche as well as the past.

As well as providing 'sensible transcendence' in the mother archetype, Jung also supplies a symbolic and plural grammar of gender in his writings upon alchemy. Through the idea of the projection of inner psychic contents, Jung read alchemy texts as if they were records of dreams. Alchemy depends upon a gendered language of a masculine sun and a feminine moon, or 'Sol' and 'Luna'. Irigaray's sensible transcendence calls for a language of fire and water in order to 'melt' (put theoretically, to deconstruct) the phallic solidities that masculinity has accrued in Western culture.[27] This is not an essentialist assigning of solidity to masculinity, fluidity to the feminine. Rather it is a strategic attempt to enable women to articulate gender identity by cracking open the binary structure that keeps culture masculine.

Jung's alchemical language of Sol and Luna is similarly not an essentialist fixing of gender identity, but instead an undoing of binary forms. Alchemy *is* a grammar of melting, heating, dissolving, coagulating in new combinations. Gender is an integral part of this fiery, fluid process. Mercurius, usually depicted as an active, potent, masculine figure, is also fiery, watery and feminine.[28]

There is a very real sense in which Jungian alchemy enables a radical revision of gender in both the imaginary and the symbolic. It offers particular resonances for all three French feminists.

Hélène Cixous and Jung: écriture feminine and the theatre of subjectivity

Explicitly indebted to Derrida, Hélène Cixous's project is to undo the logocentric ideology of binary oppositions and to seek a new 'feminine language' of multiplicity and *différance*. Dialogue can immediately begin with Jung when Cixous argues that binary oppositions demonstrate death at work by suppressing the plural feminine. Jung's complex uses of binary terms as both deconstructive (the feminine as unknowable other) and essentializing (the feminine not existing except for the reflection of Jung's anima) are brought to mind.

In an early essay, Cixous defines two psychic economies at work in culture and theory: the gift and the proper.[29] The former is a deconstructive space in which meanings cannot be fixed or structured into a hierarchy. The latter, the realm of the proper, is the drive to classification, rigid binary theories and hierarchy. It becomes essentialist when linked to a male's fear of castration. I would connect the gift and the proper to Jung's deconstructive unconscious and phallic anima respectively.

Cixous has made the greatest impact on feminist theory in what she has called 'écriture feminine'.[30] In the first place, the idea of 'feminine writing' is indebted to Derrida in writing as subject to *différance*. This entails writing as a continual slippage of meaning, the undoing of theoretical claims to secure signifying and to a unitary gendered subjectivity. Écriture feminine as a *deliberate* embrace of *différance* is a writing that undoes patriarchal binary oppositions. It rejoices in spilling meaning.

To call this writing 'feminine' is to define it as a radical challenge to philosophy and culture, not something that can be contained or comprehensively described by it. So 'feminine' here is the unknowable, inappropriable other. Écriture feminine corresponds therefore to Jung's archetypal imagery as the signs denoting an unconscious as the 'feminine' absolute other.

This argument rests upon Jung's unconscious as feminine because it is characterized as 'other' to 'masculine' Logos-oriented conscious-ness. The unconscious is also feminine because that is what does 'not exist' within Jungian theory, just as his psyche continually exceeds and challenges ego-theorizing.

However, Cixous also associates écriture feminine with the space of the pre-Oedipal imaginary, the realm of the as-yet-ungendered, boundless, pre-Oedipal mother. This enables her to speak of écriture feminine as the maternal source. She uses the language of myth and the Bible in order to imagine the 'feminine' here as signifying all pos-sible subject positions. As the attempt to recapture the fleshly fusion with the mother, écriture feminine is also of the body, the writing of the mother's milk.

Again, there are distinct possibilities for such post-Lacanian think-ing to draw out feminist potential in the ideas of Jung. As noted, écri-ture feminine as *différance* is close to the 'writing' of archetypal images, which work through difference from each other and infinite deferral of a single logocentric fulfilment of the meaning potential of archetypes. When Cixous links écriture feminine to the maternal body in the imaginary, she still has to invoke the resources of the sym-bolic to seek out the repressed plurality of meaning in language. For Cixous, the imaginary cannot simply be represented in art or writing: it is the state of being lost to everyone as post-Oedipal subjects. Liter-ature and art can only *indirectly* represent that lost paradise of unbounded subjectivity. It must be remembered that it is the Oedipal splitting of the subject into the symbolic that allows any form of lan-guage and representation at all.

Common to the French feminists is the idea that religious myth represents cultural attempts to recapture the state of grace and per-sonal fulfilment, lost forever in the imaginary. Jung would largely agree with them, yet there remain crucial differences. His imaginary is the numinous kingdom of archetypal imagery and *it does not merely belong to the past history* of the person. Integral to Jungian psychol-ogy is the pressure from archetypal imagery to push the dreamer forward, to structure the future destination of the person and not just the repressed past.

Therefore it is necessary to perceive both similarities and differ-ences in Cixous's use of myth, song and poetry to search for and direct attention to the maternal plenitude cut off by the acquisition of language. Jungian alchemy is just such another narrative grammar designed to show the creative activity of the unconscious both as source and challenge to the symbolic of language and culture. Like myth to both Cixous and Jung, alchemy is a grammar of unconscious processes, reshaping subjectivity and gender.

Of course, another 'difference' between écriture feminine and Jung can be spotted here in that the Jungian symbolic diverges from the Lacanian one. As I noted earlier, the proactive autonomous role of androgynous archetypes means that Jung's symbolic does not exclude the feminine from signifying. The effect of archetypes is to make the female body as capable of powerful symbolization as Lacan's phallus. Just as the dominant role of Lacan's phallus is a cultural fantasy from a Jungian perspective, so the feminine is always potentially *there* in the Jungian symbolic, even if cultures have traditionally discouraged feminine representation.

One could argue that Cixous's mythological renderings of écriture feminine are, like Irigaray's sensible transcendence, an attempt to formulate something akin to the Jungian symbolic – one in which both sexes (and non-binary notions of gender), can be equally represented. Despite the binary pretensions of 'grand theory', the Jungian symbolic – continually in process with the deconstructive 'feminine' of the Jungian unconscious – is able to discard logocentric binary oppositions in favour of the inherent multiplicity of archetypal images.

Écriture feminine has a related dual sense in Cixous's work: it is representation striving to make overt Derridean *différance*, and an evocation of imaginary maternal fulfilment. Cixous believes that this writing is more native to women. Similarly, the Jungian unconscious is 'feminine' as the unknowable irreducible other to Jungian theory (producing *différance* in archetypal images), and is 'feminine' as the first structuring of archetypal energies in relation to the pre-Oedipal mother's body in infancy.

As well as using myth and poetry, Cixous has also cited the theatre as the space in which the language of the body can challenge the verbal language of the patriarchal Lacanian symbolic.[31] In the theatre, gesture, image, voice and echo can undermine the conventions of traditional forms of narrative by showing how speakers constitute and contradict each other. Cixous uses the theatre to represent subjectivity as a dramatic process that can acknowledge *différance*: the gendered self is constituted through *performance* and cannot claim either fixity or authenticity.

Without wishing to overemphasize a link with Jung here, it is fascinating to discover his similar move to consider subjectivity as an internal theatre. There is a difference in that Cixous is stressing gender as culturally performed, the subject interacting with social-psychic shaping pressures. By contrast, Jung downplays the influence of culture in his descriptions of archetypal drama. He implies that he sees performing gender as purely internal. However, psychic imagery is emphatically *not* isolated from social influence in Jungian theory.

Jung becomes theatrical in portraying active imagination, his therapeutic technique in which the conscious ego is encouraged to relax vigilance and permit the unconscious to direct fantasies. He suggests that this state should be regarded as a play in which the ego ideally shifts from observer to actor. The director is, of course, the creative unconscious. 'If the observer understands that his own drama is being performed . . . He therefore feels compelled . . . to take part in the play . . .'[32] Differences between Cixous and Jung here are more marked than in the surprising degree of correspondence between écriture feminine and archetypal 'writing'. Cixous works in a real theatre as a cultural space, in order to deconstruct gender identity and specific powerful theories such as psychoanalysis. Jung, by contrast, describes a form of therapy that concentrates upon the inner world as theatrical. He believes that this inner drama should be embraced in the cause of personal authenticity achieved through individuation.

However, both Cixous and Jung suggest that subjectivity and gender can be imagined *performatively*. Cixous pushes the idea towards *différance*, Jung towards logocentric notions of authenticity. Nevertheless, the Jung striving for 'authentic' subjectivity through ever-more profound unions with the archetypal unconscious is only the Jung of grand theory. In this mode he demonstrates a logocentric attachment to terms such as individuation as having a fixed meaning. Given the radical persistence of the Jungian deconstructive unconscious, Jung's theatre of gender and being can be seen to echo productively with Cixous's theatre of the feminist application of *différance*.

Julia Kristeva and Jung: the semiotic and women's time

To Julia Kristeva, the feminine is defined as that which is marginalized by the patriarchal symbolic.[33] It is not an unproblematic gender to be lived out by persons in history. Following Lacanian strictures, Kristeva has particularly scrutinized the pre-Oedipal imaginary in which the infant exists in a non-differentiated bonding with the mother. Kristeva names this state of maternal fusion the 'semiotic'. Upon entry into the symbolic, the semiotic is repressed, yet remains within to disturb and challenge symbolic representations. Kristeva perceives the working of the semiotic in poetry and modernist art.

The semiotic is structurally linked to the mother's body. It is the pre-Oedipal maternal, so it must contain the potential for both genders, as it is *before* symbolic definitions and the understanding of gender as an exclusive binary. Therefore the semiotic is not 'the feminine'. Close in some respects to Cixous's 'écriture feminine' in its pre-Oedipal nature, Kristeva differs from Cixous in consistently detaching her pre-Oedipal maternal from femininity as a gender. The pre-Oedipal semiotic is a *position*, prior to symbolic signifying, to which both genders can seek a relationship.[34]

Of course, once the semiotic 'speaks' comprehensibly in writing or in art, it has entered the symbolic, the home of language and aesthetic conventions. As a result, the semiotic maternal can only be discerned in a 'double coding': it persists in forms of art and culture that permit its chaotic influence to disrupt, pierce and thwart symbolic conventions. In an early demonstration of Kristeva's severing of the semiotic from gender or bodily sex, she finds examples of semiotic pulsations in the writing of male modernists.

It is useful to take a pluralist approach to Jung and Kristeva, one that examines the 'differences' as well as the echoes between the two theorists. The chief distinction to be made between Jung and Kristeva is that of the paternal symbolic. For Jungians, the symbolic is archetypal as well as paternal; indeed, the phallus becomes a wholly *cultural* signifier, not a uniquely privileged one. Archetypes are androgynous, as in the pre-Oedipal mother, yet archetypes take a more active role in birthing the ego than Kristeva's pre-Oedipal semiotic. In Jung, Oedipal splitting is far less determining for subjectivity. In effect, the Jungian symbolic has a more intimate relation to the semiotic than does a Kristevan/Lacanian one.

The maternal function in Jung may well be distorted by a symbolic dominated by cultural conventions of a patriarchal inheritance, but it is not forever non-figurable. His maternal is only non-figurable in so far as it is pre-Oedipal. Jung's maternal does more. What is repressed at the Oedipal stage remains in the psyche as a proactive maternal that will continue to nurture and woo the subject throughout life. The Jungian symbolic is as capable of being maternal as paternal. What is repressed and non-figurable is only the pre-Oedipal mother, which is merely one dimension of the mother archetype.

Later Jungian symbolic images of the mother need not refer to the paternal function in two senses. First, we do not need to regard the phallus as privileged amongst the archetypally influenced images shaping the ego. Secondly, symbolic images of the mother need not refer *back* at all. They may be in touch with unconscious/semi-otic energies driving subjectivity *forwards* into individuation. Instead of pointing backward to the pre-Oedipal mother, psychic archetypal images also point to future intimations of the numinous self.

Of course, once Jung *writes* about archetypal images of the mother, they become even more lodged in the symbolic, for now they are images translated into *words*, and are subject to further cultural distortions in the conventional representation of 'mothering'. To the extent that Jung wrote in a patriarchal culture, then, the symbolic of his texts is weighted towards the paternal.

Nevertheless, archetypal images *as psychic images* (before being translated into symbolic words) could be regarded as more productive unions of semiotic and symbolic. In so far as psychic images partake of the person's cultural experience, they are insertions in the symbolic; in so far as they are regarded primarily as signifiers of the unknowable deconstructive unconscious, they are semiotic (and, to Kristeva, pre-Oedipal).

In 'Women's Time', Kristeva provides an understanding of the maternal semiotic in historical and cultural terms.[35] She argues that the symbolic has been devoted to the conception of time as linear in art and philosophy. It has produced the idea of 'history' as a succession of recordable events. The linear narrative of time is 'masculine' because the symbolic is paternal and because of historical privileging of the male.

Against linear time, she sets 'women's time' as cyclical and monumental. 'Women's time' is the time of the maternal semiotic, since the idea of the person existing in a linear history ending in death is gained only with entry into the symbolic. It is also the time of *women* in the sense of their desire to be mothers. Reproductive time takes on characteristics of circularity and eternity.

Kristeva is not essentializing all women *as* mothers, as 'mother' can have a variety of cultural positions. Instead she argues that this link between women and the semiotic maternal needs to be theorized lest feminism become a substitute for religion rather than an agency for political change. Previously, she suggests, feminism has worked with time as masculine and then time as feminine. Now it is necessary to deconstruct the binary.

Early feminism sought equality under the law. It wanted women to become equal subjects in masculine linear history. A second wave asserted female difference and separatism. Women's union with archaic cyclical time tends towards a religious rather than a political movement.

Unlike Irigaray and Cixous, Kristeva distrusts the language of religion and transcendence. Jungian goddess feminism would appear to be exactly what she is arguing against in 'Women's Time'. Instead, she desires a feminism that would insert into history a radical refusal to accept the subjective limitations of linear time. She ends by calling for an end to the binary opposition of gender by describing it as metaphysical in the Derridean sense. Binary gender is an object of belief, not an inherent logical necessity. Rather than attempt a revolution based upon the fabrication of 'a scapegoat victim as a foundress of society',[36] we should analyse within each subjectivity 'the potentialities of victim/executioner which characterize each identity, each subject, each sex'.[37]

To Jungians, Kristeva's 'solution' to gendered time sounds very like individuation. Kristeva's radical refusal of gendered identity in time involves coming to terms with one's internal violence (the Jungian shadow?) and the capacity to play the victim. What is fascinatingly implicit in Kristeva's thinking here is the way mothering allows her to think of psychically evolving subjectivity as *prospective* (like Jung's). Women desire to have children *in the future* and imagine a future for them. They psychically prepare for mothering as prospective, even if fuelled (for Kristeva) by backward-glancing pre-Oedipal stirrings. Rather than simply assimilate Jung to 'Women's Time', I need to look further at Jung, the feminine and time.

Interestingly, Jung associates the feminine in the unconscious with non-linear time. The anima is immortal and outside time, he concludes.[38] Of course, Jung's identification of the semiotic with the feminine in the importance he attached to the anima is not Kristeva's position. To take Jung's feminine further, I return briefly to Jung-in-deconstruction. There his 'feminine' semiotic is both radical and essentializing with a deconstructive 'feminine' unconscious and anima generalizations of women.

The immortal anima is supposed to be a male's major figure of the unconscious and his feminine. Jung did not write a great deal about the psychology of women, but his treatment of the Demeter–Kore myth bears reading with 'Women's Time'.[39] This is the story of the carrying-away of Persephone by Pluto, the god of the underworld. Demeter, her mother, the goddess of the harvest, eventually rescues Persephone. Jung sees the myth as a narrative of women's more organic connection to cyclical time, through the psychological effects of mothering. 'The conscious experience of [mothering] produces the feeling that her life is spread out over generations . . . which brings with it a feeling of *immortality*. The individual's life . . . becomes the archetype of women's fate in general.'[40]

Like Kristeva, Jung has a sense of a maternal time as cyclical, archaic, immortal, residing in the unconscious and in a mother's psychic bonding to maternity. Unlike Kristeva, Jung reveals cultural slippage in his 'eternalism', the way in which his theorizing is affected by outmoded styles of gender that he considers 'natural' and so 'eternal'. For example, here his theorizing of maternal time becomes collapsed into the 'fate' of all women. No combination of masculine linear history and feminine myth and eternity for Jung's women! The Jungian symbolic may be theoretically *capable* of supplying a feminine and maternal function. That does not mean that Jung can be relied upon to provide it.

Jungian feminisms might offer two responses to this brief incursion into the large and complex work of Kristeva. The first response is constituted by goddess feminism, which Kristeva would emphatically reject. Exclusive seduction by women's time is separatist, essentialist, intrinsically disengaged from multiple notions of cultural difference. She regards it as likely to produce oppressive forms of social organization based upon woman-as-scapegoat.

In mitigation, one could argue that goddess feminism's gendering of the Jungian symbolic need not be construed in an essentialist manner. The myth of the Great Goddess is an inflated casting of the pre-Oedipal mother as immanent in nature and the psyche, so *prior* to splitting into two opposing genders. It can lead the psyche *prospectively* to plural forms of gender identification.

A second Jungian response to Kristeva relies upon the more deconstructive take on the Jungian symbolic. Feminist deconstruction and 'French Feminisms' unite in the recognition that Jung's psychology is devoted to the (impossible) task of thinking in the 'other'. Jung's work insists upon the privileging of the 'deconstructive', uncontainable unconscious even within his most ambitious attempts to construct fixed propositions for his 'grand theory'.

What this chapter has tried to show is that Jung thinking-in-the-other is intimately involved with the feminine in two key ways. Jung's feminine is the principle of the unconscious as unknowableness, the irreducible metaphysics to be found in any theory, even that of deconstruction. And the other feminine, stalking both grand theory and personal myth, is the lapse into misogyny and essentialism, usually in generalizing from his anima to make reductive pronouncements on women.

Such 'eternalism' within Jungian theory could be viewed as a patriarchally distorted symbolic invading the proper sphere of the semiotic and unknowable. It should not prevent future research into Jung, deconstruction and post-Freudian feminism. I am arguing for a feminist research that respects the differences between the theories. Such feminisms seek strategic temporary linkings in echoes and correspondences; all in pursuit of the elusive feminine.

Concluding summary

Jung's theory of archetypes establishes a relation to both structuralism and deconstruction. Most suggestive for feminism is the Jungian affinity with deconstruction. However, there are also crucial divergences between Jung and deconstruction in both grand-theory and personal-myth modes. Applying deconstructive notions to Jung produces a feminine of radical indefinability *and* an essentialist idea of women.

Psychoanalytic feminist theory (via deconstruction) offers a number of perspectives on Jung and gender. Post-Freudian criticisms of masculine-dominated thinking in psychoanalysis – such as Irigaray on Lacan's phallus, and Cixous's realm of the proper – can be used to understand the essentializing anima. On the other hand, Jung can provide an alternative, more gender fluid and a more semiotically infused symbolic to that of Lacan and post-Freudian feminism.

A Jungian feminism influenced by both deconstruction and post-Freudian feminism is able to imagine more 'feminine' forms of theorizing. It offers connections to transcendence derived from the maternal body (Irigaray), écriture feminine and performing gender (Cixous), the semiotic as maternal realm and non-linear women's time (Kristeva).

FURTHER READING

For structuralism, poststructuralism and deconstruction

Barry, Peter, *Beginning Theory: An Introduction to Literary and Cultural Theory* (Manchester: Manchester University Press, 1995).
An accessible introduction to these complex areas.

Wolfreys, Julian (ed.), *Literary Theories: A Reader and Guide* (Edinburgh: Edinburgh University Press, 1999).
A more demanding introduction containing essays by major theorists, including Derrida.

On Post-Freudian feminism

The beginner with the three French feminists could not do better than to look at these three readers. They all have particularly helpful introductions.

Cixous, Hélène, *The Hélène Cixous Reader*, ed. Susan Sellers (London and New York: Routledge, 1994).

Irigaray, Luce, *The Irigaray Reader*, ed. Margaret Whitford (Oxford: Blackwell, 1991).

Kristeva, Julia, *The Kristeva Reader*, ed. Toril Moi (Oxford: Blackwell, 1986).

On Jung

Jung, C. G., 'The Psychological Aspects of the Kore', *CW* 9(i), pp. 182–203. Rare and interesting instance of Jung's concentration on women as separate beings and not just bearers of the anima.

Rowland, Susan, *C. G. Jung and Literary Theory: The Challenge from Fiction* (London: Macmillan, 1999; repr. London: Palgrave, 2001). This book reads Jung in a feminist, political and deconstructive manner in relation to contemporary literature.

6

Postmodern Jungian Feminisms

Here Mercurius in feminine form is the Queen, and she is the 'heaven' wherein the sun shines.

(Jung, *Mysterium Conjunctionis 13*, 1963)

The sublime . . . is where woman goes beyond her proper boundaries and gets out of place.

(Lynda Nead, 'Getting down to Basics', 1997)

This chapter makes a case for Jung in postmodernism. It assesses the potential for Jungian contributions to a number of postmodern feminisms in terms of the body, the sublime, narrative and the Gothic. Jung's work on alchemy is introduced before being explored in the context of postmodern debates on the body and gender.

I aim to explore the ways in which gender becomes the point where Jung most resists the postmodern, where he is most fixed in oppositional certainties. Nevertheless, careful scrutiny of Jung's writings cannot simply conclude that he is anti-postmodern on gender since his feminine is both essentialist and anti-essentialist – here sublime.

The chapter outlines the role of gender in the transition from the Enlightenment of the eighteenth century to the contemporary era of postmodernism. This is a prelude to looking at the issues for Jung in postmodernism when focusing on the vexed matter of his feminine. A key emphasis will be Jung's neglected but surprisingly postmodern-friendly notions of the body. Particular attention is given to his key notion of the psychological 'subtle body'. I go on to compare and contrast the Jungian subtle body to the discursive body of Judith Butler. Such arguments are designed to allow for the possibility of a postmodern Jungian body.

A postmodern feminist Jung may also be discerned in the notion of the sublime inherited by postmodernism from the Romantics. This, I suggest, may provide a Jungian gender as a site continually open to political and social transformation.

A reversal of the sublime unknowability of postmodernism is its proliferation of narratives as provisional and experimental. For such a contribution to feminism, Jungian concepts can be regarded as a *performing* (not a theoretical) narrative structure in goddess feminism and feminist novels.

The final sections of the chapter suggest that, although Jung has a lot to say to postmodernism, from the point of view of gender he can be more properly described as a Gothic author. This suggestion rests upon Jung's tendency to challenge, explode, and yet persistently revisit binary narratives when addressing masculinity and femininity. I end with a note about eco-feminism and cyberfeminism. Is there a future for Jung in feminism?

Introduction

The previous two chapters looked at the history of 'feminism' as it developed into an alliance of 'differences' rather than a single body designed to represent one category of 'women'. A dual pressure inspired this new diversity, that of politics on the ground and of theory in the academy. An increasingly complex politics between women, due to growing recognition of differences of class, sexuality, race and ethnicity, began to disrupt feminism as a seamless body. Simultaneously, feminist thinkers were investigating the impact of theories such as poststructuralism, deconstruction and psychoanalytic feminisms after Lacan.

Politics and theories converged on the realization that a belief in a conscious self as stable, knowable and of fixed gender, and as the foundation for true knowledge of the world, was no longer tenable. Post-Lacanian psychoanalysis and deconstruction not only exploded the myth that there are two unchanging genders of feminine and masculine; they also dispute the notion that there is *anything* fixed and securely knowable about the human subject. And if who I am is not a foundation for knowledge, if conscious assumptions have no guaranteed status, then knowledge and beliefs about the world become both problematic and unstable. Western society enters postmodernism.

From the perspective of the needs of feminism, a crucial characteristic of postmodernism is that it applies to the condition of society and culture.[1] Blending theories and social practice, postmodernism

is where social experience becomes indistinguishable from the construction of ideas. Indeed, in postmodernism it is impossible to say
whether social fragmentation and incoherence *produces* postmodern
thinking or is *produced by it*.

I am not suggesting that the pre-postmodern Enlightenment had no
purchase upon feminism. Indeed, all Western feminist movements are
indebted to Enlightenment narratives of human freedom and equality.
Rather, the condition of feminism in postmodernity is the requirement
to hang onto the Enlightenment heritage of political goals in a pluralist society in which 'women' can no longer be regarded as a simple
grouping. Postmodern pluralist society needs to explore anew the
implications of the term 'postmodern' and 'feminist'.

Moreover, where there is no one set of rules, art and aesthetic practices take on a new significance. Since postmodernism is about the
absence of secure rules and fixed points in philosophy, culture *and*
society, it is unsurprising that postmodern theories themselves do not
fit together to make a coherent agreed whole. Art and aesthetics are
the human constructs that have always been generated from the
borders of philosophical and social consensus. Therefore art in postmodernism takes on the task of embodying or representing the point
at which diverse and often contradictory ideas, cultural practices,
social needs and capitalism collide and take material form.

In this situation, one of the most fertile areas for postmodern feminism can be found in works of art, or, in the instance of C. G. Jung,
at the point at which a system of ideas strays beyond scientific boundaries. Jung's work can be said to show affinity with the postmodern
when it ceases to claim itself as a secure foundation for a fixed knowledge of the human subject. Jung speaks to postmodernity when he
renounces 'grand theory' and enters the territory of metaphor, speculation and the literary.

Postmodernism is characterized by the waning of the power of
'grand narratives'. These are those systems of knowledge whose heritage goes back to the eighteenth century, the period known as the
Enlightenment in Western culture. Grand narratives were designed
to organize and ground knowledge and scientific enquiry in secure
philosophical foundations. They include the notion of scientific
empiricism (grounding science in material evidence) and ideals of
human progress embedded in a belief in Western civilization.[2]

Of course, to make the sweeping generalization that postmodernism 'is characterized by the waning of the power of grand
narratives' is in fact to offer yet another grand narrative – that of
'their' pervasive decline. This reveals the extent to which postmodernism is complicit with the modernity that preceded it. The decline of

grand narratives could be regarded as yet another instance of the apocalyptic narrative of 'ending' that distinguishes both Christianity and Marxism.

My purpose in this chapter is to explore the ways in which Jung both counters and facilitates postmodernism, with the emphasis on gender. Much of his reductive pronouncements on the feminine can be aligned with his pre-postmodern Enlightenment credentials. On the other hand, his proto-postmodernism offers something positive and energizing to the postmodern field. Postmodern thinking is an arena that has too often been dominated by post-materialist nihilism.

When I refer to Jung's drive for 'grand theory', I mean the moments in his writing when the work both purports to be grounded in the 'big' grand narratives, such as when he refers to his 'empiricism' (see chapter 5), *and*, crucially, when he claims to provide a grand narrative himself in Jungian psychology. Jung arguing that his psychology is a viable account of culture, religion and human problems (at least the important ones!) is Jung, the man of the Enlightenment modernity. His 'grand theory' adopts the status of a grand narrative.

Nevertheless, as I have shown, there is also the Jung of personal myth. This is the Jung who admits the 'personal' into the construction of a psychology. Linking the two Jungs is the core proposition of the absolute otherness of the unconscious to theorizing of any kind. Both grand theory and personal myth are fatally disrupted by Jung's metaphysical conception of the unconscious as a generative source of the conscious self.

This unconscious is 'metaphysical' in the religious sense when Jung regards it as having a transcendent religious role in the psyche of human beings. It is also metaphysical in the Derridean sense in that it remains a foundation to Jung's system of ideas – one that Jung regarded as self-evident from his descriptions of the autonomous psyche (his word was 'objective'). In Derridean terms, Jung's unconscious is a 'supplement' – an idea brought in to provide a *ground* for all the other concepts.[3]

There is a particular consequence to having as a metaphysical supplement the radically disruptive and *unknowable* unconscious. That consequence is a very 'postmodern' foundation to Jung's theorizing. If the unconscious is truly unconscious, as Jung frequently insists, then it must deny the grand theory the status of a grand narrative, with the crucial exception of its own founding 'presence' as a metaphysical residue. If what is unknowable is most important, then the theory's claim to know *definitely and authoritatively* such concepts as archetypes is radically undercut. In effect, the founding presence for

Jungian psychology (as grand theory and personal myth) is a founding absence.

The disruptive effect of the unconscious means that no theoretical proposition can claim to be 'the truth'; it is at best a provisional and metaphorical attempt to describe a particular situation. Despite the desire to flirt with the grand narratives of Enlightenment modernity, what is particularly suggestive for a Jung in postmodernism is to be found in the writing. The self-conscious sense of the lack of a secure comprehensible grounding to theoretical arguments is woven into his works. 'For, when we say that the conscious and unconscious unite, we are saying in effect that this process is inconceivable.'[4] Postmodernism and gender make more complicated demands upon Jung. His treatment of alchemy and his notions of the body's contribution to psychic life are good perspectives from which to assess Jung's contribution to postmodernism and gender.

This final chapter will argue for Jung as a valuable thinker in postmodernism and as a potential partner in postmodern feminisms. Unsurprisingly, given the experience of previous chapters, gender is also where Jung tends to concentrate his least postmodern pronouncements. These are to be found in his essentialism on the nature of women that pretends to a foundational knowledge, and his retention of a characteristic Enlightenment structure. Jung takes directly from Enlightenment grand narratives the prejudice that desirable qualities of reason and logical thinking are to be gendered as masculine *oppositionally against* an 'outside' of feminine irrationality.

Despite these very apparent limitations for Jung in postmodern feminisms (and, of course, feminism cannot be 'one' in postmodernism), as I suggested earlier there is a very real chance that his writing could also be a 'partner', but not a prime mover, in postmodern feminist theory. The moments where his psychology most acknowledges its limits, where the unconscious is most subtly evoked in the writing, in alchemy and the body, are moments when Jung's essentialist prejudices are rendered unviable *within* his work.

One example of the potential for a postmodern Jungian feminism is the use of his ideas to provide a narrative form for art, such as a novel. This would be to use Jung as a technology of aesthetic representation without importing his work as grand theory. Such art could not invoke his psychology as a vehicle for straightforward essentialist truths. Jung contributes a method of structuring that does not claim to bestow fixed foundations of knowledge.[5]

In doing so such novels are using the anti-foundationalism latent in Jung to cut away his own essentialism on gender, in particular his descriptions of the anima. Interestingly, it is not necessary to shift to feminist artists to discover Jungian ideas being used as a postmodern narrative strategy. Jung himself does so, sporadically, in the texts of alchemy, and in his ghost story (see later).[6]

The penultimate section of this chapter will suggest that from the point of view of feminism, it may be helpful to link Jung to the Gothic rather than to over-identify him with postmodernism.[7] In its ambiguous relationship to both the Enlightenment and postmodernism, and its repeated struggles with 'the feminine', the Gothic may provide a home for Jung and all his feminine ghosts.

Jung on alchemy

Alchemy was the attempt to turn lead into gold. It was understandably a popular pastime in periods of history when philosophical and religious ideas suggested that this was possible. Flourishing in Western Europe in the medieval and early modern eras, alchemy is known to have existed as far back as the first century CE. Although alchemy attracted crooks and those merely seeking a fortune, the devotion of serious alchemists to their experimental work yielded a number of scientific advances. Alchemy is recognized as the forerunner of modern chemistry, from which the latter derives its name.

Such is the popular view of alchemy. What is less well known is alchemy's philosophical and religious dimensions.[8] Whereas Enlightenment and post-Enlightenment thinking separates mind from matter, regarding chemicals and metals as inert, 'dead' substances, alchemy believed in a continuation between what was material, what was psychological and what was sacred. Mind, matter and spirit are conjoined. The alchemist's world was animated: the divine spark resided in matter, deep in the human soul and in the transcendent godhead.

Transforming lead into gold, on one level a highly profitable operation, to the true alchemist was the refining of the divine spirit out of the prison of base matter. Base lead, known as the 'prima materia' or basic substance, could be made to yield a holy golden form, often called the philosopher's stone. The whole operation would simultaneously serve to refine the soul of the alchemist. It was the aim of alchemy to achieve the higher divine and philosophical form of both the prima materia of metal and the base melancholy mettle that is the untransformed human soul.

When reading alchemy texts, it is impossible to tell whether alchemists believed that they were making actual chemical gold, or whether such language is a metaphor for some divine reality, or both. Literal materiality and metaphorical theology are not alternatives.

Rather, alchemists lived in an ensouled world where the divine was not only 'up there' and 'separate' (transcendent); it was also immanent in matter and the human mind.

Although it might appear that alchemy lives in an entirely different dimension from the fragmentation and unbelief of postmodernism, this is not really the case. What might interest postmodernists in alchemy is that this pre-Enlightenment 'science' refuses to split consciousness off from matter. It therefore runs counter to Enlightenment empiricism, the scientific grand narrative also challenged in postmodernity. In alchemy the observing consciousness is inevitably caught up in material processes, just as postmodern science asserts that the observer affects the phenomena observed. Similarly, of great interest to Jung was alchemy's insistence that the process must also take place in the alchemist's own soul.

Jung came to believe that alchemy was, in fact, a projection of what he had identified as individuation.[9] Alchemists were so deeply involved with the matter in their test tubes because they had projected their own unconscious contents upon them. When alchemists talked of substances dying and resurrecting, uniting and dissolving, they were doing the equivalent of self-analysis in facilitating their own individuation. In this sense alchemy texts are the equivalent of dreams as records of psychic material. The only difference between dreams and alchemy is that alchemical work is projected *externally* onto matter.

Where two people are involved in alchemy, the process is equivalent to an orthodox Jungian analysis. Transference and countertransference is mutually acknowledged and used as a starting point for psychic development.

I have used the word 'equivalent' in describing Jung's aligning his ideas with alchemy because, on the one hand, Jung could be quite 'grand theory' about alchemy, regarding it as 'proof' of his concept of individuation. On the other hand, the lack of fixity and grounding in alchemy writings makes it difficult for Jung to employ alchemy as 'scientific' evidence of his psychology's universal validity.

Jung's alchemical works possess a consciousness that his ability to theorize is *reliant upon* alchemical writings as much as it is an *explanation* of them. He says that alchemy offers him 'a treasury of symbols'[10] of the psyche and that it suggests 'symbolical procedures'[11] for the crucial uniting of opposites. Furthermore, alchemy has 'made it possible for me to describe the individuation process' in a way that case material could not.[12] Consequently and paradoxically, Jung can claim to be more 'Jungian' when writing about alchemy than when describing his own clinical work with patients. Alchemy enables him to elaborate upon the endlessly varied process of individuation in ways that actual cases of real people do not.

This is a small but significant shift in the depiction of the foundations of a psychology. Is it to be founded upon clinical study or upon mystical readings? Of course, Jung does not reject his clinical-based theorizing, nor the drive to grand theory. However, when he suggests that alchemy provides more comprehensive *evidence* rather than case material's 'mosaic of bits and pieces without beginning or end',[13] he opens up a 'difference' between alchemy and conventional underpinnings of psychology. Such a shift is significant in the context of anti-foundational, anti-empirical postmodernism.

Jung wrote with confidence that his ideas could account for alchemical manifestations *but not wholly explain them*. The unknowable unconscious remains the bottom line. It defeats absolute and knowable theories of the psyche, so that one day his psychology will be defined as 'metaphorical and symbolical', as he believed alchemy to be.[14]

A last word on Jung's alchemy introduces the Jungian body. Jung divided the individuation processes in alchemy into three stages. First, a union with the unconscious would be structured oppositionally through gender as the psyche offers a figure of the 'other' as the other gender, the anima/animus. This union is typically described as a 'marriage', made into a sacred marriage through the numinous powers of the unconscious. In a second stage, the psyche would experience union with the body. Then, in a further denial of the Enlightenment severing of mind from matter, the psyche would unite with the outer world.[15]

Although Jung regarded alchemy primarily as the projection of individuation, he also used it to speculate about the ultimate identity of psyche and matter. This is a theme familiar to postmodern science, as Christopher Hauke explains in his invaluable *Jung and the Postmodern*.[16]

Jung on the body

Theorists suspicious of the anti-foundationalist stance of postmodernism have often turned to the body as a source of secure meaning. Surely the body provides grounds for some truths now that the mind and subjectivity are no longer reliable? Feminists can be tempted to resort to the sexed body as an unproblematic source of truth. The corporeal is so self-evidently fixed in contrast to the instabilities of postmodern gender.

Such feminist thinking has been countered by Judith Butler's assertion that knowledge of the body is discursively constructed.[17] That is to say, the body may be a stable 'thing' in the world, but our understanding of it is subject to all those slippages of language and systems of ideas that pollute other apparently self-evident 'truths'. Beliefs about the meaning of bodily contours are just as much constructed by the languages of gender, race, power, medicine, science and philosophy as those treacherously mutable terms, feminine and masculine.

Judith Butler's work on postmodern bodily sex can be usefully compared and contrasted to the Jungian body. First of all, I will introduce Jung's notions of the body.

Like the postmoderns, Jung did not regard the body as a self-explanatory source of meaning. The Jungian body is neither a governing nor a founding principle. Indeed, Jung referred to the body as metaphysical because it cannot be known unmediated through the active and creative psyche. Therefore to regard the body as a ground for knowledge would be an act of faith that can never be proven; hence the body as metaphysical.[18]

Always psychologically constructed (because mental apprehension of the body comes via the psyche), the body is not an objective source of truth. In this contention Jung might be surprised to find himself in the company of postmodern feminists. Jung felt that the body had to be understood paradoxically both as a separate system with its own needs and laws, *and* as vitally engaged with the psyche. The Jungian body influences the psyche yet can never be a ruling factor. This is because, for Jung, the unknowable unconscious is always primary. Making the unconscious the most central idea in his psychology is another way of asserting that the body can never be objectively known. Unconscious processes in the psyche inevitably intervene in the mind's visions of the body.

The structures of the psyche, such as the archetypes, are both material and immaterial. As material, they exist in the body at the level of instincts. As immaterial, they possess a numinous transcendent form: they are not dependent upon the body nor upon impressions received from the external world for their existence.[19] To put it another way, archetypes have two poles; their bodily instinctual pole is in dialogue with their numinous and autonomous aspects.

Neither the body nor the numinous dimension controls the other, although they are vitally interrelated. Indeed, the body is required by the ego to give it 'ground' in order that it may be more integrated with the unconscious rather than overwhelmed by it.[20] The body grounding the ego should not be confused with grounding the psyche. Nor can the body ground Jungian psychology as a system of ideas, because the ego is not the foundation of Jung's reality nor of his theory. That foundation is always the unknowable unconscious.

What potentially connects feminism and Jung on the body is the notion of the 'subtle body'. This is the body as psychically conceived or imaged. The psychological contribution of the body to a sense of personal identity is like the body in dreams; it has already been psychically processed. And the subtle body is also connected to social pressures (see later in this chapter on Jung's ghost story). Even though Jung tended to play down the role of culture in the formation of psychic images, his subtle body is still one that culture intervenes in constructing because of the cultural input to archetypal images. The subtle body is made of archetypal images that are registering bodily impressions.

The Jungian subtle body is much in evidence in his alchemical writings. Here Jung's extensive treatment of, and reliance upon, alchemy is both helpful and unhelpful. It is helpful in that Jung's lack of interest in the cultural and historical dimension of alchemy texts means that his own social prejudices do not intrude. This in turn is also unhelpful in giving the false impression that individuation can be separated from a person's own history and culture: it cannot.

Alchemy provided Jung with a grammar of psychic symbols, not the justification for his subtle body as innocent of cultural inscription. Archetypes, with their bodily and numinous dimensions, supply part of the structuring of the archetypal image-as-body realization, a subtle body. Personal history and culture also play a role, although they can never be the governing factor in a Jungian paradigm (a place reserved for the creative, unknowable unconscious). Despite Jung's own interests, the Jungian subtle body remains related to cultural ideas and competing social practices.

What is especially fascinating about the Jungian subtle body is that it is not a creature of the body, nor of the mind; it represents the union of both. Therefore the subtle body transcends that characteristic Enlightenment binary splitting of body away from mind. The subtle body is that point where mind and body meet, and one cannot be given priority over the other. Neither mind nor body can be 'translated' into the other. Therefore 'words' cannot ever completely describe nor evoke the subtle body, for they are the creatures of the conscious ego. Only symbols will do, for: 'The symbol is neither abstract nor concrete, neither rational nor irrational, neither real nor unreal. It is always both . . .'.[21] Now it is time to consider the challenges to Jung represented by such terms as 'Enlightenment', 'postmodernism' and 'feminism' before seeking a postmodern Jungian body.

The Enlightenment, postmodernism and feminism

The term 'Enlightenment' refers to the period in the eighteenth century when the philosophical, political and scientific grand narratives of modernity became established. Particularly significant was the characterization of Western societies as embarked upon a linear narrative of civilized 'progress'. This belief was buttressed by grand narratives of empirical science and of human freedom and equality. In turn, these were based on notions of a common human 'essence'. Since postmodernism counters, fractures and problematizes the intellectual heritage of the Enlightenment, it is worth exploring its assumptions a little further.

The Enlightenment as an intellectual movement has a number of defining characteristics. They can be summarized as follows:

1. Human beings possess a stable, coherent, conscious identity or 'self', characterized by rationality. 'Reason' is the superior quality that enables the human self to develop a privileged insight into itself and into non-human nature.
2. Reason structures philosophy. The resulting philosophy can provide objective, reliable and universal foundations for knowledge. Reason therefore supplies knowledge about human beings and the world that is 'true' and stable.
3. History, culture and the body do not affect reason's capacity to provide objective knowledge. In this way, reason is 'transcendent' and universal. Reason is connected to possibilities of autonomy and freedom.
4. Knowledge grounded in reason is politically neutral. Conflicts between truth, knowledge and power can be settled by appealing to reason.
5. Science is grounded in reason and so provides a model for knowledge. Therefore, science is politically neutral and socially beneficial.
6. Language offers an unproblematic window onto the world. It is a transparent medium for reason and representation: language and reality correspond. Correct uses of language make the world present to consciousness. Language does not construct reality.

Postmodernism challenges all the above Enlightenment beliefs. Grand narratives that uphold ideas of the supremacy of reason, its transcendence of the body and history, the neutrality of science bolstered by empirical practices (repeatable objective experiments) – all these have been weakened by or proved vulnerable to postmodern criticism. A particular point of dispute is the way the Enlightenment constructed its principles. Enlightenment grand narratives rely upon binary structures. For example, mind is defined as being wholly distinct from the body, the observing scientist must be wholly separable from the world studied and, crucially, reason must be cut off from the irrational.

Typically, the Enlightenment used gender as a means of positioning the necessary binaries: masculinity was associated with transcendent mind, femininity with the messy reproductive body. In clichéd terms this becomes men doing the important job of 'thinking' while women are assigned a lower position of sex and reproduction. The male scientist or doctor operates *upon* not *with* feminine nature or passive (so feminized) patients. And, of course, reason is gendered as the supreme quality of masculine consciousness while the irrational is defined as deviant and feminine.

Three related intellectual movements criticized Enlightenment grand narratives and moved Western society into the postmodern. These are psychoanalysis, feminist theory and postmodern philosophy. All three dispute the fixed binaries upon which Enlightenment thinking depended. Psychoanalysis questioned the absolute split between rationality and irrationality by showing the shaping role of the unconscious even in the rational waking self. Feminism attacked gender binaries while postmodern philosophy provided the means to challenge dualistic thinking of all kinds.

Postmodern theories are characteristically deconstructive (see chapter 5). They undo hierarchical binary oppositions that condense around the core Enlightenment belief of superior masculine reason *created by* expelling and suppressing feminine unreason.

Instead of all-encompassing grand narratives, postmodernism provides competing discourses. Here the term 'discourse' is taken from the work of Michel Foucault.[22] A discourse is a body of knowledge that is also a social practice. It is, therefore, a form of social power. Discourses provide ways of thinking and of constructing meaning. They do not just describe; most importantly, discourses *constitute* subjectivity, social relations and knowledge of the world.

A discourse is emphatically not politically neutral. Rather, it is part of the social, historical and power relations out of which it arises. Foucault believed that social reality consists of competing *and* mutually constituting discourses that *produce* power, society and subjectivity itself. Postmodern discourses are deconstructive in that they can offer no foundations for knowledge outside their own structures. In this they challenge the fundamentals of the Enlightenment's grand narratives.

Feminism, postmodernism and Jung

Feminism has an ambiguous relationship to the Enlightenment and its postmodern opponent. On the one hand, the tendency of the Enlightenment to rest upon a gendered hierarchy of masculine reason above feminine irrationality has stimulated feminist theories dedicated to promoting a postmodern era. On the other hand, it is from the Enlightenment that the modern world has inherited ideals of emancipation, freedom, autonomy and equality. Feminists want some of that, too. The argument that postmodernism *per se* is not going to fulfil the feminist project can be substantiated by looking at the way the gender binary of Enlightenment modernity persists in some postmodern thinking.

Some postmodern philosophies continue to delight in irrationality as feminine. In what appears to be a mere reversal of the existing hierarchy, the feminine other is now valued and given the privileged position as the location for that elusive, partial, postmodern 'truth'. 'She' is postmodern truth as a veiled woman.[23] From the Enlightenment to postmodernism, 'truth' has changed sides. From being the property of masculine reason, it is now placed in the embrace of the feminine other.

The postmodern self may be radically dependent upon this irrational, unrepresentable 'truth', but the continuing confinement of the feminine to the otherness of representation is not an empowering development for women in the political and social sphere. Postmodernism's quaintly traditional keeping of the feminine as other does not go unchallenged by feminist theory.

Postmodern feminism has to be both postmodern and feminist. There can be no simple collapse of the two terms into each other. The production of diverse yet allied feminisms, replacing a single feminist movement, is a symptom of postmodernism. It is also a desire continually to rethink the terms 'postmodern' and 'feminism' and their relationship. Feminist postmodernism has to negotiate a relationship to Enlightenment narratives of autonomy and freedom as well as to those narratives of masculine transcendence resting upon 'feminine' inferiority.

In this story of the Enlightenment, postmodernism and feminism, C. G. Jung has a place. Christopher Hauke has convincingly described Jungian psychology as a discourse *for* postmodern societies.[24] Focusing on the challenge to reason as the foundation for true knowledge, Jung criticizes the characteristics of Enlightenment modernity. Reason is not the source of truth for Jung, since subjectivity and knowledge of reality are dependent upon the other, the unknowable unconscious. History, culture and the body do affect the conscious mind's understanding of the world in the moulding of archetypal images that also influence conscious perception. As with postmodernism, none of these offers fixed or secure grounds for 'truth'.

Similarly, Jung does not use scientific or philosophical grand narratives to anchor his psychology in 'universal' truths. When he speaks of 'philosophy' in writing about his psychology, he does not suggest that it can supply a neutral foundation for knowledge. Rather, Jungian psychology slides into the category of personal myth because Jung's reason, situated in the ego, is dependent upon *his* other, the interventions of the superior unknowable unconscious. Jung never pretends to a reason shorn of 'personal' factors.

Therefore Jung's attempts to structure his theory as a grand narrative, what I have called 'grand theory', can never wholly be separated from the drive to personal myth *because* the most crucial proposition of the unknowable unconscious means that Jung cannot hold to Enlightenment principles of a superior, truth-perceiving reason. From this it is possible to argue that Jung's affinity with postmodernism lies paradoxically in his foundational proposition of the unconscious. What Jungian theory rests upon (its metaphysical residue – see chapter 5), the unconscious, is unrepresentable, *unwritable*, because it is inconceivable to the ego. If the founding presence is a founding absence from the writing, then for Jung, as in postmodernism, language is not a reliable and transparent window onto meaning, truth and the world.

Yet, as I suggested earlier, Jung is not wholly postmodern. In his drive to grand theory, he desires both to connect with and to imitate Enlightenment grand narratives. Most significantly from a feminist point of view, Jung is most deeply a man of the Enlightenment in his retention of oppositional thinking about gender. Indeed, gender becomes the principal means by which oppositional thinking is expressed in Jungian ideas. It is hard to imagine how the essentially deconstructive process of individuation could describe opposition between conscious and unconscious without Jung's typical use of gender.

Perhaps what I have called in the previous chapter Jung's phallic anima is a product of the Jung of Enlightenment modernity. At the same time, the vitally deconstructive 'feminine' unconscious is of the postmodern Jung. Like other postmodernisms, it still persists with the other as feminine.

Jung's writings about the anima are 'phallic' when they describe her as merely the screen upon which to project what must be cast out of masculine consciousness in order to ally it with rationality and Logos. Here the anima becomes *the* important signifier for what is knowable, in the sense that it is what the masculine has (as 'his' other), but must not be (woman must 'be' his anima for him). The anima is therefore the misrepresentation of the feminine, the means of forming a binary structure: masculine–consciousness–Logos/ feminine–unconsciousness–Eros.

The phallic anima is Enlightenment Jung, whereas Jung's anima as signifier of the unknowable unconscious is his incarnation as postmodern Jung. To take Jung from postmodernism to becoming a partner in postmodern feminism, I return to the Jungian body.

Jung and the body in postmodernism

Ideas about the body in postmodernism possess four defining aspects:

1. The body is not in a binary exclusionary relationship to the mind. Body can affect the mind, mind constructs knowledge of the body.
2. The body is therefore a factor in a person's sense of conscious self, capacity for reason, gender, psyche, etc.
3. The body is constructed through discourse. It is not a neutral or objective object of study. The body is constituted *through* ideas that are connected to history and culture.
4. The body is not an alternative to reason. As it is not transcendent of history, psyche and culture, it cannot itself provide objective grounds for knowledge or truth.

For postmodern feminism, Judith Butler in *Gender Trouble* and *Bodies that Matter* has explored the role of the sexed body in the formation of gender and psychic identity. She particularly criticizes the feminist tradition of dividing off bodily sex from cultural gender. This attitude regards bodily sex as a neutral background upon which cultural gender is constructed and inscribed. Butler deconstructs the sex/gender binary by arguing that sex can never be neutrally 'known'. Rather, bodily sex is discursive in the Foucauldian sense of being constituted through discourse. I only know the reality of my body through the cultural discourses that construct the significance of my body to me. Therefore gender, and even the sense of being a self, an 'I', is bound up with the cultural construction of the body.

This is not to suggest that the body is simply discourse. Bodies *matter* in two senses: they are important though discourse in forming the ways I understand myself. Also, they are part of matter, they have a physical being beyond conscious registration. To Butler, bodies are part of a materialist conception of reality as a lived relation of social production and domination. The body is only *knowable* through discourse; it nevertheless exists beyond the discursive.

Butler places the discursive and non-discursive body in a continuation of a materialist view of social reality: 'language [making up discourse] and materiality are not opposed, for language both is and refers to that which is material, and what is material never fully escapes from the process by which it is signified.'[25] In placing the discursive sexing of the body at the heart of identity formation, Butler suggests that gender is performative. This does not mean that there is an 'I', a self that precedes gender and somehow decides to take up a gender role. On the contrary, 'I', the self, is constructed through the discourses of the body that *replace* sex by gender.

In effect, there is no separation of sex and gender. Gendering discourses produce the effects of sex by a repetitive citing of the body that is also a siting of it within (and constituted by) gender relations. To reverse conventional assumptions, society does not have two genders because there are self-evidently two different sorts of human bodies. Rather, persistent duality in thinking about gender constructs a sense of two absolutely different types of body to justify the desire to retain binary inequalities.

Moreover this is not a question of a single external power swooping upon the developing child. It is a construction of the body as material through repeated referencing and citing. The matter of the body is not a straightforward surface. It is 'a process of materialization that stabilizes over time to produce the effect of boundary, fixity and surface we call matter'.[26]

What is of particular concern to Butler, and where her discursive body explicitly takes on the feminist postmodern project, is her view of gender as a regulatory practice. Gender is performative (not an essential 'truth') and reiterative. It constitutes the 'I', so there is no choosing subject. What circumscribes gender and subjectivity is the inbuilt structuring of discourses to produce a heterosexual norm. Heterosexuality is hegemonic, meaning dominant, when regarded as the norm and the desirable base for subjectivity and sexual relations.

However, the discourses of sex–gender cannot simply reproduce heterosexuality as a fixed stable human condition. Because gender discourses are performative and reiterative, they are not working to some pre-existing 'perfect' model. Therefore, performative gender inevitably produces gaps and fissures in the norms of heterosexuality. Gaps open up because discourses do not operate in static conditions.

They function in conflict with other competing ideas and social practices.[27]

Performativity, therefore, is not the repeated stamping of the same meaning on inert bodies. There is no single external stable 'ground' to produce gender uniformity. Rather, the repetitive citing of gender discourses reveals the instabilities within the dominant construction of male/female as heterosexuality. By the attempted reproduction of heterosexuality, performativity actually constructs bodies that expose the boundaries of heterosexual discourses.

These boundaries have to be formed by designating some sex–genders as 'other' or outside the 'norm'. Heterosexuality *requires* that some bodies fail to make the grade, are unrecognizable, even unthinkable. Such 'abjected or delegitimated bodies' fail to count as bodies at all.[28]

One example of the way Butler makes use of her analysis is in a challenge to Lacan's idea of the phallus as a uniquely privileged signifier. This has the consequence in Lacanian thought of causing the feminine to be unrepresentable. In such a system, lesbian sexuality, for example, is by definition, not thinkable, unless, as Butler suggests, a 'lesbian phallus' is conceivable.[29] Butler removes the Lacanian phallus from its binary opposition masculine/feminine by challenging the assignation of the male body's castration anxiety to the wholly discursive yet uniquely privileged phallus. This then suggests a phallus that may be transferable to other, multiple body parts, since castration anxiety need not be limited to fear of the loss of the penis.

The phallus remains a signifier, but is no longer the privileging of heterosexual masculinity. It has also lost its unique sense of organizing the signifiable. Merely one signifier amongst others in the lesbian exchange, the phallus is neither the originating signifier nor the unspeakable outside.[30]

Where Lacan relies upon the feminine body as abject and repressed, Butler takes a postmodern feminist stance that bodily discourse is constitutive and non-foundational. Her body is permeable to deconstruction in order to argue for a speakable body of feminine desire.

Jung, the body, and the work of Judith Butler

With the aim of looking for echoes and correspondences between the work of Butler and Jung, it would be wrong to suggest that there could be a complete meeting of the two theories. More hopeful is the prospect of comparing and contrasting two very different philosophical starting points on gender and bodies to seek out possibilities for a postmodern Jungian-influenced feminism.

Jungian psychology is without a theory of discourse, nor is it based upon materialism as the productive consequence of power relations. Nevertheless, the absence of such ideas in his work is not the same as absolute incompatibility. Given that archetypal images are affected by a person's culture and history, a gap opens up in the Jungian psyche for material discourses to shape subjectivity.

What remains a radical, irreducible difference between Jung and theories that privilege the role of cultural discourses is that, for Jung, the unknowable unconscious is an autonomous intervening factor. Such a 'metaphysical' unconscious independence is foreign to Butler's world.

However, this irreducible difference does not appear so vast if we put Butler's postmodern sense of the instability of discourses next to Jung's deconstructive unconscious. For both theorists, what is 'known' in the psyche is unstable and provisional. For Jung this is because the unconscious is the paramount reality, the unknowable 'ground'. What the conscious self 'knows' or believes to be true is continually undercut by the unconscious other. For Butler, conscious being is unstable because gendering discourses are unable to fix heterosexuality without the production of an abject other. In turn, the excluded and deviant body–gender persistently undermines the stability of the heterosexual construct.

Specific differences persist between Jung and Butler. The feminist is rooted in post-Marxist materialism, Jung in the unconscious as transcendent of knowledge – in both senses 'metaphysical' (see the introduction to this chapter). We could apply Butler's ideas *to* Jung and suggest that Jungian psychology is yet another gendering discourse that relies upon the 'other' that it, itself, generates. Jungian theory *produces* the unknowable unconscious that it relies upon as its 'ground' so that it may shore up the gender oppositions that maintain its bias towards heterosexuality.

Even more pertinent from a Butlerian point of view is the phallic anima as an abject feminine. As the feminine acts as the boundary to be continually negotiated and reconstituted in Jungian psychology, then it corresponds to Butler's criticism of the way powerful discourses expel the feminine beyond the signifiable as deviant or abject. Butler provides a valuable perspective on Jung's misogyny.

Ironically, however, it is not properly postmodern to take one discourse (such as Butler's) as a 'higher truth' upon which to refashion another (such as Jung's). It is possible to do more than this with these two thinkers. True, Jung does try to emphasize oppositions in the psychic unions of individuation. He does employ gender, abjecting the feminine in order to do so.

Nevertheless, unlike the psychoanalytic tradition that Butler draws upon, Jungian subjectivity is not predicated upon a 'lack' (castration anxiety) in its relation with the other. Rather, the Jungian psyche is structured upon multiple, goal-directed unions. Wooed by the unconscious towards a perfect union, the ego develops an ever-closer intimacy to the deconstructive unconscious. Here, gender as anatomical oppositions inevitably breaks down. Individuation depends upon *compensations* not necessarily structured as *oppositions*. The unconscious always produces an *excess* to the discourses structuring the ego. Therefore the Jungian symbolic is more intimately involved with unconscious processing, more fluidly gendered, and not dominated by the phallus as masculine signifier.

Crucially, the Jungian symbolic is also connected to the body, since archetypes have a bodily dimension. The Jungian subtle body is the body formulated in the psyche: it is made out of the instinctual and numinous aspects of archetypes and a person's cultural experience (their exposure to the discourses of sex–gender in Butler's terms).

Although it is not possible to say that Jung and Butler could ever sit across a table and agree, there is a distinct resemblance between Butler's postmodern discursive body for feminism and the Jungian subtle body. The resemblance is strong in the postmodern aspects of Jung's subtle body. These reside in the refusal to grant the body, or culture, or transcendent archetypes, or even Jung's theory itself, the status as a secure, universal ground for meaning and knowledge. Jung's subtle body occurs in a deconstructive web of psychic and cultural structures.

Of course, the Jungian body is furthest from Butler's postmodern feminist body when he uses bodily shape or gender clichés to structure otherness as pure opposition. The Enlightenment/grand theory Jung of anima/animus and Eros/Logos as gendered binaries has nothing to offer postmodern feminism.

It is the alchemical subtle body that is most suggestive of the potential for a postmodern feminist body in Jungian writings. This is not to argue that the grand-theory drive to gender opposition does not also lurk in the alchemy texts. Indeed, at one point Jung justifies the more diffuse 'luna' consciousness of women (in his view) by saying that this quality is just what women need to manage a family![31]

Yet in the alchemy writings Jung does what Butler calls for. He interrogates the abject and excluded body to reveal it as the constituting boundary of heterosexuality that must be renegotiated. The abject that has been cast outside in the construction of the hetero-

sexual union, the sacred marriage, must be embraced and included.
Reconstructing the abject continually to redraw boundaries between
self and other is urgent in Jung's alchemy, because the individuation
psyche cannot rest on the heterosexual model of sacred marriage of
two genders. Psychic union has to go on and encompass the body and
the discursive world.

So it is unsurprising to find in the alchemy texts the body figuring
as abject, an animal or incestuous, taking the psychic imagery of what
is commonly excluded from heterosexual norms. As Butler shows,
heterosexuality can only be structured and represented through such
exclusions. This is as true for Jung as it is for psychologies such as
Lacan's.

Where Jung reveals feminist value is that, in his work as a whole
and on alchemy in particular, there is a recognition of the limitations
of heterosexual opposition. What is cast out, what is structured as an
abject body, must be reconfigured *within*. Alchemy's multiple psychic
unions aim for a subjectivity in a web of interdependent connections
with gender, body and external reality. Simple heterosexual opposition is not the goal of alchemy; and Jung's alchemy cannot exclude
social discourses, since they are inevitably present wherever the ego is.

Jungian alchemy's subtle body is where Jung is pushed beyond his
neurotic gender oppositionalism to a body viable for postmodern
feminism. It is where the resemblance to Butler's sexed body performing gender is most marked. His writings on alchemy provide a psychic
grammar for renegotiating the abject body: when he writes of
dragons as the abject feminine, they are simultaneously revealed as
protean, mutable psychic images, ripe for transformation. Gender,
subjectivity and the body are a matter for continual psychic re-
formation in which social discourses can never restrict or congeal
identity.

Gender and the postmodern sublime

Postmodernists face a stark choice upon the overthrow of the stable
human self characterized by transcendent reason. They can either
pursue the partial fragmented consciousness of postmodernity,[32] or
they can turn their attention to what the Enlightenment shuddered to
contemplate, the unrepresentable irrational other.

A focus on the irrational is justified by postmodernism's realization
that it is this despised and 'feminine' sphere upon which knowledge
and truths now rely. Turning to the irrational and unrepresentable is
to invoke ideas of the sublime.

Just as there is a continuity between Enlightenment hierarchy of masculine reason/feminine irrationality and postmodernism's fragmented self versus feminine irrational and fragile 'truths', so too for the sublime. Visions of a postmodern sublime draw upon the sublime described in the period of the Enlightenment and Romanticism.

Shadowing Enlightenment certainties, the Romantic sublime speaks of pain or pathos felt in the gap between what can be conceived and what can be imagined or represented. The sublime is what defeats the capacity of reason, consciousness, aesthetic or philosophical categories to represent. It runs counter to the Enlightenment confidence in reason and language as sufficient resources to represent or secure truth.

There is a sense of fullness or presence in the Romantic sublime in that religion provides a ready supply of what can be conceptually thought (such as the notion of God), yet not completely imagined in all possible dimensions. Nor can religion be fully represented in writing or in art.

Unsurprisingly, if associated with the divine, the sublime is an 'other' that is gendered masculine. Conversely, the category of successful aesthetic representation, the 'beautiful', is small and feminine.[33] In placing 'big' important notions such as religion outside the competence of rationality, the sublime challenges Enlightenment suppositions. Of course, any challenge does not extend to disputing the use of the feminine to signify inferiority.

The postmodern sublime shares the Romantic characteristic of exposing the limits of language and of art: this sublime similarly resides in the attempt to represent or invoke what cannot be represented. Lacking the Romantic sense of (divine) presence, the postmodern sublime is to be found in the *failure* of the fragmented contemporary self to constitute truth, or even itself, as a stable entity.

The sublime 'is what dismantles consciousness, what deposes consciousness, it is what consciousness cannot formulate, and even what consciousness forgets in order to constitute itself'.[34]

As a consequence of the weakening of grand narratives, the sublime is the 'gaps' left between systems of knowledge as they fail to account for the postmodern condition in its entirety. In postmodern sublime art, neither the artist nor the viewer can be said to master the work.[35] There is no author in the sense of a point of authority or absolute control over meaning. From such a perspective postmodern theorists cannot be authors. Their works are sublime as they struggle with and fail in representing the 'veiled woman' of postmodern truth. Here the ghost of Jung hovers as I would suggest that his psychology too is a postmodern sublime in its inability to represent its highest 'truth', the unknowable unconscious.

Invoking the veiled woman brings gender into the postmodern sublime. Postmodern theorists rework the Romantic sublime for postmodernism to account for the elusive intensities of contemporary culture. They are particularly concerned with the destabilizing effects of late capitalism. Lacan and psychoanalytic thinkers come at the sublime from another direction, that of the phallus. Given that in Lacanian theory the phallus is a uniquely privileged signifier of the symbolic, it also marks a border beyond which is the sublime. What is absolutely repressed and unrepresentable is Woman. A Lacanian take on the postmodern sublime genders the unrepresentable as feminine.

Of course, representations of women do feature in culture and therefore in the symbolic. But are they represented for themselves or for masculine desire? Lacanian theory has proved so influential for feminist theory because it appears to account for the way women are represented as objects in culture. If the feminine is required to 'be' the phallus (the object of desire) for the masculine, then this could explain why the feminine seems unrepresentable as anything other than a mirror for masculinity.

There are two responses to this feminist impasse. One is to attack the privileging of heterosexual masculinity in the symbolic. This can be done by Judith Butler's scrutiny of the postmodern body, by Jung's more gender fluid symbolic and by his postmodern feminist-friendly subtle body. Another way is to see if the feminine in the sublime, the unrepresentable, has anything to offer. Could Jung contribute to a postmodern feminist sublime?

Jung, gender and the postmodern sublime

Reading Jung within the history of the sublime, I would like to argue that Jungian psychology provides a transition from the Romantic to the postmodern sublime. Jung's tendency to associate his archetypes (in particular the self) with the numinous and religious, as traces of a divine presence in the psyche – this is his Romantic sublime incarnation. On the other hand, the conscious criticism of Enlightenment rationality, acknowledging the limitations of language and of theory, the focus upon psychic images as the primary reality – all this pushes the work into the postmodern sublime.

What makes Jung's writing especially resonate with the postmodern sublime is the bringing of the unrepresentable and unimaginable into the heart of his theory: the founding presence as a founding absence. Both Jung and politically oriented postmodern critics regard Enlightenment rationality as partial and oppressive. For both, the sublime is invoked to value what is other to the conscious mind.

Like the Lacanian sublime, Jung feminizes the unrepresentable, either through the proliferation of the phallic anima, or by structurally feminizing the unknowable unconscious. Also, like Lacan, the difficulty for feminism lies in the tendency to think in oppositions.

Yet, while Lacan is very insistent upon the masculinity of the phallus, Jung is unable to maintain the feminine nature of the unconscious in an essentialist or literal manner. Nor can the (phallic) anima be permitted to control the representation of the feminine. As previously argued, the phallic anima distorts representation of the feminine in Jung's *writing*, not in the implications of his ideas. This is because his unconscious is fluidly gendered. Moreover, the unconscious is not restricted to gender oppositions in providing compensatory images to thwart the ego's desire to control meaning.

Christopher Hauke describes Jung as theorizing the sublime in the concept of the transcendent function.[36] Conflicts between conscious prejudices and unconscious energies may give rise to psychic images that 'transcend' the opposition or try to represent the differences in a non-rational manner: the ego does not 'win' such conflicts. What is most important about symbols supplied through the transcendent function is that they must be considered sublime. They are not to be reduced to words or any narrative satisfactory to the ego. These psychic symbols have a true home only in the irrational and unconscious.

To reduce such a symbol to a simple narrative cause – for example, to say that a religious symbol is the *result* of a sexual trauma – is to strip off the healing sublime powers of the unconscious. In Jungian therapy, the psychic symbol must be treasured for its sublimity, beyond trusting in the tenets of the theory itself. It is paradoxically to operate simultaneously within and without Jungian theory, in the postmodern sublime.

From the point of view of feminism, ideas of the sublime expose a valuable 'gap' in Jung's writing, between the representations of women and of the feminine. As chapter 2 showed, Jung did not work with an idea of gender as cultural. Instead, he tended to collapse gender into bodily sex, so did not view gender as particularly susceptible to cultural change. This is particularly to the fore whenever the work mentions women. The anima comes to dominate the representation of women, hence its phallic nature.

However, the signifying of the feminine in Jung is not wholly under the control of the phallic anima, because that would be to deny the sublime nature of the Jungian unconscious. If we take Jung's two feminines, we see a feminine of men figured by the anima and a feminine of women that becomes obscured by the seductive fascinations of the anima to the male theorist. Yet non-grand-theory Jung is also a postmodern sublime Jung aware of the limitations of theory and language to represent reality. This Jung has to offer a gap between the feminine as abject (what is cast out of masculine consciousness to create its superiority) and the feminine as truly other, so subliminally liberated from conventional representation.

Postmodern sublime Jung admits of his theories, 'nothing offers the assurance that they may ultimately prove correct'.[37] Consequently, although the feminine may be driven in the writing towards Jung's cultural prejudices, it cannot be restricted in representative potency. Jung's feminine in the sublime can point to an unrepresentable divinity or to knowledge not yet imaginable. For example, in alchemy, Jung concedes, reluctantly, that the feminine can stand for Jesus in the inability to restrict powerful images entirely to the masculine.[38]

Jung's postmodernism in the sublime is an opportunity for a feminism if feminine images and signifiers are regarded as *potential* rather than descriptive. What I mean by this is that the feminine could become a sublime marker. The term 'feminine' could be a floating signifier, without secure, complete, or mastering definition. It is then up to culture and political transformations to create new, changing meanings for the feminine in an ever-evolving representative culture. Such developing significances can never be whole, complete or *satisfactory* lest fulfilled desire inhibit the capacity of the feminine to be re-created.

There can be no prior restriction of meanings for this feminine, no allotting of who may or may not participate in its changing meanings. The signifier 'feminine' would become the site of continual social, political and philosophical transformation.[39] Jung's sublime unconscious can provide the theoretical justification for such a feminist postmodern dream.

The role of Jung in such a postmodern sublime feminism can never be overwhelming, since his drive to grand theory stamps the binary structuring of gender and the phallic anima all over his works. It is the postmodern sublime *within* his theory, freely open to the feminine because his symbolic is androgynous not phallic, that produces a possible partnership with feminist thinking.

It is worth ending this section by stressing the crucial difference between Lacan's masculine phallus of theory and Jung's phallic anima of 'writing'. In Jung's *theory* the feminine should have equal access to the symbolic owing to the gender fluid nature of his originating unconscious. A slippage in his *writing* collapses 'his' personal myth anima into, first, the anima of all males in grand theory, and, secondly, the psychology of all women. The struggle to evade this essentialism in Jung's works should not be confused with the anti-essentialist core of Jungian concepts. Jung's postmodern sublime *is* a resource for a continual reinvention of the signifier 'feminine'.

Postmodern Jung as a feminist narrative form

Another role for Jung in postmodern feminism is as a narrative without foundational pretensions. This can be done in two ways. Either Jungian ideas are cast as a fictional structure by removing them from the power claims of the discourse of psychology, or Jung's work can be reframed as a local, historically contingent narrative. His psychology is deprived of the status of the grand narrative of grand theory by being redefined as the product of a particular set of social, medical and gender discourses. I have suggested the possibilities of this second move in previous chapters when exploring Jungian theory's far from innocent relationship to Spiritualism and late-nineteenth-century notions of occult femininity. Now it would be useful to consider Jung as a postmodern narrative in a fictional context.

An already existing body of Jungian narratives of gender can be found in the proliferating stories of goddess feminism as described in chapter 3. These texts do not define themselves as postmodern. On the contrary, they amplify Jungian concepts to suggest a grand narrative purporting to 'explain' culture, gender and religion. Despite this, a postmodern Jungian feminism could 'recycle' these works as exercises in speculative fiction and performance. Goddess feminism performs narratives of the feminine in that it allows readers (and analysts and analysands) to *experience* a new story of being. It is possible to experience these stories at a profound psychological level *yet retain the sense that they are fictional*.

My model here is fantasy literature. Readers have deep responses to it without regarding it as objectively 'true'. Such stories have feminist value by attempting to show to readers what it might be like to live outside traditional patriarchal religious structures and conventional gender roles. Goddess feminism can be read self-consciously as fiction that is also an experiment in subjectivity through the act of

reading. For postmodernism, goddess feminism is the fantasy literature of psychology.

Here the term 'fantasy literature' signifies that goddess feminism
exists at the boundaries, those interesting feminist postmodern
margins, of psychology and literature. For psychology, 'fantasy' literature has clinical overtones. Fantasies are motifs of the unconscious.
Literature describing them is about a 'reality' that is not the shared
reality of social interactions. 'Fantasy literature' in psychology
addresses experiential questions of subjectivity in the 'personal
myths' of real human subjects.

On the other hand, from the perspective of 'the literary', fantasy
literature is deliberately and deeply speculative and fictional. Feminist fantasy literature is the attempt to imagine women and the
feminine beyond the social constraints of both existing societies and
the dominant genre of literary realism. In claiming to offer a window
onto the world, literary realism is profoundly the product of the
Enlightenment, since it regards language as a stable and transparent
conduit for truth. Fantasy literature is postmodern in that it uses
language to conjure visions of other worlds without asserting their
empirical reality. It does not offer social truth to readers, but rather a
chance to experience in fiction *different* narratives of society and
gender.

I am suggesting that a postmodern Jungian feminism treats goddess
feminism as an exploration of the boundaries between literature and
psychology. Such feminism would need to pay attention to the act of
reading: to read fiction is to submerge and reimagine subjectivity
through narratives not claiming the authority of truth. Indeed,
reading fiction is to experience subjectivity as not 'grounded' at all.
Goddess feminism in the postmodern is a study in the efficacy of
fictions in *performing* the conscious self.

If literature coming out of psychology can be seen to explore the
boundaries between psychological theory and feminist fiction, then so
can some postmodern feminist novels. *The Wild Girl* and *In the Red
Kitchen* by Michèle Roberts and *Alias Grace* by Margaret Atwood
are novels that address profoundly the role of the feminine in Jung's
grand theory. They investigate *fictionally* (and so are postmodern in
not pretending to set up a new grounded truth) the historical context
of the phallic anima, the potentials for Jung in a feminist sublime and
as a postmodern narrative form. I refer the reader to these remarkable
feminist works and to published Jungian analysis of them.[40]

In a further attempt to take Jung into postmodern feminism, I
now consider his relation to the Gothic – an aesthetic movement also
dedicated to exposing the limits of Enlightenment rationality.

Jung's feminine and the Gothic

The Gothic stems from the literature of ghosts, medieval castles and wicked tyrants that began to appear in the late eighteenth century. Like the Romantic sublime, of which it is a part, the Gothic shadows and disputes the Enlightenment stress on reason. Also like the sublime, the Gothic continues, modified, into postmodernism.

The characteristic medieval motifs of eighteenth-century Gothic gave way in the following century to Gothic spectres discovered haunting the domestic settings of Victorian realism. Ghosts, the uncanny and tyranny are discovered in the modern city of Jekyll and Hyde or in the tormented ferocity of Heathcliff on the Yorkshire moors.[41]

For postmodern souls, the Gothic now focuses upon the nightmare of technology and its assault upon the modern self. The endless labyrinths of eighteenth-century castles reappear in the horrific inability to escape the multiplying unrealities of cyberspace.

The Gothic is a literature of excess. In particular it exceeds those comforting Enlightenment boundaries that placed irrationality outside reason, the natural excluding the supernatural, realism over fantasy, self versus other and masculine in a binary superiority to feminine. It offers an aesthetic of emotion, principally fear, to criticize Enlightenment norms. Nevertheless, like the Romantic sublime, the Gothic is not in simple opposition to the Enlightenment. It also shores it up by allowing an outlet for the irrational that is ultimately recuperated. Reason gets restored in Gothic stories even if they gain their terrifying potency by showing its total breakdown in the course of the narrative.

The Gothic gives a cultural shape to the sublime. It provides two psychological modes of terror and horror. Whereas 'terror' signifies the expansion of the conscious self under sublime pressures, for example, in the erosion of borders between natural and supernatural in a ghost story, 'horror' means a reverse direction of recoil and even self-fragmentation.

The Gothic challenges the Enlightenment suppression of the other, yet serves to restore existing norms by expelling the terrifying sublime by the end of the work. It was a method by which Enlightenment society dealt with its great need to eradicate the other *produced* by the worship of reason as the foundation for truth. The desperate mutations and persistence of the Gothic can be read as a symptom of the continual efforts required to maintain Enlightenment binary structures. In postmodernism, the Gothic becomes the characteristic genre of the fragmented self and the horror of the sublimely unrepresentable technological society. Its chief manifestation is cyberpunk.

So what of Jung in this aesthetic movement? Given the above description, Jung can easily be co-opted as a theory to *explain* the Gothic. Individuation and the role of the shadow in supplying horrifying challenges to the ego that are finally incorporated into a greater attachment into the other – such concepts can be used to organize the Gothic. Jung's grand theory offers a coherent form of literary criticism of the Gothic, able to account for even its wildest excursions. This is to use Jungian psychology as a superior form of knowledge to literature. It entails taking Jung in grand-theory mode only. Jung is employed as a grand narrative of literature. There is an existing tradition of Jungian literary criticism that does precisely this.

Two related issues are immediately apparent. It is not postmodern to take one form of knowledge as self-evidently and absolutely superior to another. My argument about fantasy literature suggested a mutual relationship between literature and psychology for a postmodern feminism, not a reducing of one into the other.

Secondly, taking Jung only as grand theory, to become a grand narrative of the Gothic is to ignore all the dimensions of personal myth in his writing. It is to ignore also that even grand theory problematizes the very notion of a single comprehensive theory in the founding concept of the unknowable unconscious.

What is far more productive for Jungian feminisms is to remember that Jung's own work comes out of ghostly encounters with the feminine and to situate him as a Gothic author in his own right. Consider, for example, his use of the medieval in alchemy to criticize the privileging of Enlightenment reason. This tactic is analogous to the role of medieval architecture in a Gothic novel. Jung's delving back in intellectual history in order to go forward in criticizing over-reliance upon rationality is a thoroughly Gothic preoccupation. In fact, Jung's treatment of gender is peculiarly Gothic.

Jung as a Gothic writer on the feminine

The Gothic uses the sublime in terrifying or horrifying form to release and reconstitute those gender boundaries that align the feminine with the irrational. Given this characteristic, Jung belongs to the Gothic in three ways.

1. For Enlightenment Gothic, the way Jung recuperates rationality for the masculine in the (phallic) anima is wholly typical. Both

Gothic novels and Jung's writings explode the hierarchy of masculine reason constructed out of the suppression of the irrational
as feminine, only to reconstitute it in a more tenuous form.

2.   Jung participates in postmodern Gothic through his postmodern
sublime that recognizes the limits to theories made by the ego. He
does this by offering a representation of the postmodern self as
radically dependent upon the other. The peculiarly Gothic flavour
to Jung's postmodern sublime lies in the strained horror of
his relations to the feminine, as polluting the desired coherent
masculine self. This fear of the feminine other is signified in
particular by the hypnotic recurrence of the feminine ghosts.

3.   Native to the Gothic is that it belongs to the aesthetic and in
particular to the literary. Texts self-consciously aware of their
literary nature are a Gothic characteristic.

Jung's works flirt with the literary in ways that are integral to
the understanding of his ideas, even to their constitution as 'theory'.
The continual renegotiation between personal myth and grand
theory, the key recognition of the unknowability of the most important concept, the unconscious, means that Jung's psychology is characteristically a literature of the psyche devoted to registering its
sublime energies. His use of myth signifies a notion of narrative where
'story' as fiction or as a theoretical expression meet in a continuum.
Indeed, literary construction can be Jung's only means of framing a
theory, as in the generation of his 'personal myth' (see chapter 2).

My conclusion is that, on matters of gender, Jung is more thoroughly a Gothic author than he is a postmodernist. This is not to deny
his value for postmodernism or even for postmodern feminisms.
Rather it is recognition of Jung's persistent returns to reductive binary
structures that aim, like the narrative closures of Gothic novels, to
recuperate and re-establish control over gender conventions.

Jung's ghost story: an example of Jung as Gothic

Late in life, in the course of writing a preface to a book on the
paranormal, Jung told his own ghost story.[42] He claimed to be
describing events that actually happened to him in England thirty
years earlier.[43]

Staying in a rented country cottage with a male colleague, Dr X,
and attended by female servants, Jung could not sleep. He became
convinced in bed at night of a terrible yet unattributable smell.
Unable to solve the puzzle, Jung decided that it most resembled an

open carcinoma in an elderly woman patient, whom he had treated years previously.

After the sickly smell, Jung was next kept awake by an obstinately dripping tap. No such tap could be discovered. He began to suffer a feeling of lassitude and torpor. The following weekend a loud knocking and the impression of a dog rushing around the bedroom compounded the assaults of the smell and tap. At the same time, Jung began to realize that the female servants were afraid of the cottage. They confirm his suspicions that it is believed to be haunted.

Noises and smells continued until the ultimate horror. In bed, Jung opened his eyes: 'There, beside me on the pillow, I saw the head of an old woman, and the right eye, wide open, glared at me. The left half of the face was missing below the eye.'[44] Jung 'leapt out of bed with one bound' and moved to another bedroom.[45] He had no more disturbances. Yet he allows the story to end only when the scepticism of Dr X is banished. Challenged by Jung to sleep in the cottage alone, the mocking Dr X is similarly plagued by mysterious noises. The sceptic is forced to concede and give up the accommodation. Jung concludes his narrative by remarking on his own pleasure at defeating the colleague who had laughed at his fear of ghosts.[46]

What makes this small tale an example of Jung's Gothic is what he does next. He gives his own commentary, absorbing the unnatural events into an explanation fitting his psychology. All events can be accounted for in a proper 'Jungian' manner apart from an excess. He cannot explain the dripping tap!

Therefore this minor text is Gothic in its sublime spectres defeating the resources of reason *and* in its tiny victory over that child of reason, grand theory. The tap remains an unassimilable excess. So how does a classic literary Gothic genre, the ghost story, fare in the structuring of psychology?

One way of reading this ghost story is as an intriguing example of the Jungian subtle body. Jung explains the smell, the knocking noises and the 'dog' as the unconscious psyche mapping the body onto the exterior surroundings. The hyper-aware unconscious, sensing that a sick person was once in the bedroom, manifests itself in a variety of bodily sensations. The unconscious produces the body as a sick smell, as 'torpor' that Jung says is a physical registering of fear, and turns the internal heart beat into hearing a 'knocking' on the bedroom walls. It also conjures up a dog as an image of its 'nosing' out of illness. As a climax, the creative unconscious generates an optical hallucination based upon the incomplete memory of an actual cancer patient.

The psyche therefore uses the medium of the Gothic tale of the haunted house – the ghost story – to map the body. Fascinatingly, it is impossible to attribute a fixed origin to all these phenomena. Is the origin in the body, in the physical senses sniffing out at a subliminal level the odour of a sick person? Or is this the psyche, stressed by 'foreign' surroundings, provoking bodily responses? More generally, is the literature of the ghost story marking Jung's body or is his body giving rise to the genre of the ghost story?

Gender is also a feature of this Gothic adventure. What is suggestive here is the way the abject feminine body is used to constitute the masculine healthy body and mind. Afflicted in body and mind, Jung cannot sleep. More terrifyingly, he cannot be sure of his sanity when unable to define apparently exterior phenomena that appear only to him. Sickness, in both Jung's body and mind, becomes conflated with the occult as feminine in the final vision of the old woman.

Jung then breaks with his afflictions by *leaping out of bed* to escape proximity to the sick feminine. He is not going to lie down next to and *in the same position as* a sick female ghost.

Jung leaps literally in the body. Yet he also makes it a mental and conceptual leap, because it is after his *physical demonstration of bodily difference* that he can both sleep and put most of the ghost story into his own theoretical categories. He makes a distinction both by means of his body, and in his theory, to construct a difference that is also a difference of gender. The body is not only understood in terms of Jung's theory; it seems to contribute to its construction. In this ghost story the body is a dual apparition. The body is both an object to be accounted for by theory and that which seems to generate the theory.

The ghost story serves as a deconstruction and a resituating of himself in a reassuring binary of sane male theorist versus sick feminine patient. In this sense it is a revisiting of his founding séance text, built in a similar fashion around his medium cousin.

Here in the ghost story is an example of how the Jungian subtle body can be formulated as masculine authority through reinscribing boundaries that place the feminine in the abject. The abject is not only what is despised; it is what the subject can never quite cast out of itself in its own formation. The visionary part-face of the ghost woman provides a poignant demonstration of the gender fragilities of the Jungian ego. It tellingly reveals the master's inability to write of women as whole subjects!

Like Gothic narratives, Jung's own ghost story is built upon the erosion and recuperation of boundaries between natural and supernatural, masculine and feminine. In the story, the feminine is the memory of the sick patient, the ghostly vision, and the servants who believe the house to be haunted. Jung's gender trouble is that he is suspended between masculine authority allied with the rational and sceptical in Dr X, and the otherness of the occult coded as feminine and inferior in status. Additionally, he is on foreign territory (England), where he himself and his psychology are not *at home*, not accepted as natural or rational.

The leap out of bed is the bodily dimension of the leap into theory. It is his need to restructure his own gender boundaries on the model of male authority – the masculine theorist *of* the occult feminine, not participating in it. This is an entirely Gothic narrative twist, where sublime chaos becomes male rationality controlling and defining the feminine irrational/supernatural.

It is entirely typical of Jung to conclude with a triumph over masculine scepticism in Dr X yet also to leave some excess in a dripping tap! On the one hand, the ghost story illustrates very neatly Judith Butler's argument about masculinity, subjectivity and heterosexuality formed upon the suppression of the feminine body as abject. On the other hand, what Jung's Gothic writing does here is to *replace* a theory of Enlightenment reason that dismisses all otherness (the scepticism of Dr X) with a theory constituted by feminine otherness within and without. Feminism can yet be grateful for Jung's dripping tap!

Within the attempt to reassemble Jungian theory, the tap represents a loose thread, a sign of limitations and the persistent pulsation of the postmodern sublime as the failure of a single coherent set of propositions to account for all phenomena. The dripping tap imports a sense of fiction in the construction of Jung's masculine mastery upon the apparatus of the ghost story: it is the aesthetic refusing to submit to the philosophical-scientific.

The final effect of the aesthetic form of the ghost story is to emphasize that, although the feminine is finally abjected, it is not reducible to a single, fixable *cause*. The feminine ghost cannot be firmly assigned to either Jung's tired body, or his anxious psyche, or his professional vulnerability, or his alien status, or his relationship with the servants. Possible explanations remain various and phantom, even within the umbrella cast by the bringing-in of Jung's theoretical ideas. Together with the foreign body in the theory (the dripping tap), the unfixability of the feminine other is the haunting presence of the unknowability and inexhaustibility of the unconscious. It tells us that the phallic anima (abject old woman) is also a fiction and that Jung's feminine is also sublime.

By taking grand theory into the aesthetic, Gothic Jung opens up a discursive space for the feminine sublime. Put simply, Gothic Jung puts the meaning of gender beyond the reach of existing and future conventions to close off possibilities. The aesthetic form of the Gothic provides a suitably 'fantastic' home for all Jung's feminine ghosts.

Postmodern Jungian feminisms: a note about eco-feminism and cyberfeminism

In an era of plural feminisms, Jung has a contribution to make to postmodern gender. His work can aid a feminism of the postmodern body, postmodern narrative, feminist attention to the sublime and the Gothic.

Eco-feminism (stressing the relationship with nature) and cyberfeminism (concerned with the interface with technology) are two movements likely to be important in the ecologically imperilled and computer-enhanced twenty-first century. The traditional Jungian feminism described in chapter 3 is already a mainstay of eco-feminism.

Cyberfeminism refers to the loss of the so-called natural non-cultural body and stable self in a postmodern era. For these post-modernists everyone is a cyborg, because bodies and subjectivities are discursively deconstructed. Cyberfeminists seek to undo inequities of gender and work towards political transformation in postmodern society.

Inasmuch as Jung could provide a postmodern feminine sublime, may his shade hover above cyberfeminism and send his feminine ghosts into cyberspace.

Concluding summary

Jung's definition of the unconscious challenges Enlightenment reason in ways that make his work useful to postmodernism. However, gender is where Jung is at his least postmodern. There he desires to hang onto oppositional structures characteristic of the Enlightenment that align masculinity with rationality, femininity with the irrational.

Despite the grand-theory drive to binary positions, Jung's oppositional thinking is not his only position on gender. The effect of the founding concept of the unknowable unconscious is radically to undercut the claim of *any* theoretical proposition to have objective authority. Consequently, there is a gap in the theory from which to argue for postmodern Jungian feminisms of the body, narrative and the sublime.

'Personal myth' is friendly to the project of feminist postmodernism with its acknowledgement of the limitations of theory. 'Grand theory' is Jung's Enlightenment cloak. It can still participate in feminist postmodernism if grand theory's structuring of the unknowable, sublime unconscious is allowed to deconstruct gender certainties.

From the point of view of feminism it is more correct to describe Jung as a Gothic writer than a postmodernist one. This is due to the complex interweaving of grand theory/personal myth. The interplay of these two related but distinct impulses articulates the desire first to embrace the feminine as irrational and occult, and then to shore up the role of the masculine theorist.

FURTHER READING

Jungian alchemy

Schwartz-Salant, Nathan (ed.), *Jung on Alchemy* (London: Routledge, 1995).
An intelligently introduced and thematically arranged selection of Jung's work.

Postmodernism, feminism and Jung

Barry, Peter, *Beginning Theory: An Introduction to Literary and Cultural Theory* (Manchester and New York: Manchester University Press, 1995).
For the absolute beginner on postmodernism, Barry's chapter is a useful starting point.

Docherty, Thomas (ed.), *Postmodernism: A Reader* (London: Harvester Wheatsheaf, 1993).
Challenging and wide-ranging collection, not for the faint-hearted. It contains Lyotard on the sublime and an in-depth section on feminism.

Hauke, Christopher, *Jung and the Postmodern: The Interpretation of Realities* (London: Routledge, 2000).
The book on this subject. Hauke combines intellectual depth with a user-friendly style. Good on Jung's postmodern limitations on gender. Highly recommended.

Kemp, Sandra, and Squires, Judith, *Feminisms: A Reader* (Oxford Readers; Oxford: Oxford University Press, 1997).
Invaluable collection of extracts from feminist work published between 1980 and 1997. Strong on postmodernism and feminism.

The postmodern body

Butler, Judith, *Bodies that Matter: On the Discursive Limits of Sex* (London: Routledge, 1993).

Not an easy read but worth persevering for those who already have the theoretical basics of Freud, Lacan and Foucault. Highly influential in feminist theory.

Jung and the sublime

Hauke, Christopher, 'The Phallus, Alchemy and Christ: Jungian Analysis and the Sublime', in Petruska Clarkson (ed.), *On the Sublime in Psychoanalysis, Archetypal Psychology and Psychotherapy* (London: Whurr Publishers Ltd, 1997), pp. 123–44.
Accessible and clearly argued essay from a clinical perspective. The feminist implications of the sublime are not Hauke's subject here.

On the Gothic

Botting, Fred, *Gothic* (London: Routledge, 1996).
No mention of Jung, but an entertaining and thought-provoking introduction to its subject.

Jung, C. G., *Psychology and the Occult* (Ark Paperbacks; London: Routledge, 1982), contains, 'Foreword to Moser, On Spooks: Heresy or Truth?', pp. 143–52.
Jung's ghost story. Reveals fascinating gender structures.

Notes

CHAPTER 1   THE LIVES OF C. G. JUNG

1   The best works on the relationship of Jung and Freud are: John Kerr, *A Most Dangerous Method: The Story of Jung, Freud and Sabina Spielrein* (New York: Alfred A. Knopf, 1993), and William McGuire (ed.), *The Freud/Jung Letters*, tr. Ralph Manheim and R. F. C. Hull (London: Hogarth Press and Routledge & Kegan Paul, 1974).

2   Aniela Jaffé was originally to be the 'author' of *MDR*. After Jung took over the early parts of the text she remained as 'editor'.

3   *MDR*, pp. 26–7.

4   For Emilie Preiswerk Jung's early life, see Ronald Hayman, *A Life of Jung* (London: Bloomsbury, 1999), pp. 8–38.

5   *MDR*, p. 23.

6   The best of the biographies to date is Hayman, *Life*.

7   *MDR*, pp. 52–5.

8   Hayman, *Life*, pp. 13–14.

9   *MDR*, pp. 125–7.

10 Jung's doctoral dissertation, *On the Psychology and Pathology of So-Called Occult Phenomena*, originally published in Leipzig 1902, now in *Psychiatric Studies*, CW 1, pp. 3–88.

11 Jung refers to the work of Freud in notes in his doctorate: CW 1, pp. 56, 77–8.

12 Hayman, *Life*, pp. 58ff.

13 Ibid, p. 35.

14 F. X. Charet, *Spiritualism and the Foundations of C. G. Jung's Psychology* (New York: State University of New York Press, 1993). See also Richard Noll, *The Jung Cult: Origins of a Charismatic Movement* (Princeton: Princeton University Press, 1994).

15 For Jung and Kant, see Charet, *Spiritualism*, p. 287, and Hayman, *Life*, pp. 220–8.

16 Hayman, *Life*, pp. 55, 64.

17 Ibid., p. 82.

18   Ibid., p. 109.
19   *Symbols of Transformation* was first published in 1911–12; now in
     CW 5.
20   Hayman, *Life*, pp. 136–7.
21   See Kerr, *A Most Dangerous Method*.
22   Jung, 'The Psychology of the Unconscious', in *Two Essays on Analytical
     Psychology*, first published 1917, rev. 1926, 1943; now in *CW* 7.
23   *MDR*, pp. 194–225.
24   Ibid., p. 203.
25   See Charet, *Spiritualism*; Kerr, *A Most Dangerous Method*; and
     Hayman, *Life*.
26   *MDR*, pp. 215–16.
27   Jung, *Septem Sermones ad Mortuos*, privately printed 1916 and pseu-
     donymously subtitled 'The Seven Sermons to the Dead written by
     Basilides in Alexandria, the City where the East toucheth the West'. It
     was privately printed in 1925 in an English translation by H. G. Baynes
     and is now available in Robert Segal, *The Gnostic Jung* (Princeton:
     Princeton University Press, 1992), pp. 181–93.
28   *MDR*, p. 216.
29   Hayman, *Life*, p. 226.
30   Ibid., p. 284.
31   For details of Jung and the Nazis, see Hayman, *Life*, and Andrew
     Samuels, 'National Psychology, National Socialism, and Analytical Psy-
     chology, Reflections on Jung and Anti-Semitism, Parts 1 and 2', *Journal
     of Analytical Psychology*, 37 (1992), 3–28, 127–48. A revised version
     of these articles appears in Samuels, *The Political Psyche* (London:
     Routledge, 1993), pp. 287–336.
32   Jung, 'Wotan' (1936), first published in *Neue Schweizer Rundschau*
     (Zurich, 1936), now in *Essays on Contemporary Events, Reflections on
     Nazi Germany* (German edition, 1946; London: Kegan Paul Trench
     Trubner, 1947; ed. Andrew Samuels (Ark Paperbacks; London: Rout-
     ledge, 1988)). *Essays* also in *CW* 10, pp. 177–243.
33   *CW* 10, p. 166.
34   Ibid., pp. 165–6.
35   Ibid., p. 165.
36   Ibid., p. 152.
37   Freud uses the terms 'Aryan' and 'Jewish' in a letter to Ferenczi of 1913,
     quoted in Andrew Samuels, 'National Psychology, Part 1', 8–9.
38   'Racial layers', never a mainstream part of Jungian psychology, are to be
     found only in Jolande Jacobi, *The Psychology of C. G. Jung* (London:
     Kegan Paul Trench Trubner, 1942), p. 33, and Jung, *Seminars on
     Analytical Psychology* (1925), now in *CW* B, p. 133.
39   Jung, 'The Role of the Unconscious', *CW* 10, and Samuels, *The Politi-
     cal Psyche*, p. 311.
40   *CW* 10, p. 13.
41   Hayman, *Life*, p. 382.
42   Ibid., p. 317.

43 *Answer to Job* is to be found in CW 11, pp. 355–470; *Mysterium Conjunctionis* is CW 14.

44 *MDR*, p. 320.

45 Additional material for this section is taken from Maggy Anthony, *The Valkyries: The Women around Jung* (Shaftesbury: Element Books, 1990).

46 Ibid., pp. 55–63.

47 Ibid., pp. 80–1.

48 Ibid., pp. 64–9.

49 Ibid., pp. 44–54.

50 M. Esther Harding, *Woman's Mysteries, Ancient and Modern* (1935; New York: Harper & Row Colophon, 1976).

51 Anthony, *The Valkyries*, pp. 37–43.

52 Linda Fierz-David, *Women's Dionysian Initiation: The Villa of Mysteries in Pompeii*, tr. Gladys Phelan and with an introduction by M. Esther Harding (Jungian Classics Series II; Dallas, Tex.: Spring Publications Inc., 1988). This was completed shortly before the author's death in 1955 as *Psychologische Betrachtungen zu der Freskenfolge der Villa dei Misteri in Pompeii: Ein Versuch*, mimeographed in Zurich, Switzerland, 1957, by the Psychological Club of Zurich.

53 Another perspective upon this argument is given in my book, *C. G. Jung and Literary Theory: The Challenge from Fiction* (London: Macmillan, 1999), esp. chs 2 and 5.

54 For the history of Spiritualism, see Charet, *Spiritualism*, and also Diana Basham, *The Trial of Woman: Feminism and the Occult Sciences in Victorian Society* (London: Macmillan, 1992).

CHAPTER 2   INTRODUCING JUNGIAN THEORY

1 C. G. Jung, *Modern Man in Search of a Soul* (London: Kegan, Paul, Trench, Trubner, 1933; Ark Paperbacks, London: Routledge, 1984), p. 132.

2 Ibid., p. 136.

3 *MDR*, p. 210.

4 For the 'personal myth', see ibid., pp. 17, 195, 224.

5 Ibid., p. 224.

6 *CW* 9(i), p. 79.

7 Jung, *Modern Man*, p. 2.

8 See the early and later editions of *Two Essays on Analytical Psychology*, now in *CW* 7.

9 Andrew Samuels, *Jung and the Post-Jungians* (London: Routledge, 1985).

10 C. G. Jung, *Aspects of the Feminine* (Princeton: Princeton University Press, 1982; Ark Paperbacks; London: Routledge, 1982), p. 50.

11　Ibid.
12　Samuels, *Jung and the Post-Jungians*, pp. 210–12.
13　Jung, *Aspects of the Feminine*, p. 171.
14　Ibid., p. 61.
15　Ibid.
16　Ibid., p. 96.
17　Ibid., p. 20.

CHAPTER 3　　THE GODDESS AND THE FEMININE PRINCIPLE

1　M. Esther Harding, *Woman's Mysteries: Ancient and Modern* (1935; New York: Harper & Row Colophon, 1976).
2　Emma Jung, *Animus and Anima* (Woodstock, Conn.: Spring Publications, 1957).
3　Ibid., p. 23.
4　Ibid., p. 4.
5　Linda Fierz-David, *Women's Dionysian Initiation: The Villa of Mysteries in Pompeii*, tr. Gladys Phelan and with an introduction by M. Esther Harding (Jungian Classics Series II; Dallas, Tex.: Spring Publications Inc., 1988), p. 64.
6　Irene Claremont de Castillejo, *Knowing Woman: A Feminine Psychology* (Boston: Shambhala, 1973).
7　Hilde Binswanger, 'Positive Aspects of the Animus', *Spring: A Journal of Archetype and Culture* (1963), pp. 82–101.
8　Ibid., p. 87.
9　Ann Ulanov, *The Feminine in Jungian Psychology and in Christian Theology* (Evanston, Ill.: Northwestern University Press, 1971).
10　Ann and Barry Ulanov, *Transforming Sexuality: The Archetypal World of Anima and Animus* (Boston: Shambhala, 1994).
11　Ibid., p. 2.
12　Marion Woodman, *Addiction to Perfection: The Still Unravished Bride* (Toronto: Inner City Books, 1982).
13　Marion Woodman, *The Owl was a Baker's Daughter: Obesity, Anorexia Nervosa and the Repressed Feminine* (Toronto: Inner City Books, 1980).
14　Polly Young-Eisendrath, with Florence Wiedemann, *Female Authority: Empowering Women through Psychotherapy* (New York: Guilford Press, 1987).
15　Polly Young-Eisendrath, *Hags and Heroes: A Feminist Approach to Jungian Psychotherapy with Couples* (Toronto: Inner City Books, 1984).
16　Claire Douglas, *The Woman in the Mirror: Analytical Psychology and the Feminine* (Boston: Sigo Press, 1990).

17 E. C. Whitmont, *Return of the Goddess* (New York: Continuum Publishing, 1982), 128.
18 Harding, *Woman's Mysteries*, p. 105.
19 Toni Wolff, 'A Few Thoughts on the Process of Individuation in Women' (1934), *Spring* (1941), 81–103.
20 Erich Neumann, *The Origins and History of Consciousness* (Princeton: Princeton University Press, 1954).
21 June Singer, *Boundaries of the Soul* (New York: A. Knopf, 1972).
22 June Singer, *Androgyny: Towards a New Theory of Sexuality* (Boston: Sigo Press, 1976).
23 Ibid., p. 8.
24 Ibid., p. 10.
25 Claremont de Castillejo, *Knowing Woman*, p. 42.
26 Ann Ulanov, *The Feminine*, p. 13.
27 Ginette Paris, *The Sacrament of Abortion*, tr. from the French by Joanna Mott (Dallas, Tex.: Spring Publications, 1992).
28 Ibid., p. 27.
29 Sylvia Brinton Perera, *Descent to the Goddess: A Way of Initiation for Women* (Toronto: Inner City Books, 1981).
30 Christine Downing, *The Goddess: Mythological Images of the Feminine* (New York: Crossroad Publishing Co., 1984).
31 Ibid., p. 4.
32 Marion Woodman, *The Pregnant Virgin: A Process of Psychological Transformation* (Toronto: Inner City Books, 1985).
33 Ibid., p. 10.
34 Linda Schierse Leonard, *Meeting the Madwoman: An Inner Challenge for Feminine Spirit* (New York: Bantam Books, 1993).
35 Linda Qchierse Leonard, *The Wounded Woman: Healing the Father–Daughter Relationship* (Athens, Oh.: Swallow Press, 1982).
36 Nancy Qualls-Corbett, *The Sacred Prostitute: Eternal Aspect of the Feminine* (Toronto: Inner City Books, 1988).
37 Jean Shinoda Bolen, *Goddesses in Everywoman: A New Psychology of Women* (New York: Harper & Row, 1984).
38 Whitmont, *Return of the Goddess*, p. viii.
39 Anne Baring and Jules Cashford, *The Myth of the Goddess: Evolution of an Image* (Harmondsworth: Viking, 1991).
40 Ibid., p. 158.
41 Ibid., p. xi.

CHAPTER 4   JUNGIAN FEMINISMS?

1 Andrew Samuels, *Jung and the Post-Jungians* (London: Routledge, 1985), pp. 210–12.

2   James Hillman, 'Anima', *Spring: A Journal of Archetype and Culture* (1973), 97–132, 'Anima II', *Spring: A Journal of Archetype and Culture* (1974), 113–46.
3   Hillman, 'Anima II', p. 140.
4   For more on the archetypal psychologists, see Karin Barnaby and Pellegrino D'Acierno (eds), *C. G. Jung and the Humanities, Towards a Hermeneutics of Culture* (London: Routledge, 1990), pp. 307–40.
5   James Hillman, *Healing Fiction* (New York: Station Hill Press, 1983).
6   James Hillman, *Archetypal Psychology: A Brief Account* (Dallas, Tex.: Spring Publications Inc., 1983), p. 13.
7   On the relationship between James Hillman and Robert Bly, see David Tacey, *Remaking Men: Jung, Spirituality and Social Change* (London: Routledge, 1997), p. 91. See also Hillman and Bly, 'Creativity Symposium', in Barnaby and D'Acierno (eds), *C. G. Jung and the Humanities*, pp. 153–61.
8   Two core mythopoetic men's movement texts are Robert Bly, *Iron John: A Book about Men* (Reading, Mass.: Addison-Wesley, 1990), and Robert Moore and Douglas Gillette, *King, Warrior, Magician, Lover* (San Francisco: HarperCollins, 1990).
9   Robert Bly, *Iron John*, p. 4.
10 Ibid., p. 4.
11 Andrew Samuels discusses Bly's mythopoetic men's movement in *The Political Psyche* (London: Routledge, 1993), pp. 183–95.
12 Tacey, *Remaking Men*.
13 Ibid., p. 43.
14 Ibid., p. 48.
15 Ibid., p. 49.
16 Ibid., p. 69.
17 Demaris S. Wehr, *Jung and Feminism: Liberating Archetypes* (Boston: Beacon Press, 1987).
18 Ibid., p. 10.
19 Naomi R. Goldenberg, 'A Feminist Critique of Jung', in Robert L. Moore and Daniel J. Meckel (eds), *Jung and Christianity in Dialogue: Faith, Feminism and Hermeneutics* (Mahwah, NY: Paulist Press, 1990), pp. 104–11.
20 Ibid., p. 108.
21 Estella Lauter and Carol Schreier Rupprecht (eds), *Feminist Archetypal Theory: Interdisciplinary Re-Visions of Jungian Thought* (Knoxville, Ten.: University of Tennessee Press, 1985).
22 Erich Neumann, *Art and the Creative Unconscious*, tr. Ralph Manheim (Princeton: Princeton University Press, 1959), p. 82.
23 Lauter and Rupprecht (eds), *Feminist Archetypal Theory*, pp. 13–14.
24 Ibid., p. 14.
25 Carol Schreier Rupprecht, 'Enlightening Shadows: Between Feminism and Archetypalism, Literature and Analysis', in Barnaby and D'Acierno (eds), *C. G. Jung and the Humanities*, pp. 279–93, at p. 286.
26 Lauter and Rupprecht, *Feminist Archetypal Theory*, p. 227.

27 See Samuels, *Jung and the Post-Jungians*.
28 Hester MacFarland Solomon, 'The Developmental School', in Polly Young-Eisendrath and Terence Dawson (eds), *The Cambridge Companion to Jung* (Cambridge: Cambridge University Press, 1997), pp. 119–40, at p. 125.
29 See Andrew Samuels, *Jung and the Post-Jungians*, *The Plural Psyche: Personality, Morality and the Father* (London: Routledge, 1989), and *The Political Psyche* (London: Routledge, 1993).
30 Andrew Samuels, *The Political Psyche*, is a particular example of rethinking Jung in the sphere of politics, power and psychology. See also his *Politics on the Couch: Citizenship and the Internal Life* (London: Profile Books, 2001).
31 Samuels, *The Plural Psyche*, p. 104.
32 Ibid., p. 98.
33 Ibid., pp. 98–100.
34 Ibid., pp. 104–5.
35 Ibid., pp. 71–2.
36 Ibid., pp. 82–5.
37 Ibid., p. 82.
38 Ibid., p. 94.
39 Samuels, *The Political Psyche*, p. 131.

CHAPTER 5 JUNGIAN FEMINISMS IN DECONSTRUCTION AND POST-FREUDIAN FEMINISM

1 For more on deconstruction and an introduction to Derrida, see Christopher Norris, *Deconstruction: Theory and Practice*, rev. edn (London: Routledge, 1991).
2 For an introduction to Lacan, see Malcolm Bowie, *Lacan* (Fontana Modern Masters; London: Fontana Press, 1991).
3 For introductions to the work of Luce Irigaray, Hélène Cixous and Julia Kristeva, see Toril Moi, *Sexual/Textual Politics: Feminist Literary Theory* (London: Methuen, 1985).
4 For an introduction to structuralism, see Peter Barry, *Beginning Theory: An Introduction to Literary and Cultural Theory* (Manchester: Manchester University Press, 1995). For an exploration of poststructuralism, see Julian Wolfreys (ed.), *Literary Theories: A Reader and Guide* (Edinburgh: Edinburgh University Press, 1999).
5 For Derrida, see Norris, *Deconstruction*. See also Jacques Derrida, *Of Grammatology*, tr. Gayatri Chakravorty Spivak (Baltimore: Johns Hopkins University Press, 1976).
6 Norris, *Deconstruction*, p. 31.
7 A helpful explanation of the deconstruction approach to language can be found in Terry Eagleton, *Literary Theory: An Introduction*, 2nd edn (Oxford: Blackwell, 1985; repr. 1996), pp. 110–30.

8 Derrida, quoted in Wolfreys (ed.), *Literary Theories*, p. 270. The 1996 interview with Derrida can be found in full in John Brannigan, Ruth Robbins and Julian Wolfreys, *Applying: To Derrida* (London: Macmillan, 1996).

9 Wolfreys (ed.), *Literary Theories*, p. 278.

10 *CW* 9(i), p. 183 n.

11 *CW* 16, para. 537.

12 *MDR*, p. 212.

13 Jung, *Letters*, ed. G. Adler, tr. R. F. C. Hull (Princeton: Princeton University Press, 1975), vol. 1, p. 411.

14 Christopher Hauke, *Jung and the Postmodern: The Interpretation of Realities* (London: Routledge, 2000), esp. pp. 1–17.

15 *CW* 16, paras. 541, 542.

16 *CW* 9(i), p. 182.

17 Mark Currie, 'Poststructuralism', in Wolfreys (ed.), *Literary Theories*, pp. 317–27, at p. 324.

18 Andrew Samuels, *The Political Psyche* (London: Routledge, 1993).

19 Andrew Samuels, *Jung and the Post-Jungians* (London: Routledge, 1985), p. 212.

20 Samuels, *The Political Psyche*, p. 131.

21 Ibid., p. 140.

22 Ibid., p. 141.

23 Luce Irigaray, *This Sex which Is not One*, tr. Catherine Porter with Carolyn Burke (Ithaca, NY: Cornell University Press, 1985), originally published in French (Éditions de Minuit, 1977).

24 Ibid., p. 129.

25 Luce Irigaray, *Elemental Passions* (New York: Routledge, 1992), p. 1.

26 Luce Irigaray, *An Ethics of Sexual Difference* (London: Athlone Press, 1993), p. 116.

27 Luce Irigaray, *Marine Lover* (New York: Columbia University Press, 1991), p. 46.

28 *CW* 16, para. 402.

29 For more on Cixous's 'gift' and 'proper', see Moi, *Sexual/Textual Politics*, pp. 110–13.

30 For more on écriture feminine, see ibid., pp. 108–20.

31 Morag Shiach, 'Their "Symbolic" Exists, it Holds Power – We, the Sowers of Disorder, Know it Only too Well', in Sandra Kemp and Judith Squires (eds), *Feminisms: A Reader* (Oxford Readers; Oxford: Oxford University Press, 1997), pp. 269–74.

32 *CW* 14, para. 706.

33 For valuable recent work linking Jung and Kristeva, see Tessa Adams, 'Jung, Kristeva and the Maternal Realm', *Harvest: A Journal of Jungian Studies*, 48 (1997), pp. 7–17, and 'The Creative Feminine: Kristeva and the Maternal Body', in I. Bruna Seu and M. Colleen Heenan (eds), *Feminism and Psychotherapy: Reflections on Contemporary Theories and Practices* (London: Sage Publications, 1999), pp. 157–71.

34 Toril Moi, 'Feminist, Female, Feminine', in Kemp and Squires (eds), *Feminisms*, pp. 246–50.
35 Julia Kristeva, 'Women's Time', in Toril Moi (ed.), *The Kristeva Reader* (Oxford: Blackwell, 1986), pp. 187–213.
36 Ibid., p. 210.
37 Ibid.
38 *CW* 9(i), p. 199.
39 Jung, 'The Psychological Aspects of the Kore', in *CW* 9(i), pp. 182–203.
40 Ibid., p. 188.

CHAPTER 6   POSTMODERN JUNGIAN FEMINISMS

1 For more on postmodernism, see Peter Brooker (ed.), *Modernism/Postmodernism* (London: Longman, 1992).
2 The postmodern sense that 'grand narratives' are lost or waning was introduced by Jean-Francois Lyotard, *The Postmodern Condition: A Report on Knowledge*, trs. Geoff Bennington and Brian Massumi, foreword by Fredric Jameson (Minneapolis: University of Minnesota Press, 1979).
3 For Derrida and the metaphysical, see Terry Eagleton, *Literary Theory: An Introduction*, 2nd edn (Oxford: Blackwell, 1985; repr. 1996), pp. 110–30. See also Susan Rowland, *C. G. Jung and Literary Theory: The Challenge from Fiction* (London: Macmillan, 1999), pp. 17–24.
4 *CW* 14, p. 381.
5 For postmodern novels taking a feminist approach to Jung, see Margaret Atwood, *Alias Grace* (London: Bloomsbury, 1996), Michèle Roberts, *The Wild Girl* (London: Methuen, 1983), and *In the Red Kitchen* (London: Methuen, 1990).
6 Jung's ghost story occurs in 'Foreword to Moser, On Spooks: Heresy or Truth?', *Psychology and the Occult* (Ark Paperbacks; London: Routledge, 1982), pp. 143–52.
7 For more on the Gothic, see Fred Botting, *Gothic* (London: Routledge, 1996).
8 For more on the religious and philosophical dimension of alchemy, see Titus Burckhardt, *Alchemy: Science of the Cosmos, Science of the Soul*, tr. William Stoddart (London: Stuart & Watkins, 1967), esp. pp. 11–22.
9 *CW* 12, p. 482.
10 *CW* 14, p. 555.
11 Ibid.
12 Ibid., p. 556.
13 Ibid., pp. 555–6.
14 Ibid., p. 173.
15 For the three stages of psychic union in Jungian alchemy, see Nathan Schwartz-Salant (ed.), *Jung on Alchemy* (London: Routledge, 1995), pp. 150–1.

16 Christopher Hauke, *Jung and the Postmodern: The Interpretation of Realities* (London: Routledge, 2000), pp. 236–63.
17 Judith Butler's work on the sexed body as discursive occurs in *Gender Trouble: Feminism and the Subversion of Identity* (New York: Routledge, 1990) and in *Bodies that Matter: On the Discursive Limits of Sex* (London: Routledge, 1993).
18 Jung's comment on the body as a metaphysical category occurs in a letter: Jung to Henry A. Murray, 10 September 1935, in *Letters*, ed. G. Adler, tr. R. F. C. Hull (Princeton: Princeton University Press, 1975), vol. 1, p. 200.
19 For more on the body and Jung, see Hauke, *Jung and the Postmodern*, pp. 175–90.
20 Schwartz-Salant, *Jung on Alchemy*, p. 145.
21 *CW* 12, p. 283.
22 For more on Foucault, see *The Foucault Reader: An Introduction to Foucault's Thought*, ed. Paul Rabinow (London: Penguin Books, 1984), esp. introduction, pp. 3–29.
23 Patricia Waugh, 'Stalemates?: Feminists, Postmodernists and Unfinished Issues in Modern Aesthetics', in Philip Rice and Patricia Waugh (eds), *Modern Literary Theory: A Reader*, 3rd edn (London: Arnold, 1989, 1992), pp. 322–40, and Alice Jardine, 'The Demise of Experience: Fiction as Stranger than Truth?', in Thomas Docherty (ed.), *Postmodernism: A Reader* (London: Harvester Wheatsheaf, 1993), pp. 433–42.
24 See Hauke, *Jung and the Postmodern*.
25 Butler, *Bodies that Matter*, p. 68.
26 Ibid., p. 9.
27 Ibid., p. 10.
28 Ibid., p. 15.
29 Butler, 'The Lesbian Phallus and the Morphological Imaginary', in ibid., pp. 57–91.
30 Ibid., p. 87.
31 *CW* 14, p. 180.
32 For the schizophrenic postmodern self, see Fredric Jameson, *Postmodernism, or, the Cultural Logic of Late Capitalism* (London: Verso, 1991), pp. 1–54.
33 For the Romantic sublime as masculine against a 'feminine' small and beautiful, see Edmund Burke, *A Philosophical Enquiry into the Origins of our Ideas of the Sublime and the Beautiful* (1757), quoted in Botting, *Gothic*, p. 39.
34 Jean-Francois Lyotard, 'The Sublime and the Avant-Garde', in Docherty (ed.), *Postmodernism: A Reader*, pp. 244–56, at p. 250.
35 Ibid., p. 249.
36 Christopher Hauke, 'The Phallus, Alchemy and Christ: Jungian Analysis and the Sublime', in Petruska Clarkson (ed.), *On the Sublime in Psychoanalysis, Archetypal Psychology and Psychotherapy* (London: Whurr Publishers Ltd, 1997), pp. 123–44, at p. 128.
37 *CW* 14, p. 551.

38 Ibid., p. 379.
39 My attempt to make the feminine sublime a site of radical political transformation owes much to the political analysis of Slavoj Zizek in *The Sublime Object of Ideology* (London: Verso, 1989). Judith Butler in *Bodies that Matter* disputes Zizek's less than feminist deployment of gender (pp. 187–222).
40 See Rowland, C. G. *Jung and Literary Theory*, chs 4 and 5, and also 'Imaginal Bodies and Feminine Spirits: Performing Gender in Jungian Theory and Margaret Atwood's *Alias Grace*', in *Body Matters: Feminism, Textuality, Corporeality*, edited by Avril Horner and Angela Keane (Manchester: Manchester University Press, 2000), pp. 244–53.
41 Robert Louis Stevenson, *The Strange Case of Dr Jekyll and Mr Hyde* (World Classics; Oxford: Oxford University Press, 1998), Emily Brontë, *Wuthering Heights* (London: Penguin Classics, 1985).
42 I am grateful to Dr Susan Acheson for first drawing my attention to Jung's ghost story.
43 See 'Foreword to Moser, On Spooks: Heresy or Truth?'.
44 Ibid., p. 150.
45 Ibid.
46 Ibid., p. 151.

Glossary

Words marked with a * are Jungian key terms.

abject   The abject is what is cast out of the formation of psychic identity in order to produce a coherent ego. The abject stands for the maternal other that has not yet become an object. This not yet object is an abject, destined to be repressed in the structuring of the unconscious. The ego has not yet been formed into a subject–object relationship. Therefore the repressed abject remains a terrifying non-object in the unconscious that may threaten the ego. This concept is associated with the work of Julia Kristeva and Judith Butler (see chapters 5 and 6).

active imagination*   This is the term Jung gave to his therapeutic method of asking a patient to fantasize spontaneously upon an image, usually a dream image. By this method, unconscious* material may be brought into consciousness and individuation* is promoted. Active imagination is the opposite of conscious invention: it is a method of surrendering the direction of fantasies to the other or the unconscious. Most often, active imagination indicates the use of a person's own unconscious image from a dream, but Jung argued that cultural, mythical or artistic images could also be used.

alchemy   Alchemy was more than the doomed attempt to turn lead into gold. It also included philosophical and religious beliefs that held that mind, matter and divine spirit existed in a continuum. Alchemists tried to refine the soul from base matter. Gold and lead were the material aspects of substances that were equally psychological and divine. Therefore mental and spiritual work existed alongside the chemical operations that became the precursor to modern chemistry.

alchemy (Jungian)* Alchemy is defined by Jung as a projection of psychic contents, specifically the individuation* process onto the chemical activities of the alchemist. He interpreted alchemy texts as demonstrating the projection of unconscious processes and alchemists as unwitting self-analysts. Alchemists developed symbols. Jung believed that alchemical symbols enabled psychological trans-formations similar to the role of dreams in his psychology. In his view, alchemists used chemistry and symbolic language to stimulate their own individuation so that they could reach the 'gold' of union with the divine or self archetype*.

amplification* Amplification is a Jungian therapeutic technique in which a psychic image (such as from a dream) is *amplified* by linking it to a mythological motif. This serves to make the image appear less personal and so suggests something of the 'otherness' of the uncon-scious. Consequently, amplification tends to downplay questions of the personal or cultural history of a person.

anima* The anima is the archetype of the feminine in the uncon-scious of a man. In that this locates a feminine mode in the subjectiv-ity of the masculine gender, denoting a bisexual unconscious, this is a helpful concept. However, at times, Jung uses his own unconscious anima as a model for designating female subjectivity as 'more uncon-scious' than males. Remembering that all archetypes are plural and androgynous mitigates the stress of gender opposition, modelled upon heterosexuality. A male's unconscious is not purely or necessarily feminine or vice versa. (See also animus*, Eros*, Logos*, gender.)

animus* The animus is the archetype of masculinity in the uncon-scious of a woman. Like the anima, this does not lock Jungian theory into perpetual gender opposition, since the unconscious contains androgynous archetypes. Nothing can be securely known or fixed in the unconscious.

archetypes* Archetypes are inherited structuring patterns in the unconscious with potentials for meaning formation and images. They are unrepresentable in themselves and evident only in their manifest derivatives, archetypal images. Archetypes are containers of opposites and so are androgynous, equally capable of manifesting themselves as either gender or non-human forms. The archetype is psychosomatic, meaning that it links body and psyche, instinct and image. Body and culture will influence the content of archetypal images but not govern them, because archetypes are the structuring principles of an *autonomous* psyche*. Archetypes are not inherited ideas or images. When actually called upon to define archetypes, Jung insisted that they were not inherited contents. (See also archetypal images*, unconscious*.)

archetypal images*   Archetypal images are the visible representations of archetypes. A single image can never account for the multifarious potential of the archetype. Consequently, archetypal images have a metaphorical connection to the archetype. Archetypal images are always creative yet provisional and partial images of a greater unrepresentable complexity. Crucially, they do draw representative material from culture as well as shaping energy from the archetype. Therefore Jungian psychic archetypal imagery is always cultural and historical as well as numinous and psychic.

autonomous/objective psyche*   Jung believed that the unconscious was largely independent of the understanding of the ego. He spoke of an 'objective' psyche, meaning that the unconscious was autonomous. It could initiate a relationship to the ego through the desirable process of individuation*.

body*   The Jungian body is both a separate, unknowable entity and something that is vitally connected to the psyche. Archetypes are rooted in the body as well as having a transcendent spiritual dimension. For Jung, the body cannot control signifying, but it does influence it. For example, sexuality is a bodily function that can liberate archetypal energies. A sexual act may simultaneously become a rite, entering a numinous dimension that alchemists (and Jung after them) called a sacred marriage.

collective unconscious*   The collective unconscious is the common inheritance of archetypes that all human beings share. How the archetypes are then manifested as archetypal images will depend upon the particular culture and history of any individual.

consciousness*   Consciousness is that part of the psyche realized by the ego*. It is the known and knowable about every human person. For Jung, consciousness needs to be in touch with healing unconscious powers through individuation*.

counter-transference*   This refers to the tendency of the unconscious contents of the analyst to get projected onto the patient in analysis. Jung was one of the first to realize the importance of this phenomenon. (See transference*.)

discourse (discursive) Discourse signifies the idea in poststructuralism and postmodernism that knowledge is not some neutral entity separate from human society. Rather, knowledge is shaped in discourses, which are themselves social and material practices. Discourses are the argument that knowledges are also power. Discourses produce social relations and power. Disciplines such as Jungian studies have active, material, social *regulating* functions in the production of society. One of their functions may be to produce or police gender. (See chapter 6.)

dreams* Unlike the Freudian usage, dreams to a Jungian are spontaneous expressions or messages from a superior part of the human mind. They are not derivative of the concerns of the ego or necessarily about sexuality (unless they belong to the trivial class of dreams derived from the residue of the psychic processing of the previous day). Dream images are not secondary. They are a *primary* form of reality and must not be 'translated' into the mode of the ego, into words.

ego* The ego is the centre of consciousness concerned with the sense of a personal identity, the maintenance of personality and the sense of continuity over time. However, Jung considered the ego as something less than the whole personality, as it was constantly interacting with more significant archetypal forces in the unconscious. Jung tended to equate the ego with consciousness in his writings.

enantiodromia* This term expresses a core Jungian insight – that in the psyche things have the habit of turning into their own opposite. The emergence of opposites in the unconscious is a frequent characteristic of individuation*.

Eros* Eros is another of Jung's concepts based upon gendered opposites. Its other is Logos*. Eros stands for psychic capacities of relatedness and feeling with Logos as a motif of spiritual meaning and reason. Jung aligned feminine consciousness with Eros and masculine subjectivity with Logos. Since the anima* and animus* carry Eros and Logos qualities in the unconscious, this means that males tend to have underdeveloped qualities of relating, females to be inferior in 'thinking' and rational argument. The consequences for Jung's views on gender are profound. (See chapter 2.)

feminine principle*   The feminine principle is a name Jung gave to the qualities of Eros*, feeling, relationship, connectedness, which he expected were the characteristics of women's consciousness. After Jung, some Jungians expanded this archetype of mental functioning to something even more overtly metaphysical. Masculine and feminine principles exist transcendently in the psyche, and men and women have to negotiate them in order to forge a gender identity. The feminine principle may operate *within* cultures, but also exists independently of them in the human mind.

gender   Gender is a person's inner identity as feminine or masculine as distinct from possessing a female or male body. Jung tended to collapse gender into bodily sex. My own use of gender in this book is not essentialist. Gender is historically contingent and cannot be represented as somehow 'transcendent' of the culture where its particular 'style' is situated.

god-image*   The Jungian archetype of the self* is frequently represented by a divine or god-image in the psyche. This is because the unconscious self is the goal of individuation, the supreme desire of the person's psyche. Therefore it is likely to produce spontaneous divine images. (See also self*, religious experience*, individuation*.)

goddess feminism (Jungian)*   This is a form of feminism derived from *amplifying* Jung's idea that his Eros* provided a feminine principle.* Extending a notion of a metaphysical feminine principle allows for 'feminine archetypes' to be treated as if they were goddesses in the human mind. Some goddess feminists stick with the Jungian line that archetypes are a biological inheritance and do not posit exterior divinities. Some feminists have left Jungian theory behind in making the leap into a return to paganism in order to find better and more empowered models for women. A sophisticated strand to Jungian goddess feminism looks to a myth of a great goddess as a way of not generating binary forms of gender. Goddess feminism is interesting as a counterweight to the legacy of Christian patriarchy. Its weakness lies in its tendency to essentialism and lack of attention to material politics. (See chapter 3.)

Gothic   The Gothic is an aesthetic movement starting at the Enlightenment and continuing in postmodernism. It is the art of excess.

Gothic signifies what cannot be fully comprehended by reason, the conscious mind, categories of the knowable and conventions of gender. Like Jung, the Gothic is haunted by the ghostly feminine. Like Jung, the Gothic tends to recuperate gender conventions. (See chapter 6.)

grand theory* This is my term for the tendency in Jung's writings to produce comprehensive accounts of the human psyche and culture. I have taken 'grand' from the idea of 'grand narratives' (see chapter 6), which are under so much threat in contemporary theory. Jung's 'grand theory' is intertwined with his very different impulse to write in the style of personal myth*.

hegemony Hegemony means hierarchies of power in society that are often unacknowledged, so are regarded as somehow 'natural'. Hegemony describes the winning of tacit consent to unequal class or social relations.

individuation* Individuation is Jung's term for the process whereby the ego is brought into a relationship with the archetypal dynamics of the unconscious. In individuation the ego is constantly made, unmade and remade by the goal-directed forces of the unconscious. Even 'meaning' in the ego is subject to dissolution and reconstitution by the Jungian other.

Logos* A principle of mental functioning oriented towards reason, discrimination, and spiritual authority. Jung regarded it as characteristic of masculine consciousness. Logos operates in a gendered binary opposite with Eros*. Contemporary Jungian analytic practice treats Logos and Eros as equally available to both genders.

logocentrism Logocentrism is a term used by deconstructionists to indicate a pervasive belief about language that they oppose – that there is a full, present and secure meaning for a word.

materialism Materialism is the belief that social reality and consciousness are the product of the coercive economic system designed to produce material products under capitalism. It is a characteristic of Marxism.

materialist feminism Materialist feminists believe that gender and its inequities are derived from economic fundamentals, political power and capitalism. Jungian theory is ultimately incompatible with materialism of all kinds because his system contains an irreducible other (not reducible to material forces). Some overlap can occur in the sense that the Jungian body and material culture have a significant (but not governing) input to archetypal signifying.

mythology   Mythology refers to stories of gods, goddesses, monsters and divine beings that have performed a religious function in various human societies. Examples would include the mythologies of ancient Greece and Rome, Christianity regarded as a mythology and the sacred stories of particular cultures.

patriarchy   Literally meaning 'rule by the father', patriarchy is a system ruled by men. The authority of males is backed up by religious, social, political and cultural institutions. In patriarchy, a fundamental structuring principle is that masculine stands for superior, desirable, intelligible attributes, while the feminine denotes what is excluded from, or is potentially chaotic within, the system. For example, in patriarchal religions like Christian monotheism, the feminine and women stand for matter, sex and death (what has been cast outside the divine).

persona*   The persona is the mask worn by the ego in the outer world. It is the way that the ego adapts to present a coherent personality in social situations. Over-identification with the persona means that more challenging forces from the unconscious are being ignored. Individuation* means detaching identity from the persona in order to engage with the unconscious.

personal myth*   This is my term for Jung's desire to use his own psyche as the location for his theory. The Jung of personal myth disowns 'theory', meaning the foolish claim to speak for all persons (however much the Jung of grand theory will do this). The Jung of personal myth uses his own 'empirical evidence', his own psychic images as the building blocks of his ideas. (See chapter 2.)

personal unconscious*   The personal unconscious is the way that Jung drew Freudian ideas into his mature thought. What was important about the unconscious to Jung was the collective unconscious of archetypes. The personal unconscious is a Freudian unconscious created by Oedipal sexual repression. It is 'personal' because it is formed through the structuring of the ego and does not refer to the superior autonomous/objective psyche*.

phallus   To Lacan, the phallus is a privileged signifier. It represents the cultural form of patriarchy, the imposition of the Law of the Father, when a person is split by entry into the symbolic. Although it is not to be equated to the fleshly penis, the phallus organizes a person's gender upon entry to language and the symbolic. The phallus is what the masculine very ambivalently 'has' and what the feminine must 'be' for the masculine. The effect of the phallus is to make the masculine the natural home of power and meaning.

psychic reality*   To Jung all reality is psychic. I know nothing that has not already been filtered through my psychic processing or, more radically, has not been constructed as knowledge by my psyche. What the 'I' knows is *in the first place* psychic, whatever other exterior reality it might also claim.

religious experience*   Following on from psychic reality*, religious experience in Jungian theory is distinctive because to Jung all experience is mediated through the psyche and its inherited structuring principles of archetypes. Consequently, any religious feeling is located in the psyche and is a property of the supreme governing archetype of the self. Therefore, to Jung, religious experience is indistinguishable from intimations of the self. This idea of religious feeling as psychological structuring could harmonize with external religions (especially when Christ is named a self-image) but could also validate religious experience without an external transcendent God. It is not reducible to a mythologizing of bodily drives.

self*   The self is the supreme governing archetype of the unconscious to which the ego becomes subject in individuation*. Jung frequently described self-images in dreams in circular or mandala forms. He argued that Christ functioned as a self-image in Christianity. What is crucial here is to remember that 'self' for Jung means the not-known, the unknowable in the individual person. The self is to be found in the unconscious. It does not stand for the conscious personality.

semiotic   This term is used by Julia Kristeva to indicate the maternal energies repressed out of Lacan's symbolic in its very formation. The semiotic cannot signify (for then it would be symbolic). However, the semiotic haunts the symbolic as pulsations within language that sometimes can be discerned in experimental art and writing.

shadow*   The shadow is the archetypal forces of blackness, reversal or undoing. Intrinsic to the idea of a compensatory relation between ego and unconscious, the shadow is that which is denied in conscious personality. Consequently the shadow could be figured as the potential evil within everyone. Jung warned that the shadow needed to be brought into a relationship with conscious personality lest repression caused it to swell in power and break out in neurosis or violence.

sublime   The sublime exists both in Romanticism at the time of the Enlightenment and in postmodernism. In both it signifies what can be conceived but not fully represented in culture and in the mind. For example, the divine can be a concept, but many of the possible meanings of divinity are unthinkable, ineffable. Jung offers a transition from the Romantic to the postmodern sublime. (See chapter 6.)

subtle body*   The body as imaged in the psyche is a Jungian subtle body because it is formed by both bodily and archetypal ingredients. Because archetypes are of the body as well as the non-bodily psyche, mental representations of the body are both physical and psychical – the subtle body. (See chapter 6.)

symbolic, Lacan's   Lacan's symbolic means the language, symbols and conventions that organize any culture. What is intelligible is in the symbolic. The symbolic is formed by repression of the unconscious upon a child's entry into language. The phallus is the privileged signifier around which gender identity, language and representability are organized. (See chapters 4 and 5.)

symbolic, Jungian*   Jungian theory also implies a symbolic, with crucial differences to that of Lacan. Because, for Jung, the unconscious is not *determined* by repression, and contains autonomous androgynous principles called archetypes, Jung's symbolic does not necessarily repress the feminine. In the Jungian symbolic, feminine imagery can exist for itself. It is not doomed to function as a screen for masculine fantasy.

synchronicity*   Jung used this term to describe the linking of events not by cause and effect, not by time and space, but by psychological coherence. For example, if a total stranger suddenly meets a person's vital need with no apparent explanation – that is synchronicity. It refers to Jung's notion that psyche, matter, time and space are all fundamentally connected.

transference*   Developed first by Freud, transference is the idea that, in analysis, the patient will use the analyst as a screen for his or her fantasies. The analyst may come to embody a parent or a set of psychic conflicts for the patient. (See also counter-transference*.)

transcendent function* The transcendent function occurs when conflicts within the psyche spontaneously produce some powerful symbol 'transcending' the warring forces and so are able to unite them. The transcendent function produces symbols that point to the unknown in the unconscious – they must not be reduced to words, which are the ego's language.

unconscious* Jung's unconscious is his key contribution to psychology and is fundamental to all developments of Jungian theory. As for Freud, the term 'unconscious' denotes both mental contents inaccessible to the ego and a psychic arena with its own properties and functions. The Jungian unconscious is superior to the ego and exists in a compensatory relation to it. It is the locus of meaning, feeling and value in the psyche and is autonomous. It is not, however, completely separate from the body but offers a third place between that perennial duality, body and spirit. Body and culture influence unconscious contents (archetypal images), but the unconscious is not *subject* to either force. The unconscious is structured by archetypes as hypothetical inherited structuring principles.

Index